MW00928689

Smokey

Smokey, The Remarkable Life of Reclusive Inventor, Herbert Glen Irwin

ISBN 1449993575

This book is based on the personal experience of Roland B. Knott with Herbert Glen Irwin. The narrative is compiled from a lifetime of interviews with O.B. Knott, Viola Knott, Maggie Cross, and residents of Noble, LA. Some information came from members of the Irwin family. We personally interviewed those acquainted with Smokey, others by letter and email. We have visited each of his surviving workshops, houses, and property in Texas, Florida, and Louisiana. We have copies of all his inventions, drawings, US Patent Office correspondence, wrapper files, Smokey's military service record, and a few personal letters. We have supplemented information through topical and era-current newspapers, city historical records, museums, research at US Courthouses, the US National Archives, the Internet, and public record sources.

Photographs from the Knott family.

Publisher:
Echo Marketing, Fischer, Texas

Smokey

The Remarkable Life of Reclusive Inventor, Herbert Glen Irwin

By Jackie Knott

Dedicated to the village of

Noble, Louisiana, and

Autism families.

Contents

1949 – 1981

Epilogue

Preface

Sometimes the crazy old man in the town you were raised in, wasn't. Such was the case with Herbert Glen Irwin who lived in the village of Noble, Louisiana for thirty-three years in almost total solitude. None of the residents of Noble knew he was a prolific inventor and manufacturer, a master machinist, a chemist, or that he experimented with botany. Estranged from his family, even they never knew of his contribution to industry and mechanized farming in the 20th Century.

Roland's acquaintance with Herbert Irwin evolved into a lifelong absorption. I remember Roe describing the characters of his boyhood home and when he talked about "Smokey" I was stunned. He was a regular topic of conversation for over twenty-seven years. But the real search for Herbert Irwin's identity began in earnest several years ago. What began as simple curiosity escalated into compelling exploration after unearthing thirty-nine of his patents at the US Patent Office. We found an inventor of impressive accomplishments.

We attempted to interview Smokey's relatives but their lack of knowledge about their own family member was absolute. Smokey was brilliant, evasive, and purposely concealed his activities from everybody. We were left with no surviving family members who actually knew him.

Smokey so impressed people when we interviewed them sixty years later they were able to give us vivid anecdotes of their acquaintance. Still, deduction was often the only means to fill the gaps in his secretive life. Even with all Smokey's parables and halting conversations it was obvious to us Roe knew more about him than anyone. To tell Smokey's story it was necessary to be a skipping stone across the pond of the Knott family history as well.

Smokey was a complex and troubled soul. Late into this project we stumbled upon the real reason for Herbert Irwin's idiosyncrasies. This book began as a story about a recluse, then evolved into a biography of an inventor. Finally, it became a portrayal of a man who triumphed over debilitating obstacles that would have buried most people.

Roe and I feel an obsessive responsibility to this man and it is our intent to vindicate his reputation. Whatever the larger lessons are to be gleaned will be left to the reader.

Prologue

Smokey was dead – a peaceful afternoon was roused by sirens and a succession of phone calls to spread the news. Neighbors flagged each other down on the road to report what they knew about the reclusive old man who had lived among them for so long. What a shame, dying alone in that big metal building, lying in a cardboard box with no one to see about him. Crazy old man. Poor, broke, crazy old man.

The only person who knew better was Roland. He kept silent about what he knew of Smokey waiting for those things that normally take place after a death; heirs stepping forward to eulogize their deceased relative and the settling of the estate. Neither of those things happened. He seemed to pass from this life without anyone caring. It was August, 1981.

Before Smokey died, the couple living across the road from the old man kept their distance. Smokey only sought them out those last couple years because his poor health and failed eyesight prevented him from driving anymore. Unable to keep his garden or drive, Smokey reluctantly asked for transportation to a store. The shopping trips were rare, only a handful of times a year. Smokey was silent and bought very little.

The last time she took him to the grocery store Smokey bought one sack of groceries. Per his standing directive she let him out at his gate and turned around to her own driveway eighty yards away. Except for the woman telling her husband Smokey was really feeble the couple thought no more about him.

Her husband stated he glanced toward Smokey's building three weeks later and noticed his south door partially open. This wasn't normal. Smokey never left that door open, ever.

The man waited two more days and still seeing the door open walked toward Smokey's. From the side of the road he smelled the unmistakable putrid odor of death. He returned to his house and called Willis Webb, the town Marshall. Willis came immediately and was only able to enter just inside Smokey's gate because of the overwhelming stench. He retreated and called the Sheriff's office knowing this was a death the parish needed to handle. The routine investigation revealed the sack of groceries Smokey bought on that last shopping trip was inside his door, untouched. They found Smokey's remains in his makeshift bed.

*****

The last meeting Roe had with Smokey haunted him for twenty-plus years. The glimpses the old man had given him over the course of his life were intriguing enough Roe had to know more. There were too many unanswered questions. Smokey had a habit of speaking in parables and relating snippets of seemingly unrelated incidences. His reputation was full of sensation and with no actual information, the weekly *Sabine Index* newspaper had the obituary of Herbert Glen Irwin only partially correct. Roe could not let it stand. He was saddened knowing people in his hometown drove past Smokey's building and seeing his door open no one checked on him. For decades that building had been locked up tight every night. As their headlights flashed over the side of his building didn't anyone think it strange his door was open? For three weeks no one questioned, why?

Roe laid those thoughts aside and we concentrated on finding out who Herbert Glen Irwin really was. What follows reveals a troubled life rich with achievement even his family was unaware of. Smokey endured physical limitations and events that had a profound affect on his nature.

To understand this complex man one must be aware of his era, the influence of history, and the environment that produced such a gifted inventor but a disturbed soul.

1893 – 1921

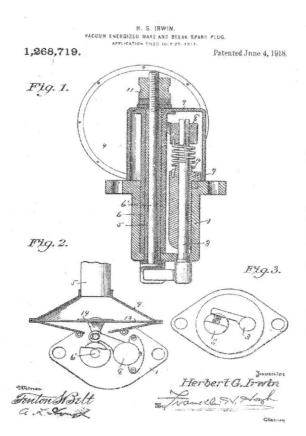

H. G. IRWIN.
VACUUM ENERGIZED MAKE AND BREAK SPARK PLUG.
APPLICATION FILED JULY 25, 1917.

1,268,719.

Patented June 4, 1918.

Fig. 1.

Fig. 2.

Fig. 3.

Witness
Fenton J. Belt
A. L. Smith

Inventor
Herbert G. Irwin
By
Attorney

Chapter One

A Mechanical Genius In The Family

Herbert's parents, Samuel David Irwin and Martha Louisa Copeland, met and married in Marquez (pronounced markay) in Leon County, Texas. The small town is centered on a railroad located almost midway between Dallas and Houston. The Cope-land family came from Mississippi and had been living in Texas as early as the 1830s, while the Irwins came from Tennessee in the 1850s. Both families migrated to Texas lured by cheap and plentiful land. The Navasota River near Marquez was the heart of some of the richest cotton producing land in Texas. Able to acquire thousands of acres, one Copeland pioneer remarked he had enough land to accommodate all his grandchildren.

Samuel's father was a successful blacksmith, as was his grandfather. The grandfather acquired land and turned to cotton farming. Samuel came into his marriage financially well prepared to accumulate land in his own right. Samuel and Martha Irwin were soon blessed with a family. Herbert Glen Irwin was born May 27, 1893 in Marquez, the first of four sons; Samuel Ruey was born in October, 1894. Felix Clyde in November, 1896, and Carmon Belle, born in September, 1897.

Tiny Marquez is divided by a railroad and most activity and business was conducted within the sight and sound of coal burning steam locomotives. The Irwins lived within

1

walking distance of the depot. Young Herbert played in his grandfather's blacksmith shop a block from the railroad. Martha's brother wrote his sister and brother-in-law about available land in north Texas and the young couple made plans to move to Antelope in 1898.

Although many families relocated by wagon the Irwins logical choice was by rail. Railroads leased boxcars for $25 per family and were the easiest way for a couple with four young children to move their possessions. The journey took them from Marquez to Fort Worth for an overnight stay. They traveled northwest from Fort Worth to Jacksboro, again by rail. The great "Tarantula Lines" centered in Fort Worth were composed of the Texas and Pacific, Denver City and Santa Fe, Missouri Pacific, Rio Grande, and New Orleans routes, all converging in a complex junction of rail trade.

A precocious five year old, Fort Worth made an impression on young Herbert. The population of the city was only 23,000, but for a child raised in a small prairie town Fort Worth seemed like a magical city. His experience up to that point was watching magnificent steam locomotives and helping his grandfather forge tools in his blacksmith shop. He knew plows, planters, harrows, wagons, and conventional farming implements. Herbert saw his first building of more than one story. He saw grand machines and the bright light of electricity. Indoor plumbing was new. This was his first exposure to large crowds of people. The massive Tarrant County Courthouse had just been completed in 1894 from red granite. It could be seen for miles atop the bluff overlooking the Trinity River.

The train from Fort Worth to Jacksboro took three hours with stops to fill the steam engine's boilers with water. Samuel Irwin bought supplies in Jacksboro and continued by wagon to Antelope in the far northwest corner of Jack County. Still an era of pioneering this part of Texas had barely been safe for settlers since the 1870s.

The arrival of the railroads opened up North Texas and connected the region to market and population centers. Martha's brother, J. D. Copeland, preceded them by several years and lived in nearby Shannon. The Copelands and Irwins were close families bound by blood and committed support to their kinsmen's success. Acquiring land was a high priority. Samuel Irwin bought 182 acres with a promissory note, two and a half miles just over the boundary line of Clay County. Samuel, Martha, and their four boys lived on this farm. Samuel found another two and a half acres outside Antelope, plus another tract of 160 acres a few miles away in Archer County. The Irwins did well enough a year later to buy a town lot in Antelope on speculation.

Antelope and Shannon are only briefly mentioned in Texas history, but in 1898 they were promising farming settlements. Antelope was situated near the west fork of the Trinity River with a population of over three hundred. It had two hotels, a hardware store, a cotton gin, a grist and flour mill, and a doctor. There was even a daily stage to Henrietta and Graham for a two-dollar fare.

Texas towns share a common romantic past of the Old West and Herbert heard tales of Indians, saloons, and gunfights. The settlers of Antelope preferred to place their future in a Methodist and Baptist Church, a school, and in businesses. The 1900-century mark brought the region out of Texas' notorious past into a more agricultural and industrial reality. Samuel readily took to the land and listed his occupation as farmer in the 1900 Clay County census. The Copeland and Irwin families were industrious, and within two generations were able to accumulate significant acreage.

A Mechanical Genius In The Family

Clay County is north of Jack County and consisted mostly of cattle ranches on free range (unfenced). Only a small percentage of the land was suitable for farming, particularly, corn and cotton. Using subsurface water for irrigation was still a consideration of the future in this region and farmers were totally dependent on the weather.

Since Antelope was only twenty miles from Jacksboro the Irwin family made regular trips by wagon for supplies. The characteristic blueprint of so many Texas towns repeated itself in Jacksboro, with a square surrounding the courthouse. Jacksboro built a grand courthouse in 1896 of native stone and granite, as were the buildings surrounding it. Due to serving a large region of ranching families, Jacksboro experienced her golden years from 1900 to 1915.

Jacksboro had a population of over 10,200 and had eighteen natural springs within a one-mile radius of the courthouse. Jack County was thickly wooded with post oaks over hilly terrain. Area ranches were commonly 7,000 to 15,000 acres. Jacksboro was where Herbert first saw an automobile. One was a homemade version made out of a buggy and engine. There were three automobiles registered in Jack County by March, 1909. Herbert was sixteen years old and was enthralled with this marvelous new device with an internal combustion engine.

Agriculture during Herbert's childhood was performed with mules and common labor. Farmers relied on itinerant laborers to pick their cotton. As with most farming families Herbert and his brothers began farm chores early. Herbert plowed with a mule and picked cotton as a young child and decided he would never be a farmer – his interest was in machines.

Two daughters were added to the family; Gracie L. was born in January, 1900 and Alta Mae in 1903. The Irwin children all attended school by 1909, even though compulsory school attendance did not come into effect in Texas until 1916. Education may not have been a priority of their parents but to their credit all the Irwin children attended public school. The population of Clay County was 17,043 with only two one-room schoolrooms in the immediate area. Herbert went to school in Antelope because it was a mile and a half from his father's farm and closer. Herbert usually walked to school but occasionally doubled up with his brothers on a horse or mule. Martha taught her children a lot at home but Herbert's formal education would begin and end in this one-room schoolhouse.

Herbert had difficulty in school and struggled with spelling. His constant daydreaming was often cause for discipline. His interaction with other children was characterized by more conflict than usual school yard pettiness. It did not surprise his teacher when after the second grade Herbert Irwin did not return to school.

Martha agonized over Herbert's frustration with school when she knew how bright he was. Herbert wasn't an easy child. She decided she must teach him fundamentals. Samuel was a successful farmer even though he did not finish the second grade, so Herbert's parents were not concerned about their son quitting school.

Martha purposed to make sure her son got an education regardless. With painstaking repetition mother and son found a method that worked for them. Martha was able to penetrate whatever it was that inhibited his learning. Martha noticed if she could draw a problem Herbert grasped it quickly. He seemed to hear sounds differently and spelled words accordingly. She made sure he had books to read and noted he could read any book she brought to the house, regardless if was an adult level book. Herbert devoured science books and absorbed chemical formulas with ease. Herbert thought the principles of physics were beautiful. Samuel watched his son master machinery and electrical principles with no instruction.

His parents knew Herbert was different from his siblings, or really, any of the children they knew of. Herbert didn't really play. He preferred being alone with tools and machinery. As a child in his grandfather's blacksmith shop Herbert learned to forge metal. Now in his father's workshop, Herbert, not yet into his teens, was making functional tools of his own design.

It is a remarkable moment every parent experiences when they blink in awareness of their child's intellect and personality. Herbert's parents saw a mere child capable of deep reasoning and an insatiable desire to find out how things worked. Herbert's endless fascination with machinery resulted in a child repairing farm machinery when his father could not. Herbert initially lacked the strength to do much of the work but certainly not the logic. By necessity, farmers are innovative and skilled in forging and mechanics. Herbert was still an adolescent when his father deferred to his son as the more talented and mechanically minded.

Herbert soon took over an outbuilding as a workshop of his own and his parents generally humored their eldest son's tinkering. Only when it interfered with his chores did they balk. Herbert constantly had to be called in to dinner or to bed when all he wanted was to work. Herbert literally would rather experiment than eat or sleep. His tinkering became obsessive.

Farmers and ranchers began asking young Herbert to repair their cultivators, plows, planters, windmills, pumps, and wagon wheels. Sometimes he would not charge the farmer if he weren't doing well but Herbert was usually well paid for his work. If a part was broken he would either fix it or make another. If it was a repeated failure Herbert would redesign the function. By his teens Herbert developed a wide reputation as a mechanical genius who could fix anything. Herbert's talent was sought after and he had no lack of work. If summoned he would readily travel miles to help someone, even to the next county.

Automobiles were the newest most modern invention of his time. Herbert began working on them building a reputation as a talented mechanic. He was asked by a Jacksboro garage to repair automobiles. Herbert seemed to instinctively know how to fix an engine and dearly loved working on them. He found himself enjoying the intricacies of the internal combustion engine and batteries more than anything else he worked on. Herbert soon found ways to improve on them.

The Irwin family was doing well in Antelope. Martha's correspondence with another brother, C. D. Copeland in Spur (Dickens County), convinced Samuel there was more suitable land to be had in Dickens and Floyd Counties. A good farmer could accumulate even more land there. In 1911 Samuel sold the tract of farmed out cotton land his father had bequeathed to him in Leon County. In 1912 he bought 640 acres in Dickens County near the tiny community of McAdoo. In 1913 he was able to buy an additional 482 acres of even better farm land in Floyd County, about fifteen miles northwest of Floydada. Samuel then sold his Antelope farm and moved his family to Floyd County. He later sold the 640-acre tract in 1916. The Irwin family was now affluent cotton farmers.

The early 1900s were ripe for an inventive mind. The tremendous need in agriculture spawned improvements in farm labor and the market was flooded with new implements. Agricultural technology was developing quickly.

A Mechanical Genius In The Family

With the invention of tractors in 1892 the 20th century saw an evolutionary change from draft animals to mechanized farming. Tractors were not commonly used until the twenties and would not outnumber draft animals until WWII. More harvesters and implements were introduced with specific functions. Previously, a farmer had been limited in how many acres he could comfortably work with mules and hired help. But the introduction of specialized farm machinery allowed expanded crop production by several hundred acres.

Herbert's tinkering progressed to serious experimentation. He had ideas for harvesting grain, cotton, enhanced spark plugs, and improved windmills. So many designs flooded his mind there seemed not enough hours in the day to prove them.

Herbert was twenty years old in 1913 and was bringing in more income to his family by repairing farm machinery and autos than he was as a contributing laborer. A family farm was the family business and all the Irwin boys lived and worked on the farm. Samuel was supportive as long as his son was bringing home income but he needed a contributing laborer to work on their farm as well. Herbert's skill and reputation brought him constant work. Inventions were all well and good but they must be put aside when the farm demanded more immediate work. There was a growing conflict with Herbert's interests and the family business. Too often his brothers worked with their father while Herbert stayed in his workshop. Herbert was reminded as long as he was part of the Irwin household he needed to be a contributing member.

When the Irwin family made their final move to their Floydada farm Herbert had no intention of going with them to become another farmer. He was compelled to invent and solutions spilled from his consciousness with almost visionary clarity. He began looking for a place that had an affluent population and a lot of autos. From his mother's correspondence with her brother, C. D. Copeland, Herbert made plans to leave the family farm and embark on his own.

With his parents strained blessing Herbert left home for Spur, Texas.

Young Entrepreneur

Chapter Two

Young Entrepreneur

Today, Spur is a small dot on a Texas map but in 1909 it was a budding agricultural community. Located sixty-five miles east of Lubbock in Dickens County it was originally part of the famed Matador Ranch, The owners sold a small portion of their land to area farmers. Spur was well financed by New York investors including the Williams Brothers and Swenson and Son. The town grew rapidly and was promoted with enough resources to have brick buildings and concrete sidewalks throughout town. The surrounding land raised premier crops of cotton and the town prospered.

The town newspaper, *The Texas Spur*, took pride in announcing the price of cotton and how many bales per acre local farmers produced. These were particularly good times for Spur.

For a community its size Spur was a modern little city over run with automobiles. Their more prosperous citizens took frequent road trips to New Mexico, California, and Colorado, all by auto. The newspaper was heavily peppered with advertisements from various garages. There were already two automobile brokers in Spur, plus an auto storage garage. By August, 1915 automobiles overtook horse and buggy transportation in the area. Many who did not own cars hired auto service to nearby Roaring Springs, Dickens, and Afton.

Young Entrepreneur

Martha's brother, C. D. Copeland, owned more than 2,000 acres and was one of the more successful cotton farmers in Dickens County. He offered to let Herbert stay with his family outside Spur. Herbert was pleased to accept knowing time in his uncle's household would be short. His uncle had a small shed he would turn over to him for "Herbert's tinkering." It was understood Herbert wasn't coming as another farm hand. He would be a self-supporting mechanic working on automobiles and his inventions. Herbert had already evaluated a recurring problem with the autos he worked on and had developed several versions of improved spark plugs.

The prosperity of the town was more than Herbert had hoped for. Affluence meant automobiles and auto owners needed mechanics. Herbert's stellar reputation had preceded him through his uncle and cousins. The ranch manager from the Matador Ranch also spoke highly of Herbert Irwin. He had done regular maintenance on their threshers as a teenager.

Herbert was an impressive young man. He was bright and capable and found immediate employment at one of numerous garages in Spur. His reputation as a great mechanic was reinforced and enhanced. The automobile industry was bursting with new companies and innovative models. Herbert worked on a wide range of automobiles in Spur; in among the many Fords were Mercers, the Winton Six, the luxurious Maxwell, and the Hudson Super Six.

When they brought their autos to him for repair, Herbert became acquainted with the researchers of the Texas Agricultural Experimental Station outside Spur. Herbert occasionally visited the facility and kept aware of the newest experimentation in agriculture. As he listened to them discuss designs for mechanical harvesters and cultivators

Herbert already had his own ideas. The TAES researchers were considered to be the finest in the country with an international reputation. Herbert proudly judged his harvester design more sophisticated and certainly more effective.

While he was working as a mechanic Herbert never stopped experimenting. At home, he had the luxury of using his father's fields, and now he used his uncle's acreage. He perfected his designs in his workshop and in the fields. Herbert only needed time to prove his many inventions. It was common for Herbert to work at the garage and come home to tinker well into the night on his own projects. His uncle wondered when his nephew ever slept. The Copelands tried to interest their nephew in socializing with their church group but Herbert only wanted to work.

Herbert stayed just eighteen months with his first employer. This was the first time Herbert had an employee employer relationship and he didn't care for it. He well knew he was hired to fix a specific problem, not overhaul and rebuild an auto all afternoon. A normal work week left Herbert little time for inventing. Neither was Herbert pleased with the amount customers were charged compared to his salary. Herbert felt his expertise was worth far more and he was confident there wasn't a mechanic anywhere as talented as he was.

Hoping for more freedom Herbert was enticed to quit and moved to another garage. He negotiated his use of the garage facilities for his own use. His customers followed him to the new garage and Herbert was relatively content at his new place of employment. Herbert saw the local paper that week and read where his boss, L. H. Gilbert, declared he had hired "the best auto mechanic in west Texas." Even though his name wasn't given Herbert knew he was referring to him. His employer needed his garage to have the reputation, not a mechanic.

Herbert wanted total freedom to work on his many projects and began saving enough money to start his own garage and repair shop. He was also saving to invest in getting his inventions patented. Besides his spark plugs and electrode cleaner Herbert had designed an attachment for an internal combustion engine to improve efficiency. Herbert decided working for anyone was a hindrance and he purposed to never work a salaried job again. He needed time and his own workshop to perfect his inventions. He wanted to give free rein to his imagination and designing.

Herbert felt he had over stayed his welcome with his uncle and told the Copeland family he would be starting his own business and would be living by himself. His uncle was glad to have been in a position to help his gifted young nephew and wished him every success. Over time the tools and machines of his profession, many of Herbert's own design, had spilled over into several buildings. C. D. was relieved to get his outbuildings back.

Herbert found a boarding house in Spur one block off Main Street on 5th Street. He chose the Dunn Building because he was able to rent the tin-faced shop in the back alley of the boarding house. He could walk downstairs to his work. Herbert moved his tools and equipment into the shop and was finally self-supporting and completely independent.

Herbert wanted his customers to know he had moved into his own repair shop. He envisioned a repair shop where he could work on virtually any and every mechanical or electrical device. Welding had always been a particular skill Herbert developed from a child and he used an improved acetylene welder he had designed.

Herbert began a series of display ads in *The Texas Spur* in May, 1917. Herbert knew all he needed was to display his name and location. The reputation of expertise attached to his name would bring in all the business he wanted.

Herbert was a young man with supreme self-confidence and he composed his display ads accordingly. The typesetter objected to his misspellings and the copy editor shook his head as the clerk related how Herbert Irwin obstinately demanded they not change one word. Herbert's brilliance in mechanical aptitude did not carry over to proper spelling. But no one had the courage to try and convince him otherwise. One of his ads spoke of his "homogenius weld." Another stated, "Cast Iron Welded By Special Aparatus." [sic]

Herbert's ads were often displayed with the largest type on the page. His first ads were simple ones but later bold letters dominated the page advertising more services.

CAST IRON
Welded by special operation. Bring in your
old broken piece of farming implement,
windmill, etc. and have it welded.
Herbert G. Irwin
at the Dunn Building.

Several weeks later he placed another display ad for batteries. If a bit rambling, the spirit of his ad was full of confident skill and ego.

BATTERY SERVICE
has been a great need of Spur since the
modern equipment of automobiles but
there has not been enough cars in this

15

community to justify a service of this
kind until recently. So, depending upon
the patronage of the car owners of this
country, I am prepared to repair and
recharge any kind of battery for your car's
equipment. For your patronage I will give
you battery service equal to any in the state.
Call and see me.
Herbert G. Irwin
at the Dunn Building.

With the boarding house and his workshop side by side, Herbert worked as many hours as he pleased, which was constantly. Customer demand evolved into cleaning storage batteries along with welding and repair work. He began to phase out auto repair except for influential customers. Herbert was bringing in considerable income for a young businessman and dearly loved having total control over his own time. The only constraint he had was space. Shunning electricity in his shop as a needless expense, he had batteries stacked and wired everywhere. He repaired them and applied them to every imaginable use. He was outgrowing his facility quickly with his many experiments spilling out over the back lot almost to the street. Passersby could only guess what he was working on.

By this time, Herbert had invented three improved spark plugs, a method to remove acid sludge from batteries, a vacuum distributor, a vaporizing attachment for an internal combustion engine, a method of repairing aluminum castings, a rotary cultivator, a receptacle for dispensing insecticide, an insecticide holder, and a garden powder sprayer.

Local cotton gin owner, S.E. Johnson Jr., corroborated with Herbert, allowing him use of his cotton gin to work on a cotton bur breaker and a separator. Herbert's mind was overloaded with ideas as he ate little and slept less.

Herbert's distinctive personality as a youngster was solidifying into something more as an adult. His discomfort at being touched as a child escalated into revulsion when people came too close to him. Herbert did not understand why but knew he only wanted to be alone. He had quit shaking hands with people for some time. Interaction was harder and he found himself less willing to engage in casual conversation. The attention of young women literally frightened him. He purposely avoided crowds of people. To solve his difficulty in writing Herbert bought a typewriter and taught himself to type his invention notes.

Most young men in his position would find any number of diversions to spend his money on. Not Herbert. He worked late into the night because this was his pastime. This was his passion and his obsession. Experimentation and solving problems consumed every waking hour. All he wanted was to work and invent and improve. The money he earned was jealously hoarded. He saw it as a means of freedom to pursue his inventions.

Herbert had heard enough tales about inventors having their ideas stolen from them. He was afraid his would be taken from him as well. He knew he must hold patents on his inventions and purposed to patent every idea he had. Instead of using Texas attorneys, Herbert thought it prudent to keep his personal business to himself. He sought attorneys in Washington DC through the U. S. Patent Office. He was fearful a delay would allow another inventor to patent a similar device before he could save enough for attorney fees. The cost to secure a patent was considerable, regardless how much income he was bringing in. Herbert had so many inventions to submit and limited funds to do all of them. He was loath to ask but decided to approach his father for help.

Samuel listened to his talented son and balked at the amount of money his son was asking for. It wasn't the cost of submission for the individual patents, but the attorney fees that were so high. Herbert had the resources to commission five inventions for patent claims but not the fourteen he wanted. Samuel could afford such an investment but he had no intention of simply giving Herbert the money. He insisted it be a straightforward business relationship, which was what Herbert wanted anyway. After weeks of haggling Samuel and Martha reluctantly agreed to finance Herbert's patent submissions – if their son would place the cotton-related inventions in Samuel's name. The understanding between father and son was they would split any profits from marketing the devices until the loan was repaid. Herbert thought they were all capable of producing income but kept what he thought would be the most lucrative for himself.

Herbert discussed the arrangement of placing the cotton bur separator, the cotton bur breaker, and the suction fan in his father's name with Stephen Johnson. The cotton gin owner was agreeable not caring what Herbert and Samuel Irwin did between them. He owned half the marketing rights and knew the inventions still needed work before submission to the Patent Office.

With his parents' help Herbert commissioned attorney Franklin H. Hough in Washington DC to begin the long process of trying to patent his fourteen inventions.

Samuel and Martha Irwin's grown children were doing very well. The farm had benefited the whole family and in one generation they were affluent cotton farmers with extensive land holdings. Samuel reflected on the many hours he had spent with Herbert in their workshop laboring over a problem. He had enjoyed that closeness with his son. Still, they had arguments over his obsessive tinkering. Samuel readily admitted Herbert was a brilliant mechanic and inventor. He did not dispute Herbert had contributed to the family farm with his innovative designs. But Herbert had also cost him. His brothers often had to do their own work and Herbert's as well. They bore some resentment for it. Over the years Herbert had ignored his share of chores and literally lived in the workshop tinkering. He had destroyed whole rows experimenting with cultivators, cotton-bur breakers, experimental cotton pickers, and a heading machine. Herbert had never offered to repay his father for his loss.

The agreement they made placing some of Herbert's inventions in his name would help pay attorney fees but still would not compensate Samuel for his crop losses. The agreement was a loan but did not include reimbursement. Herbert was a successful young man and refused to share with his parents what his income was. Samuel reasoned it had to be considerable to afford attorney fees on five inventions even though Herbert asked for help on the other nine.

Samuel felt he had invested in those inventions as well. After all, it was not Herbert's fields that were torn up, they were his. Hadn't he, Samuel, made suggestions to Herbert when he was working on a problem? Didn't Herbert try out dozens of prototype spark plugs on his own auto? How much acreage had Herbert destroyed with all his experimenting? Forty? Ten here and five there for his cultivator? How much lost income did all that represent? Their negotiation was difficult enough; Samuel didn't think the added demand to recoup his losses would have been well received. Didn't he have a right to recover some of that? Hadn't he, Samuel, contributed to these inventions with his own land?

Samuel expected Herbert to make significant profits from his inventions when he sold them. You would think his son would offer some kind of compensation. If any of these inventions were sold Samuel decided he would not only recover his loan to Herbert but would reimburse himself for losses as well. He justified his decision thinking Herbert would be mad when he eventually found out but surely he would understand. He would get over it after Samuel explained himself.

Samuel did not feel the least bit compromised with his rationale.

Young Entrepreneur

The Army Corps, One of a Few

Chapter Three

The Army Air Corps:

One Of A Few

In 1914, Herbert, along with the other residents of Spur, read about the escalating conflict in Europe. On June 28th they read of the assassination of Austrian Crown Prince Francis Ferdinand. The articles in *The Texas Spur* detailed the upheaval and riots that followed. Battles were reported each week.

The US was an ocean away from the strife with no real reason to become involved until May 7, 1915, when a German submarine torpedoed a British passenger ship, the *Lusitania*. The US counted 128 Americans among the 1198 lost in the sinking. The shock of such an attack changed conviction quickly. A fever of nationalism called for the US to enter the war. Allies were committed but now the US had lost innocent citizens in a war that was not hers to fight. Fervor grew steadily as young men spoke of fighting for their country's honor and retribution. Herbert shared much of the sentiment but continued to labor in his workshop. His life dedication leaned to his work rather than his country's politics. His obsession of the moment was perfecting another spark plug he had designed.

The automobile industry was progressing in technology and diversity by WWI. The different models and innovations consumers could choose from were increasing every year. The same could not be said of the other grand invention of all time, the aeroplane. American aviation had stagnated since 1903 while the Wright brothers were engaged in prolonged patent battles, primarily with aircraft designer Glenn Curtiss. Meanwhile, Europeans, and in particular the spirited French, continued to design and improve. The aircraft that excited pilots were all European designs while the Americans were left behind.

In 1909, a hugely successful air meet was held at Rheims, France, attracting flyers from all over Europe. The first major aerial competition in the US was held at Los Angeles and attracted few Europeans. Aviation in its first decade was marked by one record after another being established for distance, over water, and maneuverability. Most of the competition was for cash prizes and was usually won by European designed aircraft.

Using an aeroplane as a weapon of war was already being considered in aviation. The US Army Signal Corps had ordered a Wright Flyer in 1909 with two seats. One seat was for the pilot and the other for an observer or gunner. In 1911, in Mexico, exhibition pilots with the visiting Moisant Brothers Flying Troupe engaged in an aerial observation of a Mexican uprising. Within a year, aeroplanes did go into combat; the Italian Army used them in their colonial war with Turkey in North Africa. By 1912, with increasing tensions in Europe, France acquired 254 aeroplanes. The United Kingdom, Germany, and the Russians were all developing aircraft specifically for military use. Regardless of the European conflict the US felt little need to develop an air force and allocated only token funds for military aviation. American designer Glenn Curtiss soon developed a "flying boat" capable of taking off and landing in water. He sold fifty of them to England just as war broke out in Europe in August, 1914.

As badly as pilots and engineers were needed there was a crying need for mechanics as well. In November, 1915, Army Captain Benjamin Foulois led seven aeroplanes to Fort Worth, Texas. This was the entire military fleet of the U.S. Army in 1915. Captain Foulois was en route to San Antonio to establish a permanent headquarters for Army aeroplanes at Fort Sam Houston.

Many people attended the publicized event, including a judge and several businessmen from Spur. The Captain gave a talk that evening at the Metropolitan Hotel talking about the future of military aircraft and expressed to his audience the need for qualified pilots and mechanics to work on flying machines.

Afterward, the judge made a point of speaking to Captain Foulois, and told him about a mechanical genius in Spur who could fix anything. He could redesign or make parts for any engine. His name was Herbert Irwin. The Captain told the judge this was exactly the type of man the Army needed and asked the judge to please send word to Herbert Irwin. His country needed him and he would be guaranteed a place at Fort Sam Houston. Captain Foulois gave the judge his address and asked him to persuade Herbert Irwin to write him.

Herbert later listened to the summons more than a little interested. As the war in Europe raged on and with daily newspaper coverage he felt the tug of patriotism. He was still waiting on his patent attorney before offering his spark plugs to a manufacturer. He was working on numerous other projects. Still, he could not shake the call to serve. After the sinking of three US merchant vessels in March the US declared war on Germany April 6, 1917. Herbert had made his decision. He knew he had much to offer his country. His experiments would simply have to wait. Whereas the automobile had excited him as a youth Herbert's expertise ranged far beyond it. It wasn't the challenge it once was. But the engine and application that did excite him was – the aeroplane.

Herbert corresponded with Captain Foulois about working on aeroplanes, and came to an agreement with specific conditions. Herbert made demands only a talented mechanic or a pilot could make. If Herbert was to serve in the Army Air Corps it would be on his terms. He got an immediate reply stating his place was indeed assured if he would enlist. Herbert responded he would enlist as soon as he heard from his patent attorney. The Selective Draft Act was passed in May, 1917 and Herbert registered for the draft in June, listing his occupation as an automotive mechanic.

Herbert wrote his patent attorney in Washington DC to file applications on his spark plugs. He was content to wait for the research to be done on his other inventions. In early December the administrative research was completed on his last three inventions: an electrode cleaner, another spark plug, and an attachment to an internal combustion engine. Herbert knew it would take at least a year for the patents to be granted. He closed his shop and stored his tools and equipment on his uncle's farm. He left his few personal belongings with his parents, including his typed papers and stacks of drawings on his inventions. Herbert temporarily retired his experiments and nine days later took the train to San Antonio, Texas. Herbert was twenty-four years old.

Herbert enlisted at Fort Sam Houston in the Army Air Corps, December 12, 1917. Captain Foulois' aide waited for Herbert Irwin, one of only three mechanic recruits they had that month. He was told to escort Irwin through processing and to treat this man with all the deference and respect he held for pilots.

The young Lieutenant was sitting in the waiting room during Herbert's enlistment physical. The doctor left the exam room and approached the aide with his clipboard in hand.

The doctor said, "This man has just refused to let me examine him. He let me look in his mouth but that's it. He told me he's healthy and not to touch him. He means it. I barely got him to take his shirt off."

The Lieutenant remembered Captain Foulois' instructions and asked, "Is there any way to get around the exam?"

"Maybe. How bad do you want this guy?"

The Lieutenant knew recruit Irwin had some type of agreement with Foulois and well knew how much they needed mechanics. "We want him real bad."

The doctor shrugged and signed his clipboard. "You've got him. If he gets sick I won't remember this conversation."

The Lieutenant next drove Herbert to get a haircut, which seemed pointless. The Lieutenant had never had a recruit shave his head before they enlisted. The barber waived them on and they next went to gather uniforms. Herbert fingered the material thinking it was the same cotton twill as the khakis he wore at home. He could tolerate these. Herbert glared at the tailor when he came toward him with his tape measure. Herbert sharply told him he would hem his own pants. The tailor had never had a recruit say he would fit his own uniforms and turned away to the next man.

At the open bay barracks Herbert went to the far end bunk and turned his back on the other men in the room. When another recruit came forward to introduce himself, Herbert walked around his duffel bag and knelt to the floor. He acknowledged the man's introduction with a nod and gave his name. The men largely ignored the quiet loner in the corner and continued their stories about their hometowns.

Captain Foulois authorized Private Irwin to skip marksmanship training and insisted he be sent straight to the hangers. It didn't take long before the pilots at Fort Sam Houston were thoroughly impressed with this bold young mechanic. Herbert stated there was not a technician as good as he was and there wasn't a machine made he couldn't fix. They believed him.

They flew a trainer, the Curtiss JN "Jenny," before and after Herbert worked on them. The aircraft performed tighter, cleaner, and smoother than it ever had. If a pilot got himself killed it was not going to be due to a mechanical failure if Private Irwin worked on it. Herbert was quickly assigned to the 810th Aero Squadron at their Repair Depot at Speedway, Indiana. Private Herbert Irwin had been recruited for the express purpose of repairing aircraft and training other mechanics to work on aeroplanes.

Herbert was one of a handful of qualified aircraft mechanics in a branch of the Army Air Corps that was the forerunner of the yet-to-be-formed United States Air Force. Private Herbert Irwin took readily to the spit and polish of the military and enjoyed the status of instructor. He liked being able to salute a superior instead of shaking hands. Herbert attained rank quickly and was soon promoted to Corporal. The best mechanics at the Repair Depot deferred to his expertise and skill. As instructor he was soon able to have his own room and Herbert retreated in privacy. While the other men played cards, horseshoes, and tossed a baseball during their off time Herbert walked past them, oblivious to the concept of recreation. He was usually seen at the hangers late at night working on a problem with the aircraft.

Herbert was soon tapped to write maintenance manuals as an extra duty in addition to training mechanics. He established much of the service criteria for the Army Air Corps aeroplanes. Most of the manuals were on the Curtiss JN "Jenny." He also worked on the Packard-le Pere Lusac. By 1919, the Standard E-1 arrived at the Repair Depot.

Progress of the War was followed closely by those assigned to the home front and the 810th Aero Squadron kept informed of events. They cheered the Armistice affected in November, 1918. It was only a matter of time before the War was over.

It was a cold day at Speedway, Indiana on March 14, 1919. After removing his overcoat, Sergeant 1st Class Herbert Irwin stepped into the office of 2nd Lieutenant William Vogelback and gave a sharp salute. Irwin was usually dressed in fatigues and was known to prefer the company of aircraft. He rarely left the hangers but today he was in his dress uniform. Vogelback also recognized Irwin as having a gifted mind who could easily become an officer if he chose a military career. They tolerated his quirks only because he was such a brilliant mechanic.

"At ease, Sergeant Irwin. What can I do for you?"

In his quiet voice Herbert came straight to the point. "Sir, I would like to request immediate discharge."

The Lieutenant leaned back in his chair awaiting another sad tale. "Why? Family problems?"

"No, Sir. My enlistment is up in three months. I had a business in Texas. Four of my inventions were patented while I've been in the Army. A partner needs me to solve some problems with a couple we were working on. I need to return to my work."

The Lieutenant knew of Irwin's patents and of his innovative changes at the Repair Depot. There was ample reason for his swift promotions. Vogelback gave the standard answer he was instructed to whenever such a request came in.

"Well, the War is essentially over although the treaties haven't been signed yet. And, as you say your enlistment is up soon. Have you considered making the Army a career?"

"No, Sir. I'm an inventor."

"You know I don't have the authority to grant such a request but I will forward your application to Captain Emig with an endorsement. It might help if we could attach some correspondence from the Patent Office. It might expedite your request. Of course, Major Frissell has the final authority for any early discharges."

"Yes, Sir. I know. I have some correspondence."

"Good. Why don't you see Corporal Page and have him type up your request?"

Herbert was anxious to get home. "I will. How long do you think this will take?"

"Assuming Major Frissell approves it, maybe a week up to a month. You will know in a week one way or another. I don't see a problem since you enlisted instead of being drafted."

Sergeant Irwin came to attention with a salute. "Thank you, Sir."

Lieutenant Vogelback nodded and returned Irwin's salute.

"Dismissed, Sergeant."

Herbert dictated a letter to the administrative typist and left his letters from the Patent Office. He had no reason to think his request would be denied and began preparations to leave the Repair Depot. He would tell a few he was leaving only as a matter of courtesy. The 810th Aero Squadron usually had a hundred fifty men and a dozen officers, depending if they were at the Repair Depot for training. These would never be lasting relationships. This was truly goodbye for Herbert.

Eleven days later Herbert was summoned to Major Frissell's office. Herbert listened as his Commanding Officer thanked him for his contribution and wished him luck. An inventor was wasted in the Army and Herbert had no regrets about leaving.

Quartermaster 2nd Lieutenant Adolf Capelle handed Sergeant 1st Class Herbert G. Irwin his Honorable Discharge with $60 discharge and transportation pay to Dallas, plus $183.50 bonus pay. Civilian Herbert Irwin wore his dress uniform for the long train ride home through St. Louis and then to Dallas, Texas.

Herbert returned from the Army Air Corps in late March, 1919 satisfied with his contribution to his country. He had been rewarded with quickly attained rank and almost revered appreciation for his skill. That was important to him. Forget the ridiculously small monetary compensation compared to what he was used to making. He certainly hadn't volunteered for the pay. Herbert had loved working on aeroplanes. He left maintenance manuals written with such clarity later aircraft mechanics noted the precise text with respect.

Herbert took with him the erect bearing of a military man and an obsessive concern for neatness and order. He folded his uniforms and packed them away in his duffel bag absently thinking they would be useful as work clothes and shop rags. He had business awaiting him.

The Treaty of Versailles was signed June 28, 1919. The War was over. General Billy Mitchell's dramatic demonstrations of air superiority were yet to be made. Herbert Irwin left military aviation for others to debate.

Herbert's patents had been granted and he had licensed his spark plugs with a well-compensated contract. He could return to Texas with regular income and the self-satisfaction he had served his country well. Herbert's other patents were soon granted, only they did not all have Herbert Irwin's name on them. Cotton farmer Samuel D. Irwin held a few. Others were jointly in the name of S. E. Johnson, Jr. Herbert would discuss with his father the merchandising of these others when he came home.

Herbert had patented twelve inventions in less than two and a half years, while serving sixteen months in the Army Air Corps. He came home to Floydada to live with his family, eager to begin inventing again. Herbert was 26 years old.

The Army Corps, One of a Few

The First Blow

Chapter Four

The First Blow

Herbert returned from the Army Air Corps anxious to return to inventing. He stopped briefly in Spur to visit his uncle and arrange for his equipment to be transported to his father's farm outside Floydada. He had a far higher vision for his workshop and it no longer included Spur. Herbert sorely missed the freedom of his own workshop while he was in the Army Air Corps; he never stopped thinking, designing, and drafting. As much as he enjoyed working on aircraft he longed for uninterrupted, endless experimentation. Ideas flashed through his mind and they would not rest until he proved them.

Herbert had worked with cotton gin owner, Stephen E. Johnson Jr., prior to leaving for the Army. He had corresponded with him regularly about cotton-bur problems. They had corroborated and submitted a patent application together in Samuel's name. Herbert knew the improvement they were working on had only minor problems to work out before filing another patent.

Herbert had paid close attention to what was happening in the high plains of the Texas Panhandle. Oil and gas had been discovered and Amarillo was riding a wave of explosive growth. Herbert was interested because the oil and gas industry always needing welding and machine works.

In Floydada, the Irwin family was prospering. Carmon was working on the farm. The two sisters, Alta Mae and

Gracie, supported the family business with their mother. Gracie was frequently drawn to visit friends in New Mexico. Felix had married and started a steel fabricating business. Ruey leased a farm from another landowner and lived by himself. The family was somewhat indifferent to the eldest son returning home at twenty-six years of age, but they still welcomed him. Martha knew how tiresome Herbert's demands could be, but Samuel was the one who seemed truly uneasy about Herbert coming home.

The vacant bedroom was cleaned and tidied even though the bed would rarely be slept in. Herbert's lathes, drill presses, metal and band saws, batteries, grinders, castings, dies, tools, and worktables found their way back into one of Samuel's larger outbuildings. Some of the farm's seasonal implements were moved out into the weather. Samuel looked on with a frown, thinking, Herbert could at least have asked first. The other siblings discussed their elder brother, wondering how he fit in with the military's strict requirements. Herbert took his opportunity with his family while he transitioned from soldier to independent businessman again. He expected their cooperation.

The Irwins had to adapt with the addition of Herbert. He had followed his own path so totally they didn't quite know how to respond to this new dynamic – this was now a family of adults. Herbert had always been contrary but he seemed even more distant. The relationship the brothers had shared in their early lives had long lost its closeness. Although he was not living on the farm Ruey seemed to understand Herbert more than the others. But even Ruey remarked about it.

Herbert discussed the status of his patents with his father. Their business agreement had been deliberate and forthright. Samuel had been involved in several of Herbert's inventions but his contribution was more in supplying the funds for attorney and filing fees. As each of the Irwin brothers matured in their own field of endeavor, such an agreement was common with their father. Samuel helped all his sons get established; Ruey and Carmon with farming, Felix with steel fabrication and welding, and Herbert with his inventions. One shouldn't need a written contract with a father and son.

Herbert was ready to pursue inventing and regain control of the patent royalties he had placed in his father's name. When Herbert asked about selling and licensing the patents Samuel always seemed to be busy and avoided specifics. The only sales Samuel conceded to were with Steven Johnson. Along with several others in the region, Johnson used the cotton bur separators at his cotton gin. Samuel dutifully gave Herbert the royalties from them. He wasn't sure how much Herbert and Johnson communicated.

Samuel stated there was little monetary gain yet from this group of Herbert's inventions, certainly not enough to pay back the high fees charged by Washington DC patent attorneys. Samuel had made "inquiries" to manufacturers on his son's behalf but he had nothing to show Herbert yet. Samuel did not tell Herbert which patents he had sold or how much royalties they were bringing in. Merchandizing the patents had already paid back Herbert's loan but Samuel didn't quite know how to tell his son. Samuel well remembered the violent tantrums Herbert used to have as a child and the anger he exhibited into his teens, and even as an adult. His rages were horrible. Samuel did not want to provoke another one.

Herbert had watched his parents work hard to be as successful as they were. He recognized he should compensate his parents in some manner living with them and using the farm and equipment for his own. Whereas he acknowledged his father's contribution with some of his inventions Herbert's ego credited more importance to his own genius. Herbert had two more, what he considered minor inventions: a rotary cultivator and a powder sprayer. If there was any money to be made on these it would be negligible compared to his others. He gave them to Samuel in the same manner he did the first five for a total of seven inventions in his father's name. Surely, by adding these two he would be able to pay back his debt to his father and finally be financially independent. Then he would be able to pay his own attorney fees for any future inventions. Samuel readily put his name to the documents, one in July and again in mid-December. Samuel mused Herbert must be feeling enough goodwill toward him maybe he wouldn't be so angry after all.

While Herbert was in the Army, Samuel responded to several companies interested in his son's inventions. After all, they were in his name. It was certainly legal for him to sell or merchandize them. Samuel had the sense if Herbert knew how much money he had already made on those inventions his son would be furious. They *did* work together on some of them but regardless of the name on the patents there was no question these were Herbert's. Samuel recognized his own skill in welding and mechanical aptitude, but he was primarily a cotton farmer. Stephen Johnson had cooperated on the cotton-bur inventions and had equal right to them. It was only a matter of time before Herbert found out how many Samuel had sold and that the debt had been paid in full.

Martha noticed her husband's uneasiness around their son and could not understand the reason for it. She paid little attention when her son and husband were working together and half listened when they discussed business. She was more concerned with managing the farm accounts and bills. Martha knew placing the patents in Samuel's name "for Herbert" was to offset attorney fees. She was aware her husband was receiving royalties toward the debt but was vague as to details. She let Samuel handle that. Martha knew they had had a very good year and deposited the royalty checks in with the farm accounts.

Herbert's beloved routine of spending every waking hour in his workshop was reestablished. The loner was blissfully happy in the only environment he ever felt comfortable in, his workshop. The seven inventions in his father's name were all granted patents; a cotton bur-separator, a battery mud-extracting device, a vacuum distributor for an internal combustion engine, a method for repairing aluminum castings, another cotton bur-breaker and suction fan, a rotary cultivator, and a hand powder sprayer. Herbert's savings from the Army would hold him over with living with his parents. It would allow him to submit his next inventions for patent with his own funds. With no deadlines and no responsibilities the long hot summer allowed Herbert endless months of experimenting. He was more interested in his experiments right now than securing buyers for his patents.

Herbert knew his father was receiving royalties and left it up to him to tell him when the debt was repaid. Herbert was content working on multiple projects simultaneously. By December he submitted an insecticide dispensing receptacle and an insecticide holder for patent, both with his own money.

Through the winter of 1921 Herbert revisited his notes and drawings on a machine to pick cotton. He remembered the primitive "picket fence" cotton picker the Texas

Agricultural Experimental Station in Spur had developed, and knew he could do better. His two inventions separating the cotton bur and breaking the bur for a suction fan were two partial answers to an age-old problem, but Herbert was not satisfied. Even though Johnson used them at his cotton gin and they had sold quite a few to other gins, Herbert knew farmers were still dependent on laborers to pick the cotton.

Throughout the South excitement about any new mechanical picker was renewed disappointment, as hundreds of attempts were talked of and then ignored in failure. The US Patent Office was rife with "cotton pickers" but none were truly satisfactory. Wasted cotton was either left on the shrub or the lint arrived at the cotton gin so full of debris the gins refused it. There was no fully mechanical picker that did a thorough job and the industry was still dependent on cheap hand labor. There was even talk of developing a new strain of cotton that grew shorter to allow for the primitive pickers in limited use. Herbert attacked the problem with deliberate intensity, confident he could invent the first truly mechanical cotton picker.

For one whole season Herbert designed, altered, experimented, and redesigned again. He took his final prototype into his father's fields in late summer. Samuel and the other laborers were impressed as mules pulled the spindle picker between the rows gathering the lint. The picker left the dried leaves, sticks, branches, and bolls behind. When Herbert brought his first loads of cotton to Stephen Johnson's gin, the cotton was processed and baled without a problem.

Herbert sent his invention drawings and text to attorney Anderson B. Lacey, of Lacey and Lacey in Washington DC for submission in September, 1921.

Herbert then turned his efforts to a mechanical harvester for maize. He had worked on the problem on and off but now devoted most his time to it. He studied the plant and the different types of harvesters currently being used. Most tried to cut the whole stalk, and then separate the head of the plant from the stalk after cutting. Too many damaged the head and maize was still commonly picked by hand. Herbert approached it with a machine that would sever the stalk just above the ground and simultaneously cut the head off, leaving the stalk to fall to the ground. The problem of positioning the stalk properly for cutting took a year of experimentation. Mules pulled the monstrous apparatus down the rows. The geared and cogged wheels propelled the device forward, slicing a continuous blade through the stalk. The heads of the maize dropped perfectly into a holding container as the stalks dropped to the ground. It was a beautiful, complex machine.

Again Herbert used his father's livestock, his father's fields, and his father's crops to perfect his heading machine. Samuel watched and justified his selling and licensing Herbert's inventions all over again. Still, none of the weak explanations Samuel prepared for Herbert seemed adequate. Samuel said nothing.

Samuel Irwin was one of the first farmers in the region to buy a tractor. Most farmers used implements that were designed to be pulled by mules. Modifications were necessary for farm equipment to be pulled by a tractor. Herbert designed a push bar attachment for the front of a tractor that eliminated the need for modification on many of them. He now had two more inventions to submit; his heading machine and the push bar attachment. He filed the heading machine in February, and the push bar attachment in August. It had been a productive two years.

The First Blow

While making any prototype Herbert used his own acetylene welder. As he was developing his inventions he had corrected some design limitations in acetylene welding generators in the process. The cumbersome mixing of carbide and water and cleaning the tanks after every use was dealt with. The valve he designed gave a cleaner, more intense flame and made the generator safer. Regulating the carbide had been an explosive problem since its inception decades earlier but Herbert had solved that problem, too. With one application after another he would eventually incorporate each successive design into one acetylene generator. He patented these improvements as well. Herbert was looking at a highly lucrative future with just his acetylene welder.

It was December, 1921. Samuel was in the habit of going to his mailbox before anyone else pocketing his checks from several manufacturers that were producing Herbert's inventions. The envelopes from Massey Ferguson, International Harvester, John Deere, and Case were arriving almost every week. With each larger check the deception became more entrenched and more difficult to withhold his merchandizing from his son. The overwhelming truth was the debt had long been paid. Herbert may have been capable of excusing some income, but after this long Samuel was sure Herbert would be enraged, convinced his father was intentionally deceiving him.

Samuel pondered he should have renegotiated the terms of their agreement. His dilemma was in the long delay. He was caught up with spring planting and the day-to-day operations of a large cotton farm. Then, harvest. And well, he had simply procrastinated too long.

Samuel was worried about Herbert corresponding with the same manufacturers he had a merchandizing agreement with. Felix suspected his father was receiving more income from Herbert's inventions but didn't say anything. Samuel more or less confirmed it by asking Felix not to mention it to Herbert. Carmon knew but didn't want to get between his father and his brother. Samuel saw no easy way to extricate himself from a volatile situation.

A week before Christmas Herbert went through his mail at the Floydada Post Office. He looked at the letter from International Harvester corporate offices with interest. He had posted several of his inventions with the US Patent office as available for sale. Prior to this, he had received letters of inquiry from Massey Ferguson and John Deere about merchandizing.

Herbert read the letter not understanding at first. He leaned against the wall trying to digest what he was reading. The letter spoke of "similar percentage agreement," referred to patents in his father's name. The dates quoted in the letters hinted at "previous licensing." This new proposal referenced another agreement he had no knowledge of whatsoever. And, it was while he was absent in the Army. A wave of understanding washed over Herbert. The letter didn't suggest deception – it confirmed it. He recalled comments by his father and vague dismissals about the payments on his debt. The letter was making too clear sense of those comments now.

Herbert drove to the farm to confront his father and demand a valid reason how he could steal from his own son. With each mile Herbert's anger escalated until he was no longer thinking rationally. He had designed these inventions from his own intellect, his own reasoning. His father's contributions were incidental. They had made a gentlemen's agreement to fund his attorney fees and no more. He didn't *give* his inventions to him! Herbert was fiercely protective of his inventions and he was very nearly out of control.

Herbert drove into the farm yard and from the barn Carmon could see Herbert's truck skid in the dirt to a stop in front of the house steps. Herbert slammed the truck door and leaped up the steps. Carmon wondered what on earth was wrong now. Herbert's whole body language was one of severe agitation. Carmon put down his tools and walked from the barn hearing loud voices before he was halfway across the yard.

Herbert demanded to know where his father was. Martha sat at her desk regarding her son in alarm. Martha cautiously asked her son the reason Herbert wanted his father. Looking at this powerful man Martha was genuinely afraid of her own son.

Herbert began pacing and shouting his anger and accusations. Carmon walked in listening to his brother accuse his parents of deception, betrayal, and theft. Herbert's rage was frightening to behold. Carmon saw his mother back away from Herbert trying to reassure him it was all a misunderstanding. Soon Gracie and Alta Mae stood in the kitchen door watching a horrible scene never seen in this family. Sensitive Alta Mae hugged her sister crying as she watched Herbert scream his anger at his mother and brother. Brother and sisters listened in shock as Herbert threatened their father. They all felt Herbert was capable of real violence, and it was not an idle threat.

Herbert regarded his family from a completely different perspective. He did not see the fear in his family's faces. All he saw was deliberate betrayal. Carmon stood neutral, not judging any of them, which infuriated Herbert just as much. He had been horribly used and none of them blamed his father. He wheeled around and marched out, banging the door. Herbert slammed his truck into gear and drove toward Felix's house.

Martha dared not say where Samuel was or how much money she and Samuel regularly deposited in their account. Regardless of when or how much, Herbert was convinced it was his. Martha, Carmon, Gracie, and Alta Mae stood in stunned silence as they watched Herbert speed away.

Carmon questioned his mother quickly as to what was going on. Wringing her hands Martha said his father "might have" accepted more money for Herbert's patents than they had agreed upon. Carmon waited until Herbert's truck was out of sight and got into the family car and drove in the opposite direction to where Samuel really was, in town at the feed store.

Samuel wilted when Carmon told him about the scene at his house and then drove home. Herbert arrived at Felix' house in a deeper rage convinced the whole family was conspiring against him. Felix sent his wife upstairs and warily watched his brother, paying close attention to his hand in his coat pocket. When Herbert left, Felix found Ruey and together they went to their parents' home.

The family meeting that took place was hurried and desperate. None had any doubt Herbert was on the verge of violence. Martha begged Samuel to give Herbert his money back. Samuel said he could not because the farm had absorbed most of it. Martha wept as she looked at the Christmas tree in the drawing room with presents crowded under it. Felix and Carmon were sincerely concerned for their parents welfare and suggested they needed to leave Texas for a while, preferably as far away as possible. For years, California friends had invited the Irwins for a Christmas holiday. It was time to accept that offer. Alta Mae would go with them and they would leave Gracie with friends in New Mexico. Carmon, Felix, and Ruey felt if Herbert had wanted to harm them he already would have, and decided they could stay and manage the farm.

Samuel, Martha, Gracie, and Alta Mae packed quickly and left after dark in the larger of the family's two cars. Even so, in 1921 it was not a pleasurable road trip to California. The presents were abandoned under the tree and the family dispersed. Carmon wisely spent the night with Ruey while Felix kept his gun by his bedside that night.

When Herbert arrived back home the house was dark and quiet. The Christmas tree lights were off. The family car was gone. Herbert was so shaken in his rage it was days before he could think clearly. When he finally calmed down enough to speak with Carmon, he was told his parents and sisters were gone.

Herbert debated consulting with a lawyer, but Irwins did not share their business with anyone. An Irwin kept his problems private. Besides, everything he and his father had agreed upon was a verbal contract. Herbert rummaged through his father's desk and found records of checks cashed. When he had a reasonable assessment of how much money his father had withheld from him Herbert vowed if he ever found him he would kill him. His brothers denied any complicity and Herbert believed them to a degree. But he could not understand them protecting their father. It was a miserable Christmas shared only by Carmon, Ruey, and Felix and his wife. Herbert would have nothing to do with them and spent Christmas in his workshop.

After the holidays Samuel and Martha evaluated their situation and decided the California climate was agreeable enough to consider staying. Trying to appeal to Herbert's reasoning was futile. Why was he like this? Since their children were grown and making their own way, Martha and

The First Blow

Samuel recognized the family would never be an intact unit again. They also knew time would not ease Herbert's anger and sense of betrayal. California would now be their home. Samuel was fifty-six years old and had hastily abandoned one of the most successful cotton farms in the high plains, a fine ranch house, barns, accumulated tools and equipment, and left a car.

Samuel had always been good with his hands and soon opened a retail furniture store in Berkeley. He made custom furniture and at his age preferred working inside in comfort instead of the grueling life of a cotton farmer. Gracie remained in New Mexico and later married a young rancher. Pretty Alta Mae settled in with her parents and became involved in the local arts society. She was soon a popular dinner theater actress. The formally close family would never be reunited again.

Herbert had entertained the thought of moving to Amarillo for some time to take advantage of the oil and gas industry. Now that he had effectively rejected his family there was nothing to keep him in Floyd County.

Herbert held welding contracts from Amarillo businesses and made some inquiries about employment. Willborn Brothers was familiar with his acetylene welding work and had made him a standing offer. The record-breaking oil boom in the Panhandle was establishing Amarillo as the premier business hub in the nation. Capitalizing on the oil industry would give Herbert the freedom to invent more. He decided to work for Willborn Brothers long enough to reestablish himself and start another workshop and made plans to leave Floyd County with no intention of ever returning.

Herbert's eccentric personality became more detached with every year. But now his rage deepened into bitterness and real paranoia. He could not even trust his own family. The little communication he had with Felix and Carmon was eventually shunned altogether. Only Ruey demonstrated any understanding or sympathy toward Herbert.

Hereafter, Herbert would guard his work zealously and never, ever leave himself vulnerable. He would revisit this emotional scar often and consider it betrayal of the worst order. He resolved to not communicate with his family again, nor did he see his parents again.

The First Blow

1922 – 1940

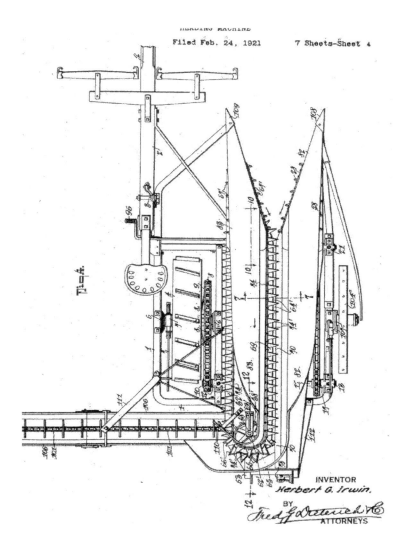

Chapter Five

The Inventor Comes Into His Own

Amarillo is centrally located in the twenty-six counties that make up the Panhandle of Texas. The railroads that arrived in 1887 brought settlers who first farmed wheat and later cotton. Some founded large cattle ranches. Amarillo owes a great deal to legendary cattleman, Colonel Charles Goodnight. Palo Duro Canyon was the heart of his huge JA Ranch and extended for miles in every direction. He owned over 100,000 cattle and was one of the first true cattle barons. The famous XIT Ranch, which bordered New Mexico, was at one time three million acres.

In 1916 Amarillo businessman M. C. Nobles drilled his first successful gas well and formed the Amarillo Oil Company, later to become Amoco. With oil and gas processing from the Panhandle Field, wide-ranging construction of pipelines followed. The oil boom brought other changes and by the end of 1919 the Panhandle not only led the nation in railroad construction but led Texas in road construction as well. Amarillo's prosperity spread across her main highways, one of which would eventually become part of the celebrated Highway 66. Amarillo's skyline changed to several multistory brick and stone buildings. Along with the oil and gas businesses Amarillo became a regional financial center.

Ranching soon took a back seat to the oil and gas industry. The population surged from 15,600 in 1920 to

43,000 by 1930. The 1920s in Amarillo were remarkable years as a sleepy Texas ranching town became an oil and gas industrial giant. The Borger Gas Field northeast of the city became a wild, thriving boomtown – Amarillo was at the forefront of the largest oil field discovery in history.

From 1925 to 1930 some 114 new gas companies formed in Amarillo. Phillips Petroleum, Shamrock Oil and Gas, and Magnolia Petroleum, all named Amarillo their headquarters. In 1928 the Texas Company expanded the oil refinery they bought from the Panhandle Refining Company and later became known as Texaco. By 1935 fifteen pipelines carried natural gas to Denver, Kansas City, Indianapolis, and Detroit.

The north and east sides of town were heavy industrial areas. Larger companies expanded to more attractive red brick complexes. They were surrounded by a gray patchwork landscape of metal workshops and warehouses. In the arid high plains metal was a particularly durable building material. Galvanized metal allowed for quick, relatively inexpensive construction as industry tried to keep pace with phenomenal growth. This sector of town was a web of chain-linked fences, loading docks, metal and pipe, and the ever-present railroad. It was first populated with draft mules and later trucks. Amarillo was a hive of intense activity and grand commerce.

Herbert had been to Amarillo enough he knew this was where his future lay. He loved the energy there. Nothing was more exciting to him than seeing machine shops lined up one after another, blocks long and as many blocks deep in the industrial district. This was the environment he thrived in; the heavy smell of steel having been ground, oil, and the distinct odor of forged metal. Amarillo in 1922 was a town of opportunity and daring venture. This was a town where innovation and hard work could make a man wealthy. If no one understood Herbert at least here they would appreciate his expertise. Herbert didn't care about the town's rich history. He only cared how he could exploit its potential.

Herbert was uniquely talented to take advantage of these surroundings. While he was still living in Floyd County, Herbert had developed a business relationship with one of the more recognizable companies in Amarillo, Willborn Brothers. Willborn Brothers supplied the oil field with monstrous oil storage tanks and was involved with natural gas line production. Such tanks required skilled welders and dependable construction that housed millions of gallons of oil. Willborn Brothers tanks were flung over the oil field landscape like so many pebbles strewn across the prairie.

The name of Herbert Irwin was already well known within industry circles as a precision machinist and expert welder. Herbert had done contract work for several other companies in Amarillo, and in January, 1922 wired Allen H. Willborn he was relocating to Amarillo. Willborn immediately offered Herbert a job as a tank welder. Herbert committed himself on one condition, that he could use his own welder. He advised Willborn he had developed an improved welder that was easier to operate, portable, and delivered a far superior weld than anything in use. Willborn agreed and offered him one of the few private rooms in the Willborn Brothers Rooming House on Tyler Street. Workers were in such high demand companies commonly provided living quarters for their employees. Rooming houses were scattered throughout Amarillo.

Herbert regarded the changes he observed in Amarillo and decided the oil and gas industry would keep him occupied for years. He had no intention of staying with Willborn Brothers for any length of time. He only wanted to establish himself and get his own workshop again. His acetylene welder was monopolizing his time, and he had several more improvements he wanted to make on it. All he needed was time and space.

Herbert drove his Ford pickup to 906 Tyler Street on a clear January day and regarded Willborn Brothers Rooms with wariness. He moved his few belongings into a room, and then drove to Willborn Brothers across the railroad tracks on the north side of town.

Herbert found C. Norton Headrick, the shop foreman. Headrick had been briefed he was to grant any request within reason Irwin wanted. Herbert chose a distant corner on the backside of the red brick building far from the rest of the noise and banging of the workshop. He did not want anyone going near his welder, his tools, or near him.

The next morning Allen Willborn was informed his new welder had arrived. He left his office to greet him along with Headrick and head welder, Earnest Simmons. They watched while Herbert demonstrated his welder. When asked how the mechanism of his acetylene generator worked, Herbert only smiled and said he had applied for several patents on it. There was little sludge on the welding seam, which testified to the skill of the technician as much as the generator itself. Most importantly, the laborious steps most welders had to perform mixing water and carbide every time the acetylene generator was used were bypassed completely and safely. All three professionals were duly impressed.

Trolleys carried hundreds of workers from the various boarding houses to the industrial complex north of town. The early morning cars traversing Polk Street were usually so loaded with men they had to stand with some hanging off the steps. Herbert Irwin never rode the trolley. He was observed leaving his room and driving the mile to Willborn

Brothers in his own car. The few men who owned cars couldn't understand the wasted cost of driving when you could take the trolley for a few cents. It was worth it to Herbert not to endure the press of crowding on the trolley.

Herbert was part of the dozens of teams assigned to weld storage tanks on site in the oil fields. As the other welders returned to Willborn Brothers and left for the day Herbert experimented on his own. At peak times a second shift arrived for smaller work in their main workshop. When this group of men left they saw Herbert Irwin still tinkering with his welder. Herbert often left as the night watchman came on duty. When the morning shift came to work they regularly saw Herbert in his corner, already working.

Besides working on site in the oil field Herbert worked as an independent contractor within the company. He took machinist and occasionally, extra welding jobs. Willborn Brothers was waiting on Herbert's improved acetylene generator, one that would save time, increase production, and improve safety. Explosions and injuries with current acetylene generators caused concern as many companies lost their best welders. The dividing line between other welders' work and Herbert Irwin's was always the acetylene generator he used.

Herbert settled into a working routine. His rooming house was sold and demolished for a new car agency. Annoyed over having to change rooming houses, Herbert moved into Willborn Brothers new one on Taylor Street.

Herbert's reputation in Amarillo was growing and he could see his own workshop was again on the horizon. He had regular inquires about his welder. With his next shop he would take advantage of the demand for precision machinists as well. He had one agricultural invention he had worked on in Floydada, a rotary crust breaker, and submitted it to his patent attorney in January of 1922. This would be his last agricultural invention. He was now completely focused on the industry around him and his energies were poured into perfecting his acetylene generator.

Herbert left Willborn Brothers after two years. His leaving was amiable and Willborn Brothers had nothing but respect for him. Herbert's first patent on his acetylene generator was granted in April, 1924. The company bought several acetylene generators from him and even asked to be a distributor for his welder.

Herbert was able to lease a small lot with a cramped shop across the street from the railroad on Arthur Street in 1925. Herbert moved once again to a rooming house on Houston Street only two blocks from his workshop. He pondered on a marketing name for his welder. It was a natural sound to him and he spelled it phonetically as he did so many words. It was not long before 801 Arthur Street was known as the manufacturing home of the "Welderz Frend."

Herbert initially made his acetylene generator himself but demand had him hiring experienced help very soon. Herbert chose his employees carefully and knew who was capable of exacting skill. Willborn Brothers used several Welderz Frend generators and their sales reps handled the sale of more than twenty-five the first year of production. Herbert became the manufacturer of his own invention.

At the same time, his machinist operation was requiring more help. Herbert was receiving orders for large ten-inch bore drills, cylinder and crankshaft grinding, pistons and rings, and drill stem fittings. Machine shops were everywhere, but not all had the equipment to machine them, or could do the technically superior work his shop produced.

Herbert squeezed as much equipment and men as he could fit into his tiny Arthur Street workshop. Irwin

The Inventor Comes Into His Own

Improvements had two distinct operations: his machine shop business and manufacturing the Welderz Frend. From 1925 through 1928 he made further improvements on his acetylene generator and filed more patent claims in January, 1925 and again in May. He filed three more in August, 1927 and another in August, 1928. Herbert had eight individual patents wrapped up in his Welderz Frend.

One particular patent claim to his welder was rejected repeatedly. Herbert was annoyed with the examiner and his many questions. Herbert had felt comfortable for years with the patent claim process and had been doing his own research and submissions for his inventions. After the fifth patent rejection Herbert hired a patent attorney. After the eighth rejection Herbert fired the attorney, believing he could defend his claim better than an attorney could.

More correspondence was passed between inventor and the Patent Office as the examiner stated, " .... it couldn't possibly work." After the tenth rejection Herbert was livid. He sat down at his typewriter and pounded out twenty-five pages of eloquent defense worthy of an attorney. He laboriously explained every detail and function of his generator. He accused the patent examiner of meaningless objection, and worse, "ignorance, pernicious skill, and sophism."

Quoting patent law by statute, Herbert cited dozens of patents by name and number to argue his position. Herbert went to the shop foreman, the owner, and head welder at Willborn Brothers, asking for notarized statements as to the proven function of his claim. Willborn Brothers had been using Herbert's welder for some time and readily agreed. His letter may have been shrill with paranoid concern for the inventor, but it worked. After four years and ten appeals

The Inventor Comes Into His Own

Herbert's patent was finally granted. Herbert gloated in satisfaction.

As 1929 progressed Herbert heard of machine shops losing business and closings but he ignored them as poor businessmen. He had more machinist work and orders for the Welderz Frend than he could supply. He heard and read about loans being called and wondered why anyone would borrow money in the first place. Investing in the stock market was a practice totally lost on Herbert. He would never trust anyone with his money. Herbert overheard troubling conversations about banks and farmers unable to sell their crops and more business closings. By October 29, 1929 Herbert well understood the significance of Black Monday. Orders were canceled and Herbert began laying off his employees as other businesses did. It became obvious he would have to close his shop. Amarillo had sunk into a deep recession but nothing compared to the devastating Depression that would grip the rest of the country.

Herbert found a farmer to store his equipment and vacated the Arthur Street workshop. Always living simply and hoarding his money Herbert had the resources to weather the Depression. He decided he needed to take a job and went to see Willborn Brothers again.

Tank welding was at an all time low and gas production was cut back, but never completely stopped. Willborn Brothers found a place for one of their more respected welders. Herbert decided he could pull through the financial crisis working and saving. As unemployment nationwide grew to 25% Herbert was skilled enough to keep a job. As fifteen million men were forced into idleness, foreclosures became commonplace. Factories closed and eventually, 9,000 banks, 40% of the national total, were closed and life savings were lost.

The Inventor Comes Into His Own

If wage earners were having the worst time of their lives farmers were in ruin. The drought that produced the Dust Bowl literally destroyed the livelihood of farmers. He watched as families with their belongings heaped on their cars came through Amarillo and continued west. Herbert saw families taking on the persona of migrants. The rails always had bums but he saw boxcars full of men. Herbert had never been without work and could not understand why these people could not make a living, He selfishly decided they had to be poor money managers or just weren't trying.

With a desperate economy, government intervention was the primary issue of the 1932 Presidential election. Newly elected President Franklin Delano Roosevelt immediately took drastic steps to stabilize the banking industry. Herbert observed what was happening on the national scene and evaluated his prospects. He thought others' misfortune could benefit him and he began planning his next step to independence, his own property and factory. He knew a person who held cash in this climate of distress could prosper.

Although he had never owned property before Herbert could see the advantages. His family had always stressed the importance of acquiring land. The other reason to take this step was the unsettling anxiety Herbert underwent every time he moved boarding houses. It was getting harder instead of easier. It must be a good thing to own your own house and never move again, never having to cope with the angst of getting used to a different environment, different colors, different noises, and different smells. If he had his own property he would always have the same routine and living arrangement. It was most appealing. Herbert had moved often because he had to. Now he would move one final time because he wanted to.

The Inventor Comes Into His Own

Herbert narrowed his available choices to a specific arrangement he had in mind. He needed a railroad to ship his acetylene generators. He needed a highway to receive supplies for his machine shop and local deliveries. He needed at least one workshop and preferably two. He would need a good fence but could build one if necessary. He wanted at least three acres not too far out of town but far enough out the property would be reasonable. He wanted outside the city limits because of taxes. Ideally, he could live and work on the same site. Herbert found five acres on Hwy 33 on the outskirts of town on the main route to Kansas City. He knew the cost to convert to his own manufacturing facility and had saved enough cash to finance his venture completely. This property had a small frame house a stone's throw from the workshop. It was perfect.

The couple who owned the land accepted the offer from a buyer who wanted an old metal outbuilding and a small frame house with no utilities. Ruth Pate and Pam Denton agreed to Herbert's insistence to sell the property to him for $10 and "other considerations." Only the three of them knew how much the property really sold for. Herbert was forty years old and had just bought his first property July 5, 1933.

Herbert moved into the small frame house with just bare bones for furniture. He didn't need or care for any because he would never entertain here. The sitting room became an office and drafting room. His bedroom had a bed, a wardrobe, a small table, and a lamp. The kitchen had a table and two chairs. He had a hand wringer washing machine on the back porch. This was all he would ever need.

The first thing Herbert did was fence the outside perimeter of his property. He built an inside fence to keep his house lot separated from the factory, allowing enough room for a garden. Production was begun before all the property improvements were completed. Herbert saw the value of hiring work done when he could use his own talents for more exacting problems. Herbert soon built his second workshop larger and taller than any he ever had before. It was made out of the heaviest gauge galvanized metal he could find, railroad metal. It was more suited to build boxcars than a workshop. His employees were all welders and machinists, and most had building experience of some kind. Herbert directed the construction himself.

Herbert's accumulation of dozens of small engines and generators supplied electricity. The newer employees who didn't know Herbert Irwin were incredulous of the work done here without commercial electricity. Content to have jobs, the men became used to the white light of carbide lamps strung in the workshops.

Herbert developed a small assembly line system for producing the Welderz Frend. He personally instructed each man and would accept nothing but work produced to his criteria. Herbert did not think about his contribution as sole owner, investor, designer, manufacturer, quality assurance, trainer, engineer, and site manager. He wanted total and complete control and he had it. No decision was made without his approval and direction.

As his acetylene generators entered the field and developed a reputation for ease of operation, orders for Welderz Frend generators came in steadily. The oil industry made slow progress to recovery. As oil production climbed and industry demands increased Herbert added more machinists. Herbert found himself with less time for inventing and devoting more effort to running his business. He had every aspect of his enterprise under tight control except one. The thing he lacked for a business of this size was a bookkeeper.

The Inventor Comes Into His Own

Herbert was making more money than he ever imagined. Numbers in a bookkeeper's column did not represent money to Herbert, but images did. He saw orderly stacks of bills he could visualize and measure. He had laboriously figured his cost to produce one Welderz Frend and priced it to insure a high profit. He pictured how many sheets of metal it took to make a welder. He knew how many hours and how many men it took to build a Welderz Frend. He knew how many gauges he needed, the pipe, and the connectors. Those images were how he figured his production and profit margin.

Herbert's practice of dealing only in cash worked well for him with many of his local customers. As pipelines extended north and eastward, he was supplying clients over north Texas, and out of state. Herbert accepted and wrote checks when he had to, knowing business protocol called for it. Accounting ledgers bewildered him and the more money he made he knew he needed a bookkeeper. Herbert hoarded his money but Irwin Improvements was outgrowing his ability to manage it. He trusted no one, and the thought of anyone knowing about his finances caused his familiar paranoia to rise.

The Inventor Comes Into His Own

.

A Second Hit

Chapter Six

A Second Hit

Herbert was too self-absorbed to notice how badly other citizens were suffering with the Depression. Compassion and understanding for those who lost everything were foreign attributes to Herbert. He simply did not see it. In his mind, if a man would work he would not be in need. As Herbert walked back and forth from his workshops to his house he hardly saw the string of cars that passed his factory every day. When he did notice them he wondered where were all these people going? And why weren't they working? With no responsibilities other than himself, Herbert had never felt the hopeless sting of defeat as so many did. If a man were skilled anyone could hold a job. Herbert turned his face from them in disgust.

As a property and business owner, Herbert should have been more attentive to those things that affected his professional life. He was well aware of industry trends but generally was not interested in national politics. As a young man Herbert paid casual interest to the political debate that brought Woodrow Wilson to the Presidency. Thinking it his civic duty and right, Herbert voted in the elections that produced Warren Harding, Calvin Coolidge, and Herbert Hoover. But none of these Presidents, nor any who followed, influenced Herbert's life as did Franklin Delano Roosevelt. Seeing his business suffer with the crash of 1929 Herbert voted for FDR in the fall of 1932, expecting better things.

A Second Hit

With the entire US banking structure in near collapse, Roosevelt called a special session of Congress within days of his inauguration. The Emergency Banking Relief Act passed, giving the President authority to regulate banking transactions, and Roosevelt promptly closed all banks. After a four-day bank holiday and evaluation by the Treasury Department, only sound banks reopened. Thousands loyal to their banks left their money in with promises of eventual recovery that never came. Life savings and whole businesses were lost. Herbert was fortunate he hid most his money and lost very little. But the experience would affect his attitude toward banks for the rest of his life.

After four years of the Great Depression over twelve million people were unemployed. Many families were homeless. FDR introduced a menu of legislation in his first 100 days that would lift the failed economy from the brink of total collapse. While Herbert immersed himself in the noise and energy of his factory, Roosevelt began his fireside chats to outline his vision for the country. Roosevelt was the first President to use radio as a political tool but the event was lost on Herbert. He never listened to radio.

It was impossible during Roosevelt's terms as President to read a newspaper, large or small, and not find commentary of FDR and his policies. Depending on what side of the political spectrum a citizen stood, the public either revered him or believed FDR was taking the country and her liberties into socialism. If you were a successful farmer in fiercely independent Texas some Roosevelt policies crippled your production, and consequently reduced your income. Regardless how many programs stabilized agriculture over the long term and benefited the masses, it wasn't hard to find a farmer or rancher in Texas who despised Franklin Roosevelt.

A Second Hit

Few Presidents exercised their will and power to the degree Franklin Roosevelt did. His three terms (barely into his fourth term, he died April 12, 1945) were responsible for the most ambitious government programs the country ever sponsored. The New Deal for Americans resulted in unprecedented legislation. FDR's domestic policies drove the political climate Herbert lived in as a citizen, an inventor, and a manufacturer.

Legislation included the Agricultural Adjustment Administration (AAA), which paid farmers to restrict their production, the National Recovery Administration (NRA) that affected wages, the Civilian Conservation Corps (CCC), the Tennessee Valley Authority (TVA), the National Labor Relations Act, sometimes referred to as the Wagner Act, which benefited labor, and the Work Projects Administration (WPA).

The Supreme Court declared a number of FDR's proposed legislation unconstitutional. There was considerable controversy as Roosevelt promoted another new bill calling for the retirement of senior judges. The bill was never enacted and the Supreme Court later relaxed its stance on several issues. With natural attrition FDR was able gain a more agreeable bench with his appointments. Many of FDR's bills were successful but in the larger scope of history, some were not. Regardless, Roosevelt's New Deal policies continue to influence modern American society today.

Two important bills passed in 1935, the Rural Electric Administration (REA), and the Social Security Act. Had Herbert paid closer attention he would have realized how much these two bills would affect him.

Herbert's was the transition generation that moved from wind power, storage batteries, carbide lamps, and small kerosene generators to commercial electricity. Herbert used dozens of small engines and kerosene generators to power his equipment in his workshops. Generators and storage batteries were as familiar to him as his fedora hat. Kerosene generators in his factory were refilled several times during the day to keep up with production. Storage batteries worked well for carbide lamps but Herbert decided he needed another source of power for expansion.

Windmills were critical fixtures on farms and ranches when Herbert was a boy. His father had several as did most farmers. Ranchers used windmills for water wells to fill tanks and troughs for their cattle on land that lacked regularly flowing creeks and rivers. Windmills were commonly used to recharge storage batteries, carbide lighting, and for small home appliances. Herbert had repaired hundreds of wind-powered generators over the years and knew the design weaknesses.

The Texas Panhandle and wind were almost synonymous. Dust was lifted into driven clouds that enveloped the landscape in a beige tempest. Wind disturbed Herbert, especially the horrible dust storms the plains were subject to. He hated them and took refuge in his house when the wind became intolerable. Herbert had played with wind power designs in the past but he purposed to invent a wind power machine to generate electricity to operate his factory.

Herbert had his own private corner in the larger of Irwin Improvements' two workshops. He worked years on the design and construction, and completed his first wind power machine in 1935. Herbert had a tower welded out of angle iron for its base and set the four corners deep in concrete. The tower reached above the taller workshop. He raised the wind power machine to the top with pulleys and installed the propeller. Herbert connected his largest generators to it and linked his storage batteries together in an elaborate conglomeration of energy producing power. He released the brake on the propeller and it began spinning in the hot Texas wind. Herbert made adjustments over the week and when the wind died down at dusk the storage batteries were charged, ready for the next day's work. Irwin Improvements was no longer limited in expansion by lack of electrical power.

The wind power machine was the tallest structure on Highway 33 and could be seen from a mile away. It generated considerable discussion by the sheer size of it. Herbert had farmers and ranchers stop and ask if he could build one for them. In a couple months he had enough orders he considered the wind power machine another product for Irwin Improvements. Herbert developed the wind power machine for his own use but the commercial potential could not be ignored.

Herbert had several variations in mind and continued to work on more design features. He could see an endless market in the thousands of ranches that dotted the Panhandle and other plains states. He was anticipating years of production.

Those rare becalmed days on the prairie were highlighted at other times by near gale force winds. The attachment Herbert designed adjusted for wind velocity. He studied his competition, doing his own marketing survey. Herbert thought he had considered everything. The one thing he did not anticipate was government intervention.

In the midst of his expansion plans Herbert read an announcement in the newspaper about the Rural Electrical Administration. It would allow cooperatives to be established bringing electrical power to the most remote farm or ranch in the country. Electricity was in every town in the nation but not in the countryside. Soon that would change.

The bill would bring electricity to rural residents eliminating the need for his invention. Isolated farmers and ranchers would no longer need his wind power machines. Many who had considered buying a better wind powered machine than the one they presently had, chose to wait for electricity. Orders were soon cancelled. These four inventions represented years of work to be tossed into the wind with one signature, that of Franklin Roosevelt. Herbert was enraged.

Still, he decided to complete his filings since the research and attorney fees had been paid. Herbert filed successive patent submissions for "wind power machines," each with a slightly different improvement. The first was October, 1936, the second July, 1938, and the third February, 1940. The same month he submitted the attachment that adjusted for wind speed.

The Patent Office was evaluating his inventions so Herbert let the laborious process continue. Trying to salvage his invention, he reasoned it would take years for ranchers to be reached with electrical power. He might be able to sell a few. Herbert did sell some but the orders were nothing compared to the thousands he had hoped for. Patents were eventually granted in 1939 and 1940. As electrical and telephone service slowly came to the most remote residents in the country all orders for his wind power machines ceased. His invention was obsolete except for his own use. Herbert stubbornly decided he would never subscribe to commercial electricity for the rest of his life.

Herbert was convinced it was Roosevelt and his meddling that took his invention's potential from him. Roosevelt was the heir of all Herbert's anger and blame. It was Roosevelt and his labor bills that had workers organizing for higher wages. It was Roosevelt who was sapping initiative from citizens with his entitlement programs. It was Roosevelt who eroded incentive from manufacturers to produce. It was Roosevelt . . . . it was Roosevelt.

With no outlet to express his rage Herbert retreated to his house. He paced his frustration out hour after hour in his small house. Herbert considered the REA a personal attack on his enterprise. His suspicious mind conceived new enemies who were conspiring to steal his work and money from him. His cynicism toward people had already been confirmed, and this loss drove him deeper into paranoia. Herbert trusted no one. His own father had first sold him out and now "they" had taken this one from him. The country he so dearly loved that had prompted him to volunteer during a war had betrayed him as well. How could Franklin Roosevelt promise so much and then legislate away his livelihood? Herbert felt betrayed by the political process he at one time had confidence in. Herbert brooded while he worked on other projects but he would never vote again.

In pure defiance of bureaucracy Herbert purposed to live in such a manner even government intervention could not control him. Herbert retreated to the only place he found comfort – the solitude of his workshop. Herbert muttered his anger to his machines, the only thing that listened in sympathy and understanding. It was weeks before Herbert could shake his depression and rise to the challenges of operating his business.

Herbert determined he would be the instrument of his own success. With renewed vigor and determination Herbert resolved to not let Roosevelt's Rural Electric Act set him back. Ignoring this second obstacle he continued to accumulate cash reserves. While Herbert returned to his labor another Roosevelt policy was brewing in the halls of Congress.

Herbert had built an upstairs office in his second metal workshop late in 1938. He could look through the windows and see his machinists bent over their tasks. He had welded the pipe foundation and the galvanized plate steps himself. He hired carpenters to build the office and walkway. He moved in two desks, one for his shop manager, two chairs, a file cabinet, and a fan. It was the barest of offices, with only a calendar as decoration in a utilitarian room designed strictly for business.

Herbert had done well managing his business after such dramatic expansion. He needed more machinists and increased production of the Welderz Frend. He had two supervisors, a manager, and a deliveryman.

Irwin Improvements employed over seventy-five skilled men now. Even with a manager, Herbert still needed a bookkeeper. He pondered and fretted for months and decided he must.

He reasoned other businesses had bookkeepers and accountants. It was a natural progression for Irwin Improvements that was long overdue. Herbert thought visually and counted in images instead of abstract numbers. His bookkeeping wasn't exact but Herbert still had a firm grasp on his profits. He would impose stringent checks and balances to monitor all his cash. Herbert needed a recommendation and one of the best businessmen he knew was his former employer, Allen Willborn.

Willborn listened as Herbert came straight to the point. He needed a bookkeeper and could he recommend someone? Herbert wanted a man who was trustworthy and who would not discuss his business with anyone. Allen Willborn knew several accountants and referred him to Sophie Roberts, assuring him she was capable and responsible. Herbert wasn't keen depending on a woman, but with Willborn's endorsement he thought he would at least try her.

Sophie was in her early thirties and knew of Herbert Irwin only by reputation. She had never married and had been a bookkeeper for one business or another around Amarillo since her teens. She was a natural mathematician and understood business. She had clients all over the county. Sophie was well regarded because of her conservative approach to finances. She believed in scrupulous bookkeeping, lawful reports, and paying the exact tax the county, state, and federal government demanded. She discouraged her clients from any questionable deductions and pushed for true profit and loss statements. Sophie had left many a client who had skimmed their company profits.

Sophie received a short typed note in the mail asking for her services. She couldn't find a phone number for Herbert Irwin or Irwin Improvements and found out he didn't have a telephone. Sophie drove out of town to the factory for their first meeting. She blinked in disbelief when she saw carbide lamps hanging overhead. Sophie thought she was walking into a factory from an earlier generation. She saw a fan wired to a generator. Everyone had electricity these days, except maybe Herbert Irwin.

Sophie's potential client regarded her with skepticism. Sophie quietly explained her philosophy and what she could provide Irwin Improvements. When Sophie said she "believed in paying taxes in a timely manner" Herbert assumed she meant the only tax he ever paid besides sales tax, property tax. When Herbert said he wanted to be sure no one could manipulate his money to steal from him. Sophie was not offended and only nodded. She was used to such suspicion. Some had it worse than others. Sophie said she would be back the following week to help set up the proper accounts for Irwin Improvements.

When Sophie arrived back at the factory she took Herbert's lever-style adding machine and asked for his payroll records and invoices. Sophie knew it would take a week to set up the account. Some of her clients were better prepared than others to convert to a bookkeeping service. A couple hours into the process Sophie thought Herbert Irwin probably had no idea how much money he was making or losing. She was wrong. Herbert's balance sheet was purely mental imagery and was not entered into columns and ledgers.

Herbert was in the workshop all morning tinkering and came upstairs midday. Herbert was uncomfortable being in the same room with a woman but equally, he wanted to watch his new bookkeeper work. He told Sophie if she had any questions to ask his manager. He answered a few questions and left.

Sophie could see Herbert Irwin had his business correspondence in fairly good order. She noted Mr. Irwin's method of dealing with invoices and paperwork, simple in and out boxes and basic files. The wooden boxes were stout enough to hold tools and she wondered if they had been used for that before. His filing system consisted of folders in stacked metal boxes instead of a file cabinet. Sophie had to employ simple organization before she could even begin setting up ledgers.

Sophie found it surprising Mr. Irwin did not have a secretary for an operation this large. She observed he did his correspondence himself and even the simplest memo was typed out. He kept stacks of telegram copies.

A Second Hit

Sophie was aware of some unspoken rules by the end of the month. Mr. Irwin would never leave his house if it was raining or storming, or dust storms. No one was ever to step inside his gate to his house. And no one was to touch his personal area of his workshop.

Sophie thought Mr. Irwin rather peculiar in some respects. She quickly dropped her pleasant, "Good morning." When she came to work the most Sophie got out of Mr. Irwin was a nod. He did not offer the courtesy of telling her where he was going when he left the office, or when he was coming back. But what really made her uneasy was when Mr. Irwin would pace the office back and forth if he was upset about something. She had heard of his rages and worked there four months before she saw him explode in anger. A driver delivered the wrong gauge sheet metal for a rush order. His reaction was dreadful and Sophie decided she never wanted to incur such wrath.

After a few months as his bookkeeper Sophie was developing a begrudging respect for Herbert. She saw his talent in the many products Irwin Improvements produced. Even though he did not speak to her at any length she recognized a man of real brilliance. The fact he invented his products fascinated her. Sophie worked two days a week and it did not occur to her to assume any familiarity with her employer. Mr. Irwin didn't invite it and he seemed indifferent to casual friendship.

There was one area of Irwin Improvement's business that concerned Sophie. As she recorded the payroll ledgers she realized Mr. Irwin was not deducting the new Social Security Tax. The tax had been passed in 1935 and it had been over two years now; plenty of time to implement the new law. If Mr. Irwin wasn't deducting it he probably wasn't sending the tax to the government. She spoke to the manager about it and he shrugged, "Mr. Irwin don't cotton to any kind of tax. The men, they don't care. They want to take home all their pay."

Sophie didn't want to approach the subject with Mr. Irwin but she must. The time cards were completed and the men were paid in cash every Friday afternoon. But she was the one keeping the books. This is what Mr. Irwin had hired her for, to keep his books and advise him about any problem areas. This wasn't just a problem; this was violation of the law. Sophie wasn't an accountant but she was certainly as knowledgeable as one. She must tell him.

Sophie could see Irwin Improvements' bank statements reflected gross earnings from those accounts that were invoiced and paid by check, Mr. Irwin was not keeping all his money in his business account. When he received checks he kept his deposits up to cover expenses but little more than that. Bank failings weren't all that far in the past and she could understand that. She assumed he had other bank accounts he didn't want her to see. She could understand that as well. She thought Mr. Irwin would be forthright about his profits when it came time to post his income tax next spring. She made no attempt to probe into it for the time being.

By the fall of 1939 Herbert had hired more employees. He would soon have one hundred machinists and factory workers. Production was at an all time high and the lingering effects of the Depression were a disagreeable memory. Herbert was satisfied with his overall operation. His Welderz Frend was his real money maker. He had lost count of how many he had produced since his earliest model in 1925. The improved product he now made enjoyed a wide reputation for ease of operation and safety. The Welderz Frend had followed pipeline construction as they snaked their way up to Denver, Chicago, Indianapolis, and Minneapolis. Herbert had shipped acetylene generators all over the Midwest, Oklahoma, Louisiana, but most were in Texas.

Herbert's royalties from earlier agricultural inventions merchandized to International Harvester, John Deere, Case, and Massey Ferguson had been accumulating for years. Some inventions he had sold outright, others he retained minor royalties that added up over time. No one knew about this aspect of his wealth.

Herbert's bookkeeper was working out well, although he disliked having anyone know that much about his business. He was still in the habit of hoarding cash and wasn't about to leave it in any bank. Use them he would but only because business demanded it.

Sophie minded her own business as much as possible in her position. When Herbert was in the office he watched Sophie quietly tap her figures on the adding machine keys and make her notations. He still wondered why he could not do that. Numbers seemed to reverse, add and subtract at will, until he couldn't make any sense of them. They were abstracts. But there was one thing he knew *very* well, how much money he had accumulated. Money was a material, real thing that held worth. He could touch it, look at it and, bury it. No one would ever know how much he had. To Herbert money was freedom to pursue his work. The more money he had the more freedom he had. Herbert was a wealthy man.

Sophie came into the office one morning and sat down at her desk facing her employer. She could not remain silent any longer and took a deep breath. "Mr. Irwin, I must talk to you about something with your payroll. I'm your bookkeeper and it is my responsibility to advise you correctly."

Herbert looked at her, immediately on guard when the subject of money came up. He could not shake the conviction someone was always seeking ways to take it from him.

"Mr. Irwin, you do know the federal government passed a Social Security tax in 1935, right?" When she received no response from him she tried again.

"President Roosevelt's tax bill? Remember all the old people who lost their savings in the banks that failed? They had no income or savings anymore. Thousands were too old to work and had nothing to live on. That's what the tax was for. For the ones who couldn't help themselves."

Herbert was seconds from rising from his chair in anger but restrained himself because Sophie was a woman. She took advantage of that moment and began again.

"Mr. Irwin, you are supposed to be withholding a percentage from of your employees' pay. It's not much, just a few dollars. You are supposed to be sending this to the federal government quarterly. The grace period is over with. I'm afraid if you don't you are in violation of the law. It is my responsibility to tell you that. I can have your next pay period in compliance with the tax and can recover it for the last tax year."

Sophie hardly got the words out before Herbert exploded. She sat glued to her chair as Mr. Irwin yelled at her. She watched him stride around the desk and begin pacing as if he had more rage in him than his body could contain. He was not screaming at her but at Franklin Roosevelt. His face was red and contorted in anger. Sophie wanted to leave but if she got up she would run into him. So she sat silently. She knew he would be mad but did not expect uncontrollable fury.

A Second Hit

Herbert stopped in the small office and glared at Sophie in that piercing gaze that so unnerved her. He hissed the word, *"No,"* and strode out the door. He was down the steps and out of the building. Sophie was a strong woman but she was shaking after witnessing such a tirade. She tried to calm herself and began work again.

Soon the shop manager came up the steps into the office and asked, "What happened? We saw the boss jump down the steps. He walked right past us and is holed up in his house."

"I told him he needed to start withholding Social Security Tax. He blew up."

"Whew, I could have told you that would happen. He hates Roosevelt."

"He may hate him but it is the law nonetheless. He told me, no."

"Well, I guess you gotta make a choice. Either do as he asks or quit. Sophie, please stay. I know one thing, he's not going to pay that tax with you or without you."

Sophie nervously fussed with her hair and went back to her ledgers. She didn't know what to do.

Herbert continued his pacing inside his house. His ranting made complete sense to him. If people would work they wouldn't run out of money. It was their fault. Roosevelt wanted workers to support someone who wasn't even kin? Nonsense! Take money out of his workers' payroll? They didn't want it. They had their own families to support. They would start demanding more money to make up for the loss in tax. No, he would not do it!

Herbert's blowup at Sophie was overlooked when he came to the office a few days later. She said nothing and wondered if he would apologize to her. Silence. He acted as if the outburst had never happened. If that was how Mr.

A Second Hit

Irwin chose to handle the situation Sophie was resigned to accept it. She did not mention the Social Security tax again even though she knew Mr. Irwin would be confronted about it one day.

Herbert continued to work his customary sixteen to eighteen-hour days. During this decade, the 1930s in Amarillo, Herbert had more interaction with people on a daily basis than he had in the past or ever would again. This was as close as Herbert would come to being a conventional member of society.

No one was really close enough to Herbert to see him drifting farther away and losing his grip on traditional culture. Herbert's behavior was a compulsory way of life. He had always been a loner and would always be one. On the surface he was still the same pleasant, successful businessman. But within his mind, Herbert was slipping deeper into an isolated world of his own making.

A Second Hit

The Gut Punch

Chapter Seven

The Gut Punch

Herbert had been manufacturing the Welderz Frend for sixteen years. The pipelines that fanned out from the Texas Panhandle took its reputation for ease of operation to the ends of the pipelines.

One of those many contractors was Oklahoma City general contractor, Leo F. Brauer. Most of his work dealt with heavy equipment but pipeline construction was part of his business as well. As familiar as Brauer was with general contracting he knew this acetylene generator was superior to others he used. He decided this welder would be an asset worth having. Brauer wrote Irwin Improvements about the possibility of licensing the welder and if the owner was so inclined, to possibly sell it.

When Herbert received his first proposal from Brauer he replied he was not interested in selling or licensing the Welderz Frend. Still, he kept Brauer's name in case he ever changed his mind. There were many oxyacetylene generators on the market, and technology was steadily moving toward new innovations in the whole science.

Herbert was a good employer in that he paid his workers on time. He was never one to give favors and although he knew some of his men for years, he was not close to any of them.

Herbert had worked with one of his employees at Willborn Brothers as a tank welder. Both had been healthy, strong, and capable of long hours and hard work then. Whereas Herbert left and became a manufacturer Delmar was older and stayed with Willborn Brothers. It was an occupational hazard for tank welders to climb on partially completed tanks to weld seams up the sides and across the top. Delmar slipped one day and fell twenty feet to the ground after hitting hard against the metal tank. It was three months before Delmar could go back to tank welding. He was never the same after that fall.

At his age Delmar was having trouble keeping up with the younger welders. Willborn Brothers was on the verge of letting him go when Delmar heard Herbert Irwin was hiring. The prospect of working in a factory appealed to Delmar. He would not have to climb those huge tanks perched on scaffolding with ropes trying to weld. He went to see Irwin Improvements. Remembering his skill Herbert readily hired him. Delmar knew Herbert was in his mid-forties because he had just turned sixty-two. Herbert walked easily up the steps to his office while Delmar limped stiffly around the dirt floor of the factory. The work was hard even though it was on level ground.

When Delmar read about the Social Security benefit bill that Franklin Roosevelt introduced it seemed like a blessing from heaven. If he and his wife had a garden and raised chickens and he took a few odd jobs they could make it on Social Security. Men in their sixties didn't often retire in that era but doing so was really attractive to Delmar. He read if he was born before 1929 he would have to work only a few quarters to qualify. Delmar paid close attention to the few details noted in the newspapers and was one of the first to sign up for the benefit at the Post Office. He had to hang on a little longer. Delmar would be sixty-five soon.

The Gut Punch

Delmar waited several months and finally a letter from the Social Security office came. Delmar was puzzled. The letter stated he had not paid into the program and was not eligible.

When the shop manager handed his cash to him every Friday Delmar realized the 1% that should have been deducted from his pay was still intact. He waited for the manager to say the reason his pay was short was because they were deducting the Social Security benefit. It never happened. Finally, Delmar asked why? When asked the manager told him Mr. Irwin didn't believe in the program.

Delmar went home thinking what does a body do if your employer doesn't take part in the Social Security? Does that mean he can't get it? Delmar was desperate enough to ask questions of some of his friends at Willborn Brothers. He learned his former employer had been withholding Social Security from their pay since 1937. This was 1939. Several of his older friends had qualified and were due to retire soon. With all the grumbling from younger workers, with the controversial Supreme Court decision as to its constitutionality, even with some employers refusing to comply, the benefit was still valid.

Reluctantly, Delmar wrote the Social Security Board. He remembered the many times Herbert had fixed his old clunker and didn't charge him for repairs. He remembered Herbert hiring him when no one else would. He had so much respect and admiration for Herbert Irwin, but Delmar thought if he didn't retire soon he would have to quit with nothing to sustain him. He had to. In his letter Delmar stated he had applied for Social Security but his employer, Irwin Improvements, did not withhold for it. Was there any way he could still get the benefit?

The Gut Punch

The second week in October Sophie was working quietly on her ledgers and Herbert was typing correspondence. One of the men came upstairs and poked his head inside the door. "Mr. Irwin, there's a man downstairs wants to see you. Says he's from the government. From Austin."

Herbert paused from his typing and thought someone coming to see him from the government must have something to do with his generator. What could they want? Maybe the Army wanted to buy his generator. That war in Europe was getting worse and this may have something to do with that. In anticipation of a government contract Herbert rose, took his hat, and followed the man downstairs. Sophie had an uneasy feeling and wondered at the pleased expression on Mr. Irwin's face. She handed the ledgers to Mr. Irwin every week and had no idea what he did with them thereafter. She was still worried about the taxes she knew he was not paying.

Herbert walked into the yard to see a man standing beside his car. The man tipped his hat and introduced himself.

"Mr. Irwin? I'm Wendell Styles with the Treasury Department." Herbert looked at the man's open wallet to see a gleaming badge on one side of the fold and an identification card on the other. Herbert was still thinking about a government contract for his generator.

Styles extended his hand but Irwin did not take it. Styles continued.

"Good to meet you, sir, good to meet you. My, you have some operation here. I don't believe I've seen this much activity in one place before. No sir, few places in Amarillo, anyway." Herbert was proud of his factory and gave a rare smile.

"I would sure appreciate a tour of your factory, Mr. Irwin. You make oxyacetylene generators don't you?"

The Gut Punch

Herbert nodded and turned toward the larger of his two workshops to show his assembly line to what he assumed was a government procurement agent. They walked inside the metal workshop with a background noise of hammers banging and metal saws screaming. Welders were bent over dozens of partially completed generators. The stench of fired metal fouled the air along with the smell of chemical. The noise was deafening. Styles tried to shout a question but gave up and just observed. He saw fogged light streaming in from the sooted windows. The carbide lights overhead gave a white light that lit up the dim workshop. Styles was impressed with the two wind powered generators that dominated the factory yard. He noticed dozens of generators provided electricity for the grinders and saws, all powered by the wind. Herbert walked slowly with his guest, mentally constructing his invention as they moved along the line of workers. Had he been capable of the emotion Herbert would have said he loved his welder. They reached the far end of the building and walked out into the bright sunlight.

"My, my, that sure is impressive, Mr. Irwin. Sure impressive. How many men do you have working here?"

Herbert proudly said, "Sixty-five on the welders. I have more men in the machine shop."

Styles said, "Do you now? Could I see that?"

Herbert walked to the shorter, lower profile old building that was on the property when he bought it. A minute inside the building, Styles jumped at the blare of a steam locomotive's horn. Styles looked through the barred, dirty glass windows to see boxcars and gondolas flying past the fence of Irwin's property, barely eighty feet from the walls of the workshop. The freight train shook the ground under them and the carbide lamps overhead trembled and swung back and forth. None of the men inside the workshop seemed to notice. Styles looked around at the various dies and casting tools, molds, grinders, forges, and the many small generators powering the tools; strange not to have commercial electricity for an operation this size. The high-pitched whine and grinding was as loud as the other building. Styles saw oil field drill bits, bores, joints, and other industry related tools he couldn't name, nor did he know what they were for. Styles took a tally of the men working in this shop.

Herbert stepped outside with Styles and they walked toward the main workshop again.

Styles proposed a statement only for clarification. "You must have another thirty men in your machine shop."

Herbert was quick to correct him. "Thirty-three. With my shop foremen and delivery man I employ one hundred men."

"Is that right? Most impressive, Mr. Irwin, most impressive. Well then, why don't we go to your office and talk? You know why I'm here don't you?"

Herbert stopped. He didn't like the change in Styles' tone of voice. "The government wants to buy my generator."

"No. No, I'm afraid not. I'm with the U.S. Treasury Department, Mr. Irwin. It has come to our attention you are not paying Social Security on your employees. Is that correct?"

In a second Herbert leaped from pride to resentful anger. Someone had turned him in, and he thought he knew who.

Styles saw the look on Herbert Irwin's face and immediately established his position of authority. "Now you can get mad all you want Mr. Irwin, but the law is the law. You can either cooperate or make it hard on yourself. Unless you can show me proof you have withheld Social Security tax on your employees, but more importantly paid it, I'm afraid the United States Treasury Department will have to take appropriate action. I have the authority to look at your books. I have the authority to freeze your bank accounts. I have the authority to seize your assets, your inventory, and your property. Now do you want to sit down and talk or do I need to bring an armed agent with me?"

Herbert looked at Styles' face and could see nothing but bureaucratic socialism: laws that hurt manufacturers and producers. They enabled the lazy to feed off the industriousness of others. It had nothing to do with him breaking any new law! Herbert wasn't the only employer in Texas not paying the Social Security tax. There were hundreds like him who thought the tax was wrong and refused to pay it. Who turned him in? *Who?*

Herbert was livid and screamed at the man. "Get out of here! Get off my property! I'm not paying Roosevelt one cent of my money. Get out!"

Styles could see Irwin was nearly out of control and decided he needed to give him time to calm down. He would come back with an armed security agent.

"All right, Mr. Irwin. I'm leaving. But I will be back with an armed agent and a warrant. The law is the law. You better think about it and if I were you I'd comply or you could lose everything. It's up to you. I will be here at noon the first Wednesday in November and you had better be here. You have until then to think about it." Styles walked to his car and drove away.

Shaking, Herbert leaped up the steps to his office. When he stepped inside the door Sophie backed away from him. He scared her when he was like this. Herbert's expression erased the times she saw him looking at her. The occasional pleasant words between them might never have been spoken.

The Gut Punch

Herbert seethed with anger at Sophie, "You had to tell them didn't you? You couldn't wait to turn me in. You think I've broken the law? I did not! It's not right!"

"Mr. Irwin, I don't know what you are talking about. I didn't turn you in to anybody. Who was that downstairs?"

"You know who it was! The Treasury Department! You told them about the Social Security tax, didn't you?"

Sophie pleaded her innocence, "No, I did not! I told you they would find out eventually but you wouldn't listen to me. Mr. Irwin, I told you they would!"

Herbert wheeled around not believing one word from her. "You're fired. Get your things and get out of here. I don't want to see you on this property again. Get out!"

For all his irrational temper Mr. Irwin firing her shocked Sophie. She saw obstinate self-righteousness in his face, which bewildered her even more. She didn't do anything – *he* was the one who didn't pay the tax! She was just his bookkeeper. She warned him and tried to reason with him and now he was blaming her. Sophie picked up her few things in the crocheted bag she carried to work. She looked at Herbert Irwin with tears in her eyes and left.

Sophie was crying as she drove back to town. If there had ever been any remote possibility she, an old maid, could marry any man, Herbert Irwin would have been him. He was so eccentric, so moody, so driven …. and so brilliant. Sophie must have been mistaken when she thought she felt a comfortable silence when they were alone in the office. She dismissed those pleasant conversations they had. It was ridiculous to have such thoughts. She laughed at herself. She had never addressed him by his first name. They had never even shaken hands. Sophie never saw Herbert again.

Herbert shut himself in his house pacing. He blamed lawyers, lawmakers, and slandered Roosevelt. He was furious at Sophie. She was the first and only woman he had ever trusted. His disappointment in her stung particularly hard. He would never make that mistake again.

Before he was to see him again Wendall Styles did some investigative work on Herbert Irwin. Styles secured a warrant and spoke to the judge. He studied Irwin Improvements' bank account and noted there was only enough in the account to operate the business. It showed little comparative activity, which indicated Irwin dealt in cash. He didn't need an accountant to know there was more money floating around that wasn't being properly validated. Too often with Treasury Department investigations it uncovered IRS inconsistencies.

Styles searched the county records and could find no liens or lawsuits. He found people in Amarillo who knew Herbert Irwin and his overall reputation was good. "Mechanical genius" was repeated several times. Generally they referred to him as "eccentric" but fair. He could be hard to work with at times. Well, we'll see how hard he is to work with faced with fines and seizure.

Styles was back at the factory, this time accompanied by an armed agent. He had briefed the man about Irwin's temper and told him not to put up with any nonsense with him. The shop manager escorted the men to the stairs and returned to his work.

Herbert sat at his desk with papers strewn in front of him. He glared at Styles and only gave a cursory glance at the man with the sidearm at his belt. Styles was pleasant, but firm.

"Mr. Irwin, I want to see your payroll ledgers. Here is the warrant. I've already looked at your bank account. You obviously make enough to pay your employees industry wage. It is my job to figure out how much you owe Social Security and I intend to do it."

Herbert pulled his ledgers from the shelf and placed them on the desk. After a few minutes Styles said, "Who does your books?"

"Sophie Roberts did. I fired her."

"Why?"

"Because she turned me in and you know it."

Styles paused and said, "No, it wasn't your bookkeeper I can tell you that. And don't ask because we wouldn't tell you who it was anyway."

Herbert didn't believe him and said nothing. He sat stifled and bound by ridiculous laws he had no power to fight. The hours ticked by on the clock. He watched Styles make notes. The other agent stood, paced, sat, and watched him. Herbert reached into his desk once and saw the agent place his hand on his pistol. The gesture disgusted Herbert. Late that afternoon Styles closed the ledgers and stretched in the chair.

"That is all for today, Mr. Irwin. I will be here at eight o'clock in the morning. I don't need to do a complete audit. I am only looking at certain entries. Your bookkeeper was exceptional. I think by tomorrow afternoon I can make you an offer to settle this. You owe the Treasury Department money – it is only a question of how much. If you want to dispute my findings you will need to hire an attorney but that is entirely up to you. Good day, sir."

Herbert sat alone in his office wondering how he could fight this. Socialist laws! If people would work they wouldn't need handouts like Social Security. If people would save their money like he had they wouldn't have lost it in the banks. That was their fault. Why should he have to support the lazy ones?

The Gut Punch

Before Styles went to Irwin Improvements the next morning, he had a short interview with Sophie Roberts. Styles wanted to verify Herbert Irwin knew of the tax and had been properly informed it was law. They outlined their discussion as to time frame and content. Reluctantly, Sophie answered his questions matter of fact as she knew she must.

Later, Styles again poured over Irwin Improvement's ledgers. This time he asked for employee records, hiring dates, those let go and others hired. Irwin Improvements earlier records weren't complete but Sophie Roberts had set up excellent files.

Herbert turned them over without protest. He was still convinced of his moral high ground and thought he had a solution to his dilemma. Herbert was going to play along with this charade until he had enough of it. Styles threat of arrest was the only thing that kept Herbert's temper in check.

Late in the afternoon Styles closed the books and spent another hour going over his notes and figures. He consulted a handbook, figured, scratched his head and asked questions. Sometimes Herbert answered them and other times he was evasive about employee overtime and compensation. The Treasury agent was annoyed with Herbert and threatened him more than once.

Styles was frustrated he couldn't pinpoint an exact figure for Irwin Improvement's profits. Styles was trying to establish potential for repayment of back tax. He had a figure in mind but knew it was not accurate. There might well be an additional case against Irwin with the IRS. He would have to rely on the Treasury Department's final option: any tax collected was better than none. They certainly didn't want to jail anyone. Prosecution was expensive and time consuming.

The Gut Punch

"All right, Mr. Irwin. You and I both know you've done a pretty thorough job of hiding your income. I'll let that pass for the moment. Most your employee earnings are fairly straightforward. I paid close attention as you've added men to your work force. You've got some names that have turned up as being paid but no record as to how much. I had to estimate and I'm pretty good at that. A conservative figure, and I do mean conservative, this is what I think you owe the Treasury Department."

Styles shoved a form toward Herbert and pointed to a figure in the middle of the page.

He continued. "This is my proposal to you: we know that's a lot of money and to show you how cooperative the government is we will allow you pay that off over three years. I have the authority to recommend penalties be levied against you but I'm not going to do that if you pay the back taxes. From your production levels that shouldn't be hard. However, in good faith you also have to start payroll deductions immediately. You will send quarterly reports to Austin verifying your compliance with the law. You do that and we'll forget about any seizures of assets."

Herbert made every effort to control himself when he looked at the figure estimation of his tax bill. *Never.* He would not pay it. His voice was tight with anger. He glared at Styles and said, "No. I won't pay it."

Styles sighed. He backed up his demand with a real threat. "Mr. Irwin, I'm going to remind you again. If you don't pay that money we'll get it one way or another. Unless you want the Treasury Department to confiscate your property and sell it off for taxes you had better reconsider. I can have you thrown in jail for tax fraud, do you understand that? I'm going to give you another week to reconsider our proposal. I'll be back the last Tuesday in November at noon.

The Gut Punch

I want you to think real hard about your options. I will sit down with you then and we will work out terms for repayment. It is up to you if this goes any further. Good day, sir."

Styles left thinking about the look in Herbert Irwin's face. He didn't see any "give" there at all. He thought of another way to persuade Irwin. Family. He knew Irwin had several brothers. He would speak with them and ask for their intervention. It had worked for him before.

Before Styles returned to Austin he called Felix Irwin. Felix told Styles he had no influence whatsoever on his brother. He doubted Herbert would even speak to him and he refused to see him. Styles again tried to persuade Felix to speak to his brother but he would not. Styles then called on Carmon.

Carmon listened as Wendell Styles explained Herbert's predicament. He hadn't seen Herbert for some time but he would try to convince Herbert to cooperate. The brothers' visit was over in minutes, with Herbert lashing out in protest.

Carmon told Styles Herbert wouldn't listen to him or anyone and the family relationship was strained. Styles literally begged this family to get involved and convince Herbert Irwin to pay the tax. For the third time he spoke to Felix, Carmon, and finally, Ruey. Sensing some influence Styles took a detour to Floydada to see this brother before returning to Austin.

Ruey sat alone in his kitchen and told Styles a similar family saga. Ruey agreed to see his brother but told Styles not to expect any change in Herbert. Styles drove back to Austin thinking, what a strange family. They lived within a hundred miles and didn't communicate? Or was it just Herbert Irwin that was different?

The Gut Punch

Together, the Irwin brothers discussed their brother's tax problems. They did not want an Irwin in jail for tax fraud. They had far too much pride for that. Reputation was everything here. That government fellow seemed like a pretty reasonable man but they also knew Herbert was supremely stubborn. The others had long given up on him but Ruey tried one last time to convince Herbert.

Ruey sat with Herbert at his small table in his house and neither said a word for several minutes. Ruey glanced around the stripped down room. His own did not look that much different and he was the only one who halfway understood why Herbert lived like this.

Ruey said, "That Treasury Department man came to see us. Herbert, if I was you I'd pay that money. The family thinks you should cooperate. Get them off your back. Pay 'em whatever they say you owe them. The country is changing."

"I will not! That law is wrong. Wrong! People ought to work."

Ruey paused. "Yeah, they should. But you and me, we wouldn't survive in jail. Don't let it come to that. I'd pay 'em."

Herbert was determined but the thought of jail chilled him. He didn't answer for several minutes. With his decision solidifying over the course of a week Herbert had thought of another way to beat the government at their own game. "I need to hide some money on your place."

Ruey was sure he did not want to be between the federal government and Herbert. "Now, I don't know about that. What if they come to me hunting it? Then I'd be in trouble. You could marry and put your money in your wife's name, you know."

Herbert blanched thinking of Sophie's betrayal and snapped back, "No!"

"Ycah, I know." Ruey knew he and Herbert would ever marry.

Herbert thought of what would entice Ruey to help him. "If you let me hide my money on your farm I'll make good on it. I don't want any part of the old man's land or money. He'll pass it on eventually. I'll sign my part over to you before I ever take a nickel from him."

Ruey pondered the risks and decided if Herbert did hide any money it would take a mighty smart Treasury man to find it. "All right. Do what you want. But don't tell me where it is. I don't want to know. And I'll take you up on that offer." Ruey slipped quietly out the door and left.

Herbert had yet another week to think about what to do. He paced in his house late into the night sifting through his options. Paying the tax wasn't one of them. He reflected on lots of things besides Social Security and finally came to a workable decision. Herbert recalled the cash he had stockpiled all these years. He was wealthy enough to do pretty much anything he wanted, wherever he wanted. He had proven his ability and success. He didn't need to convince anyone of his achievements, regardless of what the family thought of him. Herbert pondered on manufacturing in general and the effort it took to run his business. He thought of all the time he used to devote to inventing. He thought about the bad things that had happened to him in Texas.

Herbert studied his industry's trends around the nation. He had read in the Farm Journal about prospects in Florida. He read about the industry Florida was drawing due to the European war. Herbert had a plan of action and he would begin preparations immediately.

The Gut Punch

Wendell Styles was preparing to make one last trip to Amarillo and force Herbert Irwin into a settlement. The newspaper and wire were reporting ice and snow in the Panhandle of Texas. Styles thought better of the trip and sent a telegram to Irwin he would delay his trip and see him on the following Thursday.

It was the 22nd of November, 1940. Herbert walked to his house in the bitter cold agitated over the weather. Herbert knew a winter storm was descending. No one understood what these storms did to him. Maybe it was the dropping barometric pressure, but whatever it was he could not stand it.

Herbert shut himself up in his house and shuttered the windows. He had plenty of coal for his stove and enough food to last him until the storm was over. As freezing rain began to fall on the 23rd Herbert became increasingly nervous. He tried to occupy himself with drafting an idea but concentration was impossible. As was his habit during bad weather Herbert began pacing his anxiety. The floor of the room was worn down to bare wood and marked his path. His compulsion kept him pacing for hours and was only interrupted to add more coal to the stove. Herbert recognized this was going to be a terrible storm, worse than he could remember.

The tinkle of frozen rain blowing against the shutters and roof seemed like cymbals clanging. The wind whistled around the house more like a train coming through it. The storm continued into the night until Herbert paced himself into exhaustion and fell into his bed. His fitful sleep lasted only a few hours and he rose again, adding more coal to his stove. He mumbled and talked to himself by the hour. He was so upset he could not eat and paced again. Only his rhythmic pacing, step, step, step, step, step, swish of his shoe turning, step, step, step, step, step, swish, kept Herbert halfway stable.

For two and a half days the freezing rain fell over the Panhandle. It toppled and split trees. The ice brought down electrical lines, iced over roads, and locked the high plains in hard ice. Workers could not get to their jobs and equipment froze. Cattle on the prairie sought shelter on the leeside of hills but still froze to death. Thanksgiving preparations were abandoned, as it became a question of surviving the ice storm. The oil refinery was still. The white streets of the city were vacant. Amarillo was frozen and quiet. The water system failed, cemented in ice. By November 27th the temperature warmed enough the ice began melting and a silenced industrial city slowly stirred to life. People would talk of the Great Ice Storm of 1940 in their old age and remember a bitter, cold killer.

Herbert didn't leave his house for a week. It took that long to regain his equilibrium and think rationally again. He remembered reading about Florida and how beautiful the weather was supposed to be. With all the bizarre weather patterns the high plains was famous for, it had never been this bad. Herbert didn't think he could survive another winter storm like that one. His mind was made up. He would move south away from ice storms.

After Styles' last trip Herbert had gone to Ruey's farm before dark with three leather satchels of cash. There were still things Herbert was worried about. First and foremost was the most disturbing of the threats Styles had made to him – jail. Ruey was right. He couldn't survive prison; not one day, not one meal, not one hour living with another human being. The next thing that worried him was Styles digging further into his income. Sure he had hidden his profits. Everyone did. Herbert dealt in cash whenever he could and that was often. He paid income tax but nothing like he should. That was his business. And last, the whole principle in which this conflict was based. He would have to pay Social Security hereafter and support those unwilling to work, or those who had squandered their money. He would not do it.

When Styles came for their next meeting Herbert was ready for him. Styles was prepared for battle and was thoroughly willing to arrest Irwin. If he did not cooperate he had advised his agent accordingly.

"All right, Mr. Irwin. I hope you've slept on it and decided what is in your best interest. We're not unreasonable. How do you want to pay the tax? Quarterly or monthly?"

Herbert said, "You've made me a proposal and now I'll make you one."

"Mr. Irwin, you are hardly in a bargaining position."

"No? You think I have a lot of money? Well, you try and find it. I'm not paying you that. You close the books on your Social Security tax. And I never see you or anyone from your department again. I'm not paying any employee tax."

Styles smiled. "Mr. Irwin, do you think we are playing games? This is the law and if you are going to continue manufacturing you *will* pay the Social Security tax. You don't have any choice."

"Oh, but I do. I'll shut this place down and then what tax are you going to collect then? None."

Styles snorted, confident in his position. "You wouldn't give this up. You're making too much money. No one would."

"Want to bet? That war going on in Europe, it's only a matter of time before the US gets involved in it. I know. I saw the same thing before the first war. They're going to need machine shops, lots of them. No one can do work like my shop can. They're going to need my welder, too."

Styles looked at Irwin and thought this man is not bluffing. He was sure Irwin was just hardheaded enough he would pull a stunt like that. He had to wrap this case up and move on. He had spent too much time with Irwin Improvements. He had been given his guidelines before coming to Amarillo. Faced with going through seizure and liquidating this conglomeration of metal and machines, he would at least listen to Irwin. He knew some agents had foregone collection with other employers entirely and simply initiated compliance.

"Mr. Irwin, I still have the authority to seize your assets. I know we can get enough out of this place to pay your debt, especially with your equipment. But let's make this easy on both of us."

Herbert calmly said, "I wrote up an agreement. You sign this and I want that man to witness it."

Styles wasn't used to anyone bargaining with him and read the agreement Irwin placed on the desk. Herbert had typed the amount of the agreement, which obligated the Treasury Department to accept his check as full payment for all back taxes and relinquishing any claim to his property, his bank accounts, or his equipment.

The ice storm had delayed Styles a whole week and he was weary of Herbert Irwin and his stubbornness. He took the check and signed the agreement. The other agent witnessed it and stepped back.

Styles said, "All right, Mr. Irwin. I'll take it. And you're getting off cheap. But you won't be able to manufacture a bucket unless you pay the tax from now on. I'll see to that."

"No, you won't because there won't be anything left for you to tax."

The Gut Punch

Herbert stood and grabbed a bullhorn from the floor and stepped out onto the metal platform of the office overlooking the factory below. He yelled into the bullhorn so loud his voice carried over the din of noise.

"Everyone, stop! You are out of a job thanks to Franklin Roosevelt! Get out! Leave." Herbert turned and looked at Styles stunned face. Herbert stood outside the office door and pointed down the steps. "Now get out of here!"

Styles was momentarily confused as to what to do next. If Irwin stopped manufacturing and quit his machine shop operation there would be no tax revenue for the Treasury Department. He looked at Irwin's defiant face and realized he was dead serious. This man was willing to walk away from his business rather than pay the Social Security tax. Amazing.

Styles rose and took his hat convinced Herbert Irwin was nuts. There was nothing left for him to do but leave.

The men stood in hushed silence as they watched the two men walk to their car. The shop foreman gestured for the men to shut the welders down and turn the generators off. As each machine stopped the noise level decreased until the only sound was the murmuring of the men. They knew something momentous was happening, but this? One of the men had run to the other workshop and related the news. Soon more men filed into the larger workshop.

Herbert took his bullhorn again this time calmer but still agitated. "Turn your hours in. You'll draw your pay today. Don't come back. This factory is closed." Herbert retreated to his house not bothering to thank them for their hard work or loyalty all these years.

Herbert thought seriously about the offer Leo Brauer had made him almost a year before. Herbert wrote him with a counter offer. He would sell his Welderz Frend generator

The Gut Punch

only if he bought his factory, machine shop, and land as a package deal. Herbert placed a ridiculously high price on it. He established a value for his eight patents, the land, the machine shop, and the factory. Herbert was convinced the war in Europe would make his factory and machine shop valuable.

Herbert inventoried his machine shop and withheld only enough equipment a buyer could consider it a fully furnished machine shop. Over the next two weeks Herbert liquidating some of his equipment. He offered other machine shops his grinders, metal saws, band saws, oxyacetylene generators, forges, dozens of small generators, casts and dies, borers, and stacks of tools and toolboxes. There was no shortage of buyers. Every piece was negotiated for cash. He sold his machine works contracts to his competitors.

Herbert systematically emptied his factory of equipment except the necessary machinery to manufacture acetylene generators. It too, was a fully functional factory and could be started up immediately.

Herbert kept everything else, a formidable amount of machinery for one man. He looked at the dozens of partially completed generators and reserved them as well. Herbert walked through his stilled factory. The cold dirt floor was spotted and pockmarked where equipment had stood.

Leo Brauer received Herbert Irwin's offer with interest but shook his head at the price. He wanted the factory but was undecided about the machine shop. He would speak to a business partner who might be interested. Maybe they could put something together but Irwin must come down on his price. Leo Brauer wanted the Welderz Frend with its patents. He too, was convinced the US would enter the war eventually. It was the first week of December, 1940.

1941 – 1948

Filed Jan. 26, 1925   3 Sheets—Sheet 1

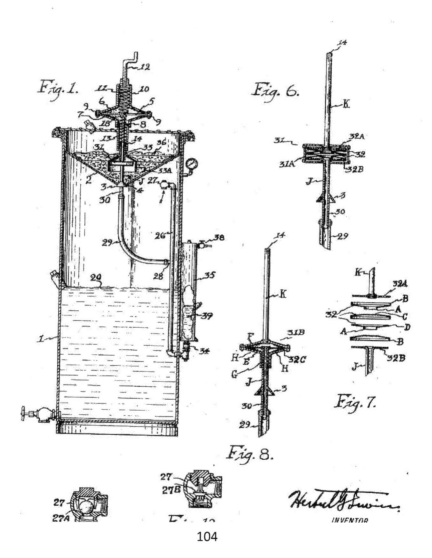

Fig. 1.

Fig. 6.

Fig. 7.

Fig. 8.

INVENTOR

104

Chapter Eight

Starting Over

Herbert had enough accumulated reasons to shake the dust of Texas off his feet, never to return. His family, the Treasury Department, imminent war, and finally, he didn't think he could handle another ice storm like that last one. He had contended with the extremes of Texas weather all his life but it had never been like that. Tolerating the extremes of weather was harder now than when he was young. Herbert reasoned a southern climate would help his stability and he would not have to endure summer dust storms and winter ice storms.

The ominous press reports of the war in Europe left him no doubt the US would be involved soon. He well remembered *The Texas Spur* prior to entering the first war and how every issue brought more warnings. Herbert kept up with his industry in trade periodicals and read where businesses where converting to wartime products.

Several articles mentioned the relationship to Roosevelt's Lend Lease proposal to support the United Kingdom in their war effort. The signs were everywhere and it was only a matter of time. Of the states with a desirable southern climate that were investing in wartime industries, Florida had risen to the top of his possibility list.

An article in *The Farm Journal* about development in Florida mentioned one of the largest landowners in the state, Consolidated Naval Stores. Herbert wrote them stating he was interested in property in the southern portion of the state. He received a list of available property and after sifting through a stack of scattered tracts he kept coming back to one particular parcel of land north of Okeechobee, Florida.

The simplified plat showed a tract of land in a sparsely settled area bordered on three sides by a state highway and secondary roads. Herbert was familiar with those elements that make for desirable property. But he knew he must physically see the land and the surrounding area. The only thing the property did not have was a railroad. That wasn't of any real importance since he had decided not to manufacture on a large scale again. The town of Okeechobee was only eight miles south from the property. If he needed to ship anything he could do so from there. He would have to go to Florida to make an informed decision.

Herbert wrote the Consolidated Naval Stores he wanted to see the property. He was referred to real estate agent and insurance man, Karl Stello. Herbert wrote Stello and made an appointment for late January, 1941 and made plans for the long trip. The only other lengthy trips Herbert had made were by rail in the Army. He liked the train itself but hated the people on it. He could not tolerate being that close to people anymore. He would drive to Florida, sleep in his truck, and eat on the road.

Herbert packed the few belongings he would need in his old Ford truck. The prospect of moving again caused him anxiety but Herbert recalled the far worse trauma of the ice storm. This would be the last time. He was sure of it.

Herbert packed a sleeping bag, a box of food, and a couple changes of clothes. Before dawn he hid a sizable amount of money in the hidden compartment he had welded inside the door of his truck. If the land was what he hoped he would buy it without hesitation. He took $10,000 cash.

Starting Over

On his way out of town Herbert stopped for gas and glanced at the December 26th *Amarillo Daily News*. An article about machine shops caught his eye. Herbert read where in 1940 the National Machine Tool Builders Association doubled their production from 1939 to meet defense demands. The Washington DC report stated the Defense Department survey wrote levels were still insufficient. They predicted an increase at least by another third, in machine tool production in 1941. Herbert bought the newspaper; this meant his machine shop was worth even more than he thought. He would set a price on it accordingly.

Herbert camped on roadsides and other than a minor mechanical problem, his four-day trip was largely uneventful. As he drove into the southern part of Florida he was enthralled with the green profusion of tropical plants, palm trees, and palmettos. Herbert couldn't help but compare the dry vegetation of the Panhandle. Herbert was generally oblivious to his natural surroundings but the green overwhelmed him. He saw cattle and sheep grazing on lush grass. He compared Texas where several acres were needed to feed a cow and calf. Pasture here could support a small herd on very little acreage. Herbert was compelled to stop when he came upon his first orange grove. This was winter but he saw orderly lines of orange trees, some still growing small greenish oranges, and other groves already picked from the harvest. A few oranges were still left on the trees.

Herbert studied the orchard and wondered what a fresh orange tasted like. He had tasted oranges grown in the Rio Grande Valley in Texas but these were different. He knew this grove had been harvested and was dormant until spring. He saw some dropped underneath on the ground. He walked to a tree and pulled a branch down. He reached up until he was able to reach a late orange and plucked it. Herbert smelled the strong citrus odor of the orange and dug his fingernails into the orange and peeled back a section of orange. He sniffed it again and cautiously ate the segment. The juice burst in his mouth with a tart sweet taste, the texture unlike anything he had experienced before. It was wonderful. Herbert returned to his truck his senses pleasantly stimulated with the new taste and smell of a tree ripened orange, remarkably, in winter. What an amazing climate.

At noon Herbert drove to the insurance office of Karl Stello. Stello rose from his desk to greet his potential client. When he asked if he was Herbert Irwin, the man only nodded. He introduced his wife Marie and Irwin nodded to her, not bothering to remove his fedora hat. Stello offered to take him around town before they went to see the tract north of town. Herbert did not answer, having already driven around Okeechobee all morning to look at what this town had to offer in the form of industry and hardware.

In his car Stello spoke with enthusiasm and attempted to fill the silence with as much information as he knew about the region and Okeechobee. The only time the real estate agent got any response from Irwin was when they crossed the railroad tracks and Irwin asked about three lots adjoining the tracks with a for sale sign. One of the lots had a workshop that fronted the street. The other lots were empty but were fenced. Stello had invested in these lots some years before and offered them to Irwin. He got no answer.

The little information Herbert gave was he was relocating to Florida from Texas. When they arrived at the property Stello listed the attributes of the land. The east side of the 1400 acres fronted State Highway 15 to Okeechobee. The north and south sides of the property fronted secondary roads that intersected the highway. They drove around its perimeters as much as possible as Stello pointed out his few neighbors. He noted sixty acres of the tract were dissected diagonally by the southern road.

Stello called this the Bimini Community, settled earlier by descendents of moonshiners and bootleggers. It received its name from the proximity to the Bimini Islands in the Bahamas, barely fifty miles from the coast of Florida. Stello explained they normally kept to themselves and were considered good neighbors regardless of how they made a living. Most the other residents raised cattle, were farmers, and had orchards. The seaside town of Fort Pierce was thirty-five miles due east.

Stello showed him picturesque Otter Creek, which split through the property. Stello assured Herbert trout, bream, and perch were caught regularly in it. He related the only time in recent history the property flooded was during the 1926 hurricane. Hurricane gates should have solved the flooding problem even though subsequent storms had not been a severe threat. Other than Texas flash floods in arroyos and creeks Herbert had never experienced a real flood before. He was not familiar with the function of a hurricane gate and the comment did not quite sink in.

The east side of the property was partially cleared but the rest was a wilderness of palmettos, palm trees, thick undergrowth, and huge hardwood trees. They drove up a short dirt drive to a grove of massive live oaks that towered above them. Spanish moss hung from the gnarled limbs. It was truly a beautiful setting. Stello called the grove the White Hammock or the Indian White Hammock. He explained the Army had a camp here during the Seminole Wars. It was a local landmark rich in Florida history, first to the Seminoles and later to the Army that was never able to conquer them.

Herbert looked around him from under the canopy of huge oaks and could hardly see the road from where he stood. Nor, would anyone from the road be able to see into the grove of trees. The lushness of the property was overwhelming. Coming from the high plains of Texas this was a tropical paradise. Herbert walked away from the trees into the sun and dug his heel into the dirt. He squatted down and sifted the sandy topsoil in his hand. Stello was not getting any signals positive or negative from Irwin and said nothing. How could he counter any objections if the man would not say anything? What was he going to do with this property? Could this man afford the land? Herbert Irwin looked around him in silence.

They drove back to town and Herbert asked to see the three city lots. Stello did not press Irwin for any commitment and opened the locked gate to the vacant lots. Herbert walked around the lots and looked inside the tiny workshop without comment.

Herbert had considered opening another machine shop in town and it was still an option though not a serious one. Even if he didn't the lots were perfect for receiving his shipment. Besides, he would need to stay somewhere waiting for the closing of the 1400 acres. It was a prime industrial location and Herbert agreed to buy the three lots if Stello would write up the cash sale deed for "$10 and other considerations." Stello agreed.

Returning to Stello's office Herbert stood at his truck and said he would be inside in a few minutes. Herbert lifted a metal plate to reveal a security box he had welded to the frame of the truck. He opened the padlocked box with a key.

Starting Over

Herbert came in and put a roll of bills on the desk saying simply, "Count it and give me a receipt." With Marie's help Stello did as he was asked while Herbert watched. He wondered just how wealthy Herbert Irwin was. As Marie typed in a blank deed for the city lots Stello finally got some worthwhile information about Herbert Irwin.

He found out Irwin was single and that he was moving his company to Okeechobee. He needed a place to store his metal and equipment while he built a workshop on the 1400 acre tract. Would he, Stello, act as his agent to receive several railcars of equipment? Indeed, he would.

Karl Stello saw nothing of Herbert Irwin after he left his office. He occasionally drove by the city lots on the railroad and saw Irwin's truck parked inside the locked gates. Stello stopped only once to tell Herbert he would pick him up on the 19th of February to take him to Sebring to close on the 1400 acres.

At Sebring, Vice-President V. G. Watters and Assistant Secretary W. H. Percy of Consolidated Naval Stores made polite conversation with Herbert Irwin and completed the transaction. Expecting a certified check, the businessmen were momentarily surprised Irwin placed a bank bag of $100 bills on the conference table. $4,159.50 cash was acknowledged in receipt, the papers signed, and Herbert and Karl Stello returned to Okeechobee.

Herbert left for Texas the same day and left his address with Stello. Herbert said he would wire him when to expect his shipment and told him to hold the railcars because he would arrive in Okeechobee a couple days later. Stello watched Herbert Irwin drive off thinking he didn't know much more about Irwin than he did before.

Back in Amarillo Herbert began the arduous task of inventorying his accumulated supply of metal from sixteen years of manufacturing and machinist work. He hired the work done from a pool of former employees. He had his typed lists in hand of how much sheet metal, how much pipe, aluminum, mesh wire, corrugated metal, angle iron, I-beams, and the thousands of odd hardware pieces, nuts, bolts, and shelves of metalworking tools he had. Herbert had always kept a goodly supply of metal on hand and when the inevitable war shortages began he made sure he would never be without metal.

Herbert began preparation for his move with meticulous detail. He pictured in his mind a systematic timetable for packing, loading, shipment, arrival, unloading, storage, and reconstruction. It unfolded in his mind as a newsreel, a finely orchestrated event. He planned it with the logistic precision of moving a military unit; only this was one man with an entourage of metal. Herbert drafted a house and workshop for Florida and developed a supply list he would need to build them.

Herbert could have liquidated his equipment completely but preferred to keep as much as he could. He didn't want to sell it and later wish he had kept it. Herbert never quite got around to selling two delivery trucks and simply parked them. Herbert had decided it would take six railcars to move him: three flat cars, two boxcars, and one gondola. He packed his precious machines on wooden pallets and covered them with tarpaulins. He made stencils and painted his pallets with, "Herbert G. Irwin, c/o K. Stello, Okeechobee, FL." On the top sheets of metal stacks he etched the same stenciled name with acid. He did not want his railcars misdirected or pallets on them stolen. Herbert went to the railroad office and reserved his shipment.

Herbert had two things to take care of before he left Texas. He decided to concoct a story he was sure his family would believe. It was common knowledge around Amarillo Herbert Irwin closed his factory over a tax problem, only no one knew the particulars. He would weave a tale of deceit believable enough he would never have to be concerned about his family again. He hated them for their duplicity and lack of understanding. The only way to make the lie work was to deceive Ruey as well. No matter. The ruse would work because none of them were around him anymore.

Late one afternoon Herbert drove to Ruey's farm outside Floydada and knocked on his door. They had seen each other only a few times in years, lately during Herbert's tax troubles. Neither greeted the other. Ruey merely opened the door and Herbert followed him into the kitchen.

Herbert did not sit and said, "I'm moving to Florida. I need to get my money now."

"When are you leaving?"

"As soon as I can arrange shipping. Maybe a week or two. I lost my patents on the Welderz Frend. I can't manufacture   anymore.

Ruey was surprised. "You lost them? To who?"

"Some California people. They sued me and won. I told the judge I invented it. He knows me. Everybody knows I did. They stole it …. they stole the trademark. They stole my invention."

"What about the Treasury Department? How did that turn out?"

"They fined me. A lot. I lost everything but I won't go to prison. Now they're after me about income tax. I'm going to Florida to hide from the law. Tell the others I lost everything. Ruey, I'll take care of you for doing this. You tell me when we need to sign papers."

Herbert turned to leave and Ruey remained seated, not expecting or offering a goodbye. "I will."

Starting Over

Herbert drove behind the ranch house in back of the barn to a path hardly wide enough for a tractor. It extended down the side of a divided four hundred acre cotton field. The weeds at the edge of the fields almost hid his truck as Herbert slowly made his way to the very end of the rutted path. There stood a small weathered shed used to store old farm implements. Herbert parked the truck close against the building so from a distance they looked like one speck on the horizon. He looked all around him and behind the barn and could see miles in every direction. The only visible structure was Ruey's house a half mile away.

Herbert propped a shovel against the wall and forced one of the sagging barn doors open. He took one last glance around and stepped over old harrows to one corner. He shoved against a rusted planter until he was able to move it several feet forward. Herbert lifted several shovelfuls until he had scraped off a rectangle of dirt two feet by three feet. A rope poked through the dirt and Herbert braced himself over the rectangle and wrapped the rope around his hands. He pulled steadily upward as the dirt fell away from a crude wooden door. The cavity under the trapdoor held three leather bags. Herbert examined the lock he had placed on the largest and noted it was undisturbed, neither was the leather cut. He lifted the two smaller bags making sure they were untouched as well. Herbert moved all three bags to his truck and glancing constantly at his truck, settled the trapdoor back into its position. He covered the spot with dirt again and pushed the planter back over the trapdoor. He tossed the shovel into his truck and dragged the barn door shut. Herbert drove away as the sun was setting. He knew exactly how much cash was in each of the three leather suitcases, not in an abstract number but a distinct image. The Treasury Department did not know. His family certainly didn't. Not even Ruey knew. His bookkeeper had barely a hint. Only Herbert knew.

At the Amarillo rail yard, six railcars were backed onto a spur to await loading. Truck after truck drove out of the chain link fence gates of Irwin Improvements. It took almost a week to load the railcars.

Herbert's beloved work routine was abandoned since he had started packing his equipment. As unsettling as the whole process was, this sabbatical was necessary to relocate. The last evening Herbert walked the length of the railcars referring again and again to his typed lists. He was told a locomotive would hook up to his railcars at dawn the next morning and would be part of a freight of eighty cars.

The next morning Herbert watched as the locomotive gently bumped into the lock on the first car and pulled it toward the freight train. Herbert left the rail yard and went to Western Union to wire Karl Stello his shipment was en route.

Herbert packed his truck with his few personal belongings and locked the gates of his factory and the home he had occupied for seven years. The railcars were loaded to their maximum but he still was forced to leave some equipment he would have preferred to take. He wished he had a larger vehicle than his Ford truck.

Herbert had told enough people the land was for sale and he knew it would eventually sell. He had written Leo Brauer if he wanted to reconsider his offer, Herbert was moving to Okeechobee, Florida. Right now he wanted to get to Florida to his grove of oaks and begin building his workshop. Herbert felt a hunger to immerse himself in his work but knew it would be weeks yet before he would have that luxury.

Starting Over

In Okeechobee, Karl Stello stood gawking at the six railcars stretched down the tracks before him. Herbert Irwin said in his telegram he would be arriving within another two days. Stello had never seen such a conglomeration of metal. Angle iron jutted up in different directions from the gondola car. The flatcars had stacks and stacks of sheet metal, pipe, and rods piled high and held tightly with metal straps. There were draped pallets crowded together. The boxcar doors were shut but he expected more of the same. The odd shipment had even garnered some attention from the locals.

Herbert arrived in Okeechobee anxious to see his metal and equipment. He walked up and down the track trying to see if any of his supply of metal had been touched. Help was easily found and Herbert supervised the unloading of his precious machines and metal. The generators, lathes, tools, forges, and pallets of equipment were safely stored inside the small workshop, crammed tight with equipment. Stacks of galvanized railroad metal were piled high in the fenced yard. Herbert wanted to build his workshop as soon as possible and sought workers with trucks to move much of the shipment to his acreage. Herbert would begin building immediately.

The Indian White Hammock changed character quickly as truckloads of pipe and sheet metal were delivered under the canopy of live oaks. The Hammock once held the camps of the proud Seminoles and later, orders of Army officers echoed in the trees. But now a structure rose under the oaks like none other in its remarkable history.

To Herbert the grove was only a secluded backdrop for his beautiful workshop. In the months of preparation for this move he designed a workshop more functional with a better layout than anything he had before. The workshop had a clerestory window across the roofline. It faced the brilliant morning sun that broke through the grove in one particular spot. The rest of the building was in deep shade. It would receive perfect light and still be shaded enough to stay relatively cool. Herbert hired several laborers to help him build the structure. The heavy shade of the oaks left the ground reasonably free of vegetation. The corrugated metal for the workshop was placed around stakes Herbert had driven in the ground. He set vertical metal pipe deep in concrete and welded the three inch pipe skeleton of the building. The few in the group who welded studied the oxyacetylene generator and observed this one could be stopped and fired without cleaning in between welding sessions. Nothing like it had been seen in the region.

The corrugated sheet metal that covered the sides fit together tightly. Local cypress was plentiful and cut for bracing. Cypress boards were bolted to the pipe and metal. Herbert had designed a sliding garage door that locked tightly into the side of the building. The workers wondered at the excessiveness and joked Irwin must be building it to withstand a hurricane.

While the workshop was being built Herbert never left the site. He set up an Army surplus tent beside it with his truck parked close between. Herbert's plans had been thorough and in less than four weeks the project was finished. Herbert had his equipment moved from town into his workshop. He decided he could build his own house at his leisure and dismissed most the workers.

Herbert had a referral from Ellis Meserve at the hardware store and contracted Hiram Padgett to build a fence surrounding his property. Padgett's workers were surprised anyone would want to fence such a large tract when most people still had free range in Florida. This fence would be over six and a half *miles* of wire fence. Herbert specified the fence would have metal posts with two layers of net wire topped by barbed wire. There wasn't another fence in the whole country to equal it. What on earth was he going to fence in there? Besides the outside perimeter of fence Herbert wanted one around his house and workshop as well. The interior fence would be built enclosing three acres of dense woods and underbrush on one side. His garden would be on the east side and his house and workshop under the grove of trees.

While the fence was being built Herbert uncrated his remaining equipment, organizing and arranging his beloved machines and tools. Foregoing sleep from one day to the next his compulsion reasserted itself. Exhausted, Herbert went back to his tent and wrapped himself in his sleeping bag, content once again.

The heavy vegetation posed two problems with the fence construction. Herbert needed to clear dozens of trees along the fence row and also for his garden. From a few feet off the road, weeds and underbrush grew thick and high. While fifteen more feet in, the subtropical vegetation was almost impenetrable. The men complained they were hired to build a fence, not clear a wilderness.

While they worked on the fence in open areas Herbert attacked the problem of how to clear the fence rows. In Texas, a rancher may have to simply run a disc over a fencerow but this was far different. Herbert imagined heavy cutting blades that would snap and cut the palmettos and drag the root and stems out of the ground. He retired to his workshop and worked into the night for two days. Herbert was blissfully happy once again to be working on a mechanical problem.

Herbert opened the garage door of his workshop and asked Hiram Padgett's crew to hitch their tractor to an odd contraption. It had three vertical rectangular metal plates, the rear ones eighteen inches high. The front one was slightly shorter, two feet tall and an inch thick. The angle iron frame was welded into a triangular shaped off set harrow to be dragged behind the mules. The forward and bottom edges of the beveled plates were formed into a knife-like cutter. There was an adjustable handle on the apparatus that raised the plates from a level to an edge-cutting position. Heavy galvanized mesh screen covered the device.

Herbert said simply, "Drag it where the fence is to be built. It will pull the underbrush out by the roots. That will fall over the screen. Raise the plates to cut through the palmettos." The fence row was cleared easily, just as Herbert knew it would. He went back to his workshop to tackle the problem of removing the stumps. He designed a levered device to be pulled by two mules. As the mules heaved against the weight it would lift underneath and pull the stumps upward. The fence construction progressed quickly.

Herbert told the fence contractor he would install his own gate and dismissed his crew. They remembered Irwin was adamant they leave exactly an eight foot opening at the drive. The few people who passed in front of the newcomer's property were puzzled when they looked at the driveway. It looked like he had continued his fence across the drive. Only if one were to stop and inspect the posts was the inside gate lock visible. Whoever this new person was he certainly didn't invite company.

The Okeechobee Feed Store was pleased to have a new customer and welcomed a new resident's business. Herbert Irwin asked numerous questions about fruit trees and gardens most Florida residents were familiar with. The owner knew Irwin was from Texas and took the time to pass on his knowledge. He was rewarded with the sale of dozens of trees, seedlings, and seeds enough for a huge garden. He put Herbert in touch with a beekeeper so he could keep bees and have fresh honey.

With his workshop and fence completed Herbert settled into a routine. He knew he had to build his house soon. When it rained he holed up in his workshop rather than his tent until the rain passed. It was a tolerable rain compared to the vicious thunderstorms that rocked the high plains of Texas. It bothered him of course, but if these were as bad as it got he could handle it.

One particularly bad storm came through that almost changed his mind. It came as a torrential downpour with heavy winds. The roar inside the metal workshop testified as to the intensity of the rain. Herbert paced his nervousness through the storm and it was over in a couple days. He emerged from his workshop thinking he must build his house right away. Herbert sloshed through the puddles to his tent in rubber boots to his workshop. Rain had leaked through his tent and as he cleaned up the mess he heard a horn honking outside his fence. Herbert lifted the flap of the tent and saw Ellis Meserve, the owner of the Okeechobee Hardware Store, standing beside his car.

Meserve yelled, "I thought I should see about you because of the storm!"

Resenting the intrusion Herbert replied, "You've seen me." He closed the flap of the tent and continued to clean up the soggy mess inside the tent.

Ellis Meserve blinked in surprise. Wasn't he trying to be neighborly? Hadn't he driven all the way up here just to check on a newcomer? This Irwin man was a strange one. He got in his car and drove back to Okeechobee.

Herbert thought about his house carefully. His frame house in Amarillo came with the property but he would never have built one of wood by choice. This house would be metal and would last him the rest of his life. He would never have to paint it or worry about termites, mold, or a leaking roof. Herbert planned for two types of adjustable windows. He poured concrete into molds he had made for the sixteen supports for his house even though twelve would have sufficed. He positioned his house forty feet from his workshop door. Herbert welded the pipe frame of the room-sized house as one complete unit with galvanized bolted struts supporting his corrugated metal roof.

The set of windows on the north and south sides had metal louvers that would adjust from a closed position to open horizontally to allow air and light. The only glass window was beside his door and he welded security bars over it. Inset under both sides of the eaves of the house he designed a vent that traversed the length of the house. He covered the vents with galvanized mesh wire to keep birds and anything else out. An inside lever opened and closed a metal cover that folded over the vents like shutters. All the window and vent frames were metal and were riveted every few inches to the walls.

The door was fashioned from galvanized metal plates molded over a six-foot by three-foot by one-inch door of plywood. Herbert screwed the metal plates to the plywood every three inches with screws. The edges of the door were completely enclosed by formed metal. The door was hung on three eighteen-inch long metal hinges in a metal doorframe. Galvanized corrugated metal covered the whole house, screwed into cypress interior supports. It was possible to shut himself up inside his house completely protected by the worst rainstorm Florida could offer. The only wood in the house besides his tables and bed was the plywood floor supported by welded metal struts. His house was a mini-fortress built to withstand anything, including a war.

Herbert had brought only the barest of essentials with him from Texas for his house. The wooden bed he had made himself years before, a mattress, a drafting table, a straight backed wooden chair, a chamber pot, his typewriter, a small iron stove, his wash machine, and a few pots and dishes. Anything that needed hanging was hung from nails and hooks suspended from the supports over his head. Herbert cooked, ate, slept, and occasionally drew designs in his house. He kept up with his experiments and typed notes. His workshop was for everything else.

Herbert's compound was complete. He took great pleasure in the design of his workshop. His house was sturdy and tight. His garden was already sprouting and would produce vegetables and fruit before long. The climate was most agreeable and he enjoyed the shade of the mighty oaks surrounding his buildings. It was quiet, secluded, protected. Herbert considered his accumulated wealth and knew he could live for decades on it even if he did not produce any more income. Herbert still had royalties coming in regularly. He owed no one. He could continue to invent and do occasional machinist work.

Herbert would live here the rest of his life and work to his heart's content.

Starting Over

Living In Paradise

Chapter Nine

Living In Paradise

As Herbert settled into his new home he found himself more content than he had been in years. He wasn't totally oblivious to the beauty around him. Sometimes the intense green of his environment was so overwhelming he retreated into the shadows of his workshop rather than work in his garden. The blandness of the high plains never intruded into his consciousness as did this subtropical setting. His senses were on overload. The real focus of his pleasure was his workshop. He had his machinery perfectly arranged, his house was comfortable. All were made to service his compulsion to work.

Herbert wrote one simple note to Ruey to tell him where he was. He did not include any details or descriptions of his new home. It was not an appeal for correspondence or company, only to let his brother know where he was. Herbert saw no reason whatsoever to contact his family anymore.

Herbert made plans to put cattle and sheep on his property to claim an agricultural exemption. The local feed store proved to be a reliable supplier of information and labor when Herbert needed it. He soon found someone to buy cattle and sheep for him. Herbert knew enough about livestock to keep them healthy and increase his herd. There was another reason as well. He wanted a readily accessible supply of pure beef and mutton.

Living In Paradise

Families down the road from Herbert Irwin wondered about a man so affluent he could afford to fence such a large tract of land. They had heard about the workshop and house made of railroad metal. Herbert did not seek out his neighbors but Dozier Smith thought it was the neighborly thing to do and came to his fence one day to welcome him. Herbert regarded the intruder with suspicion and would not allow him inside his gate. Smith decided to come back another day thinking their new neighbor would eventually realize this was a friendly and tight knit community. Smith would later rethink that.

Herbert's factory had kept him so busy he wasn't able to devote the time to growing his own food in Amarillo as he wanted. Now he could. He worked hard the first season to make a garden and purposed to prepare a large tract to grow vegetables. He bought two mules to clear his property and plow his garden. Herbert expected animals to work as he did, non-stop. Even with his boyhood experience on his parents' farm, Herbert had no sense whatsoever of the capabilities of an animal. He had worked himself to exhaustion every day of his life.

Mules are smart animals. They know when they do not have the strength to pull against a load. Many an old muleskinner paid close attention to their animals and if a mule stopped they would allow him to rest. Most mules would resume work or if it was too much the muleskinner knew he needed to use a team or lighten the load.

Herbert had plowed with one mule since early morning. Mid-afternoon the plow blade came up against a thick root. The mule leaned into its collar and when the root didn't give the mule stopped. Herbert clucked to him and slapped the reins over his back. The mule didn't move. Annoyed Herbert stepped away from the plow and gathered the reins in his hands and applied the reins sharply over its back. The mule flinched but did not try to pull. Now angry, Herbert took the reins again and with repeated strikes, whipped him. Lifting its head the animal laid its ears back and recoiled with every blow but still refused to move. Herbert yelled at the mule, furious it would not work. He flogged the animal repeatedly but the mule would not budge. In a rage Herbert dropped the reins and walked to his workshop. He came back with a pitchfork and jabbed the animal in the rump so hard the mule jumped in shock and lashed out with a hind leg. Enraged, Herbert stepped to the shoulder of the mule and with a double grip plunged the pitchfork deep into its neck and throat. The mule dropped to its knees still in harness. Blood gushed from the animal's throat. Herbert's temper had snapped and he jerked the pitchfork back and struck the mule again. It fell back on its side with all four legs outstretched in adrenalin shock. Out of control, Herbert stabbed the animal over and over again. The dead mule's legs relaxed as Herbert pulled the bloody pitchfork out of its neck, almost unaware of what he had done.

Herbert stood over the carcass of his mule. He willed his breathing to steady as he fought for reasoning. He looked at the bloody pitchfork and the glazed eyes of his dead mule. That'll fix that lazy mule. Everybody should work! Men, animals, that's what you had to do. You must be productive. You must *work!* That mule didn't deserve to live.

In calm disassociation of an act of brutality Herbert unharnessed the dead mule and took the bloodied harness back to his shop. He rinsed it in rainwater and hung it to dry. He drove his truck over to the dead mule and secured a rope around its hind legs. Herbert drove the truck over to the northwest corner of his property dragging the carcass as deep into the woods as he could. Let the buzzards dispose of him. He did not care and didn't think of digging a hole big enough to bury it. Herbert drove back to his workshop and planned to buy another mule; one that would work. Herbert was as indifferent to the loss of his mule as he was to a piece of machinery that broke down and couldn't be repaired. He would simply replace it.

Herbert's garden was flourishing and he was more enthused about his food than he had ever been. This climate was truly remarkable. His family had raised a garden and he had a garden in Amarillo, but nothing like this. His house had been so close to his factory in Amarillo he was able to taste the chemicals in his food. But now he had untainted land to grow the purest of vegetables and fruit. He planted potatoes, squash, sweet potatoes, beans, peas, turnips, corn, bell and hot peppers, carrots, radishes, cucumbers, and tomatoes. He grew blackberries and strawberries. His bee hives were buzzing with activity and he would have honey soon. He even experimented with a small patch of sugar cane and had some success growing peanuts. He planted a variety of herbs: rosemary, thyme, dill, tarragon, curry, mustard, garlic, onions, celery, and mushrooms. The variety of herbs was an exciting addition to his food preparation. Herbert was so intrigued by the new fruits and vegetables he grew he began to study the grafting techniques the farmers around him were using. He studied experimental groves testing different strains of oranges, tangerines, tangelos, and grapefruit.

Herbert saw farmers growing hemp in response to the growing shipping industry around Tampa Bay. He had studied hemp before and knew it to be a truly universal plant that was ideal for more than anchoring grand ships to docks. He planted fruit trees content to wait before they would bear. Nothing had taken his mind off machines before. Herbert subscribed to farming periodicals, immersing himself into a whole new field of study, an intriguing diversion away from inventing. He would be able to supply himself with completely uncontaminated fresh food.

Herbert's teeth were deteriorating and he began testing several versions of a smoker to make his meats tender. Herbert was hypersensitive to taste and explored herbs and their endless combination of tastes. He knew smokehouses well but wanted a portable smoker that could smoke smaller quantities to be used inside his house when it rained.

Herbert became acquainted with the sounds of his paradise and the unfamiliar bird calls. It was a whole different night sound than he was used to. Most his adult life he had lived by a railroad but now only a rare airplane could be heard. Herbert's machinery was the only noise to disturb the tranquil silence of the Hammock. One night he lay in his bed and heard a sound like nothing he had heard before. It was a high-pitched screech and then he heard the excited sound of a flock of birds fleeing, crying out an alarm. What could have scared them like that? He did not know.

Herbert made infrequent trips to Okeechobee and passed Connors Field, a small military outpost only four miles from him. He saw a new military ambulance parked outside the gate. The size of the vehicle impressed Herbert and he stopped and asked the driver if he could see it. The driver opened the doors and let Herbert examine the truck. The ambulance was spacious and sturdy enough to haul equipment. He decided the big Ford would do nicely to transport the remainder of his belongings from Amarillo. He had seen International panel trucks but the Ford was larger. He did not trust Okeechobee Motors, the local Ford dealer. Not because they weren't a reputable company, but because he did not know them.

In June Herbert wrote Walter Irvin in Amarillo and told him to order a Ford panel truck for him. Considering the heat and bugs in Florida he ordered a heavy-duty radiator as the only option. Herbert ordered the truck in green thinking his truck would be far less visible than his black one in the Hammock. The dealer wrote back the US Army was ordering hundreds of panel trucks for ambulances and that it would be September before he could deliver the truck. Herbert considered it one more sign the country would soon be at war and wired the dealership the total amount, $958, for a new panel truck.

Herbert had another reason to return to Amarillo besides getting the remainder of his belongings. Leo Brauer had written he was still interested in his factory and patents. Selling his Amarillo property wasn't important right now but Herbert knew that this was a promising prospect. Herbert knew Brauer's interest was in his welder but he insisted Brauer must buy his property and the machine shop.

Dozier Smith made another attempt to befriend Herbert Irwin. Dozier still wanted to extend an offer of friendship. He appeared at Herbert's locked gate again and honked his horn. Herbert watched Smith from the shadows but soon came out to the fence. It made Smith uneasy to see Irwin's hand in his overalls pocket. There was no doubt he had a gun in there.

"Mr. Irwin, I'm Dozier Smith. I live up the road a piece and thought I would introduce myself since we're neighbors. I wondered if there was anything I could do for you."

Herbert tipped his hat and looked at him. This man was of no use to him except for information. Herbert asked for the only information he needed.

"I need to buy a mule. Where can I buy one? One that will work."

Smith said, "I thought I saw a couple mules behind those trees over there."

"One wouldn't work. I killed it."

Smith paused not knowing quite what to respond. "You have to work with mules. You can't overwork them. You shot your mule?"

"No, I used a pitchfork. It didn't deserve to live. Mules should work. I won't stand for it."

What kind of man would kill his own mule, much less with a pitchfork? Smith thought he would be very careful around Irwin but gave him the information he asked for.

"They hold a livestock auction every week on the edge of town. You should be able to get a decent mule there. I'll tell them at the feed store you're hunting one, too."

Irwin did not say anything else so Dozier Smith wished him a good day and left.

Herbert's twenty head of sheep and seventy-five head of cattle could graze at will and retreat into the deep woods in the heat of the day. The dense underbrush scraped against their bodies and brushed the mosquitoes away. Otter Creek gave abundant fresh water. His neighbors really didn't know what Herbert had inside his fence because no one except a sheepherder had been in there since he built his workshop and house.

One day at the feed store the cattleman who bought Herbert's cattle for him innocently asked if he wanted his cattle dipped for ticks. The man backed away in startled surprise as Herbert lost his temper in an instant. Herbert wheeled and began pacing. He mumbled about the government harassing citizens, poisoning beef, and tainted water. The hapless cattleman could hardly understand the man. Several customers watched in amazement as the newcomer ranted about the dangers of poisons. Herbert

Irwin seemed to be in a delirious rage. They quietly paid for their purchases and left. The cattleman departed quickly, doubting if Irwin even knew he was gone. He made up his mind not to have any more dealings with him. Anyone that unpredictable needed to be avoided. Herbert willed himself back into an acceptable demeanor and asked the salesman to load his feed as if his tirade had never happened.

Herbert returned to the solitude of his compound convinced his cattle would not need dipping. The land was pristine, never having had chemicals dumped on it, not even fertilizer. He had studied the insects around him and saw a balance of mosquitoes, flies, ticks, fleas, ants, aphids, gnats, crickets, beetles, and exotic ones he had yet to identify. He saw a population of frogs around his creek. There were lizards, snakes, and a few small alligators. There were more birds than he could name or number with egret, heron, and ducks. Nature would keep the ecological balance. Herbert was firmly convinced his cattle and sheep would be healthy without any dipping. He always tasted chemicals in any beef that was dipped or treated and he refused to subject his to the same poisoning, especially DDT.

Herbert had an abundance of fish in Otter Creek. In the high plains of Texas the cycles of drought and flash flood did not lend itself to large fish. The stocked ponds common to Texas could not compare to the steady current of fresh waterways in the region. The water even smelled clean, not the dank odor of stagnant water. When Herbert cleaned his fish and smelled the white meat he knew the fish were untainted. The first fish he ate was a delight in taste he never thought possible. It was wonderful.

Herbert used washtubs to catch rainwater but made several over-sized aluminum tanks to increase his water supply capacity. He made a metal table to clean fish on and moved it to the creek. He made a pipe and wire clothesline, a weathervane, rain gauge, and wind gauge. It never occurred to Herbert to buy any tools he needed. He made everything whether it was a rake, hoe, scoop, an auger, tongs, a table, gate latch, drains, or convenience.

Herbert saw grouse, dove, quail, prairie hen, and rabbit and decided to trap some for food. There were a few wild hogs and he would try one later after he perfected his smoker. He had traps but made more. He was rewarded with all the wild fowl he wanted. Deer were plentiful and he liked venison if it was cooked in a particular way. He would wait another season before harvesting one.

As late summer came upon his tropical sanctuary Herbert watched his cattle settle into a routine. They would graze, water, shelter in the woods, and late in the evening, graze again until they bedded down for the night. The sheep followed their own instincts and grazed and watered in a natural separation from the cattle. One morning Herbert missed one of his sheep and went hunting it. He came upon the spot where his sheep bedded down for the night. Herbert stopped as he saw bloody entrails and tufts of wool. Someone had slaughtered one of his sheep. Herbert immediately looked around hunting boot prints. He was sure someone had sneaked on his property last night and killed it. He found prints but they weren't boots. Puzzled with the unfamiliar print Herbert settled on the most suspicious answer to the loss of livestock – someone had tried to be clever and covered their feet to make an animal print. It must be his neighbors. He would find out.

Herbert drove over to the Arnold homestead in time to see them cleaning up after butchering an animal. In the best of circumstances Herbert could be rude and he wasted no time in stating his mission. William Arnold was disgusted as

Herbert Irwin so much as accused him of stealing his sheep. Arnold walked over to the edge of his field beyond his smokehouse. He picked up the severed hind leg of the steer he had killed only hours before. The leg was cut at the hock joint.

"Does this look like sheep to you? This is *my* steer. I raised this steer and I slaughtered it just like I do every year. I don't take anything from no man. I don't need to. You know what killed your sheep? Panther! You may not have cats like this in Texas but we got 'em here. Why did you think right away it was me who killed your sheep? That was Florida panther tracks you saw. Any poacher would have gutted it and maybe took off the head. Then they would have taken the meat. That cat dragged the whole thing off didn't he?"

Herbert pondered on Arnold's answer. Panther. The logical explanation was harder to digest than the paranoid one. Maybe that was what he heard at night. Yes, Texas had cougar but the high plains didn't have much problem with them. Herbert turned and left without making an apology. It never crossed his mind. Mr. Arnold watched him leave and shook his head. That was one peculiar man.

Herbert spoke to his sheepherder and decided to sell his sheep. Once a panther identified a flock of sheep nothing would be able to keep them out. They arranged to take them to the auction and Herbert let his sheepherder go.

Herbert thought about his cattle and knew he would probably have to be concerned about panther next spring when calves were on the ground. Right now none of his herd was younger than yearlings and most were fast and strong enough to protect themselves. Still, he would make a large trap to hold a panther.

Living In Paradise

While Herbert was only concerned with his immediate surroundings there were other events happening in the world. He was disturbed Franklin Roosevelt would be his President for the third time. Herbert knew the country was concerned about the Nazis. He thought if he had to go through another war this was about as good a place as any to survive it.

Herbert embarked on a course of action to protect his supplies during a war that would assuredly bring about shortages. Herbert made gasoline and kerosene tanks and locked them inside his workshop out of sight. Remembering the supplies the Repair Depot had kept during the first war he ordered enough kerosene to last him five years. The fuel supplier that drove out to his property thought nothing of it when he made a second trip with 500 gallons of gasoline. Lots of farmers stored fuel on their property. Herbert hid several fifty-five-gallon barrels of oil in his workshop.

Herbert was afraid the government would take his hoarded metal away from him. He took sheet after sheet and hauled it in his truck to a clearing and buried it. He left enough sheets in his workshop for his numerous projects but little more than that. He buried pipe and galvanized angle iron. He hid crates of nuts and bolts. He stashed inner tubes, fan belts, and glass panes. Herbert had brought coal with him from Amarillo and heaved the fifty-pound bags into bins stored in a corner of his workshop. Between his food and industrial supplies Herbert would never have to leave his compound. Let this war come. He could survive it and it would not affect his work.

Herbert made plans to drive to Amarillo one last time to retrieve his remaining belongings and get his new truck. He might even be able to negotiate the sale of his property.

Herbert wrote Brauer he would be in Amarillo the first week of September.

Moving to Florida had been an ordeal for Herbert. The anxiety it had caused him was in deep conflict to his craving for order and routine. The logistics of moving so much material had been a monumental undertaking and it had drained him. Herbert had forced himself to make the move because he had to. He could console himself this would be the last trip he would ever make; once more and then he would never have to leave his sanctuary again.

Herbert arrived in Amarillo late in the evening on the fourth day and unlocked his gate. The factory yard and his frame house already had the deserted look of an abandoned business. Herbert had mentally separated himself from it and attached himself in mind and purpose to Florida. He had prospered here. But now all he wanted was to gather his few remaining tools and leave.

He was at Walter Irvin Motors early the next morning. Herbert could see his green panel truck parked in front. The truck was more distinctive than he would have preferred but he was more concerned about its serviceability. The salesman, Riddle, went over the features of his 1941 Ford ¾ Ton Panel Truck in Lochaven Green. Herbert looked under the hood to verify the truck was equipped with a heavy-duty radiator. He bought eight extra tires in addition to the spare that came with the truck. Herbert left his old truck and keys with the salesman for one of his former employees to pick up later.

Herbert drove his new panel truck back to his factory and examined how he could pack the spacious vehicle. He walked through his workshops picking up odd items he had left. He removed a handmade toolbox, filled it, and moved it to his truck. Late in the afternoon he removed the passenger seat to allow for two more small engines that weren't crucial to the machine shop. They were more important than a seat no one would ever sit in. Herbert threw in a few more pairs of khakis and overalls and one more pair of work boots. He laid an old mattress on the floor of the truck with his sleeping bag and spent the night in his truck instead of the house.

The next morning Herbert saw a man parked beside the locked gate. Herbert walked over to the gate thinking this must be Leo Brauer. He stood at the gate waiting for the caller to identify himself and speak.

Leo Brauer knew Herbert Irwin through the oilfield industry. Irwin was called brilliant, a genius. He also had a name for being difficult. Brauer already knew that from his correspondence with him. Irwin was adamant if he wanted the Welderz Frend he had to buy the machine shop and factory with the patents. His partner, Johnson, was willing to invest in the machine shop. It was obvious the Welderz Frend was going to be in huge demand if the European war escalated to include the US. Brauer considered the Welderz Frend was the welder of choice and he wanted that welder.

Brauer introduced himself and said, "Mr. Irwin, you know I'm interested in your welder. I know what you said in your letter and I'm prepared to offer you a fair price. I'd like to see your factory."

Herbert silently opened the gate and gave Leo Brauer a guided tour of his facility. Brauer asked questions and got the briefest of answers. He was surprised there was no commercial electricity here. Brauer was impressed at the condition of the equipment. Irwin had said he had a fully furnished factory that could be started up immediately. It was true. Still, Irwin wanted a ridiculous sum of money.

"Mr. Irwin you presented your factory accurately and I appreciate that. But what you are asking for your patents is pretty high. I can offer you market value for your facility here and no more. If I bought the machine shop and your seven and a half acres here I'd have to bring in a business partner. If you'll come down to a more realistic price we have a deal. I'm not saying it isn't worth that, I don't know. I just can't go that much. What do you say?"

Herbert listened but heard only Brauer wouldn't pay for his machine shop and his factory. Herbert had priced his property four times what he had originally paid for it. Considering the improvements, a house, two fine workshops, his machine shop business and equipment, his factory, outbuildings, and wire fence it was an ideal factory site. Herbert knew how much his Welderz Frend was worth based on his past production and he wouldn't budge an inch.

Herbert firmly named his price again itemizing each element of their negotiation.

Brauer shook his head trying to keep their negotiation light. "Mr. Irwin, I just can't invest that much in your patents. And you know this place isn't worth that. You don't even have utilities! Look at all the work I'd have to do to make this place work. Look at the money I'd have to put in this thing. No, I can't do that. If you'll meet my price I'll buy it."

Herbert did not have to sell anything and said, "You want my patents you'll pay for them. You want my factory then you'll pay what it's worth. No, I won't sell for that. Now leave."

Herbert escorted Brauer to his gate. Herbert wasn't going to waste his time and turned around and walked away leaving Leo Brauer standing outside his fence. Brauer thought Irwin was more than a little obstinate but he wanted the welder. Brauer drove away thinking he would let that crazy man think about it awhile and make him another offer later.

Herbert mumbled his annoyance and thought about his welder. He had successfully manufactured it for sixteen years. That was a pretty long run in an industry that was changing every year. His Welderz Frend would become obsolete in the not too distant future. But if the US went to war the Welderz Frend had incredible value for a manufacturer. Herbert didn't need the money and didn't care if he ever sold this property. If anyone wanted it badly enough they knew how to find him in Okeechobee, including Brauer. By sunset Herbert had his truck packed tightly with everything he wanted to take back to Florida.

His distinctive new Ford truck would be the most appropriate vehicle for Herbert's endeavors he had ever had. The olive green panel truck would be identified with him for the next thirty-five years.

At dawn Herbert drove out of his gate, locked it, and headed southeast. Herbert had closed the door on one chapter of his life and was embarking on the next one. He was completely preoccupied with his relocation as the country made preparations for Franklin Roosevelt's unprecedented fourth term of office.

By Inauguration Day in January, 1941 Herbert was vaguely waiting for the announcement the US would go to war with Germany. Herbert read the transcript from Roosevelt's Inaugural address stating the US was threatened by events outside her borders. Roosevelt committed to an "all inclusive national defense" and to greatly expand the country's military machine. And the ominous promise that the US would, "… support those resolute peoples everywhere who are resisting aggression and are thereby keeping war away from our hemisphere." In what would become a classic vision for the future, President Roosevelt concluded his speech with, "four essential human freedoms: freedom of speech, freedom of worship, freedom from want, and freedom from fear. To that high concept there can be no end, save victory."

Intent was fairly clear. The President had taken a decisive path even though one of his campaign promises was that he would not send our boys to war. In open defiance of those promises the German Embassy hung a Swastika flag of the Third Reich only blocks away. Soldiers marched in the inaugural parade and tanks were parked at intersections. This was a country gearing up for war.

Sweethearts, wives, and mothers were nervous when the first conscription of the Selective Service Act was called up in August of 1940. The second was called in December and the third was due shortly.

By March, Roosevelt was encouraging the populace to not be complacent and support her allies. He asked for increased production of armaments as aid for threatened democracies. It was a call to duty and sacrifice for ships, planes, and food. Manufacturers began converting to arms production. The US was rapidly developing into a formidable military power.

Florida thunderstorms had the same affect on Herbert as weather always had. Lightening, pounding rain, the wind – his senses were sharpened and he felt the familiar anxiety. The sounds of a storm seemed to be compounded underneath his towering oaks. Every year storms seemed to bother him more. Surely, surely there was something that would help him endure these storms so they wouldn't upset him so much. There must be some herb, some natural medicine he could grow to help him cope.

Living In Paradise

Herbert read about herbal crops in farming publications and discovered farmers in the northeastern part of Florida were growing opium poppies for pharmaceutical companies. He read of the medicinal properties that could be extracted from poppies in the form of opium that was made into the drug, morphine. It was used for pain relief and had a tranquilizing effect. The government was even encouraging farmers to grow them. Herbert ordered seed to experiment with and grew a small patch with his vegetables over the summer.

Herbert read the publications but was unsure how to process the opium. He would experiment and arrive at a conclusive dose just as he approached every problem. The first time Herbert took his pocketknife and slit the bulb of a mature poppy he watched the milk ooze out. Herbert knew the dry pods were sent to pharmaceutical companies. They processed the brown extract to pill form or, to be injected as morphine.

Herbert knew he could inject the heroin as hospitals did. Injecting it did not appeal to him at all. He could smoke the opium as they used to do in opium dens. He could snort it into his nose but he knew how sensitive his smell was. Or, he could eat it. There must be another way he could experiment with it; he would try it in his food first. After all, it was just another herb. It was just another medicinal derived from a plant people had grown for thousands of years. Herbert knew there were different strengths of the opium but had no idea how to arrive at a suitable dosage. He read the caution in his publications and knew the heroin was decidedly potent. His intent was only to help him cope with the anxieties that came with weather.

Herbert scraped the sticky dark milk from a poppy pod and took the cup back to his house. Herbert had almost a teaspoon of gummy opium against the side of his cup. When he first sniffed the milk on the pod it had a sweet scent. Now after a day the brownish gum had a disagreeable smell. He thought if it tasted like it smelled it would be bitter. He looked at the tiny amount and thought surely it can't be that powerful. He mashed the gum into a generous amount of jelly in a saucer and stirred it. Herbert spread the spoonful of opium jelly on a slice of bread. He folded the bread over and ate the jellied bread. He could readily taste the opium in the jelly. It was disgustingly bitter, but not intolerable. If it didn't work he would burn the poppies. If it did help him the bitterness would be worth it. He rinsed his mouth and spat out the water.

Herbert walked back to his garden to work the rest of the afternoon. He rarely took any medicine but expected the opium to have some affect on him within the hour. He hoed weeds for less than twenty minutes when he began feeling a wonderfully pleasant sensation. Herbert knew it was the poppies. He felt an extraordinary sense of calm and well-being, then euphoria. Herbert became flushed and a bit apprehensive with the intensity. He had no control over it and he hated being out of control. Soon his own mumbling interrupted Herbert's normally silent world. He saw people and fantastic things he knew could not possibly be real. Brilliant color, motion, waves – the most marvelous thoughts tumbled about in his mind but made no sense. Herbert dropped his hoe and stumbled back to his house and fell into his bed. He did not remember anything after that.

Herbert slowly awakened to hear birds singing and saw early morning sunlight streaming through the louvered windows. His clothes were wet with sweat. He lay there for some time analyzing what had happened. No doubt he had ingested too much opium. Herbert recalled reading that at the turn of the century opium dens were commonplace. Those people mostly smoked it. Opiates were way beyond recreation. It wasn't potent; it was hyper-potent.

Herbert had never fallen asleep before without shutting himself up in his house. His windows and door were open. His thinking was perfectly rational this morning. Late yesterday afternoon – *yesterday afternoon* he had taken the opium. Herbert sat up carefully. His mouth had a terribly bitter taste. He drank from his water bottle but could not quench his thirst.

Herbert's stomach was queasy. He sat on his bed and ate directly from a jar of pickles to kill the taste. He pondered over the attributes of this herb drug from poppies. One thing he remembered clearly was the euphoria he felt before the drug overwhelmed him. That was the most incredible feeling in the world. If he could capture that feeling, that dosage, he felt he could better tolerate storms. That was the optimum affect. He would have to be very careful with this opium medicine. The next thunderstorm Herbert would be sure to have opium gum in his house and use far, far less. He would experiment and soon he would be able to arrive at a proper dosage. Maybe there was a better means to take it. Or process it. After this experience injection didn't seem to hold the revulsion it initially had. He needed to do some more research. *Finally, he had a medicine to help him cope.*

Herbert had his opportunity a week later to try his poppy medicine during a storm. The first time he had taken it on an empty stomach. The second time he knew he had still ingested too much. He did not hallucinate the third time but he still could not function. That was what he was after; serenity, but still able to function.

Herbert decided to try injection and experimented processing the opium into heroin. Making a syringe was easy. He read where lemon juice would break down the gum and he tried that. The fourth and fifth times he almost had it right. A syringe was so much easier to control the dosage. By winter Herbert had arrived at the exact amount he needed.

Herbert did not identify it as such but he could feel the tug of addiction. Only his violent hatred of taking any medicine and his obsessive determination to always be in control stopped him from using more heroin. Now he understood the warnings in the farming publications. He could readily see why poppy production was controlled. This was his storm medicine. Herbert resolved he would never take it unless he needed it. With all his obstinate determination and good intentions Herbert's unsettled mind would often depend on his heroin.

There are two types of heroin users – most are destructive and hopelessly addicted. They lead lives of despair. Some die from overdoses. Then there are some like Herbert who become lifelong users of heroin. For whatever reason, some are able to partially manage it. But they never stop using.

Living In Paradise

Chapter Ten

Eden Turns To Hell

In Amarillo, Leo Brauer watched machine shops convert from oil field work to defense contracts for the government. Although he initially wanted Herbert Irwin's Welderz Frend, he now wanted his machine shop and factory just as much. He knew a machine shop would provide lucrative contract work throughout an inevitable war. Brauer thought he would try again and wrote Irwin with another proposal; more than he had originally offered but not what Irwin wanted.

Herbert rejected Brauer's offer for the third time with a letter telling him not to bother him again unless he would meet his price.

By September, 1941 President Roosevelt was openly admonishing Hitler over the radio the US would protect her naval and merchant vessels. He made warnings to Germany and Italy any infringement would be "at your peril."

The news was now commenting about the treatment of ghetto Jews and labeling. When Poland was invaded six thousand Jews were killed but a concerted "final solution" was still to be implemented. In Bucharest, arrests and slaughter of Jews was openly and systematically eliminating a city's whole Jewish population.

The upheaval in Europe was in sharp contrast to the tranquility of the Indian White Hammock. Whereas Herbert felt he needed to contribute to his country in the first war, at

147

his age he felt this was a young man's war to fight. His only thought was continued engagement of his craft. He wanted to work on his projects and wanted peace for himself. It would take a deaf and blind man not to see the US was gearing up for intervention in the European war. Herbert was neither and prepared to survive a war as he stockpiled as many supplies as he could.

By November Herbert had witnessed the citrus harvest in the orchards around him. He had watched farmers bale three cuttings of hay off one hay field. He saw cattle grow fat with grass that was still green and growing. His personal garden had given him jars upon jars of canned vegetables and fruit that would give him enough food to last him well into the next season. He had spent hours canning his food and was able to give all the exact attention he wanted as to spices and preparation. He built shelves in his house to store his food and secure bins to hold onions and potatoes. It gave him pleasure to look upon the neat rows of colorful jars. He studied drying fruit and built racks and experimented with them all summer and late into the fall.

When the Japanese attacked Pearl Harbor December 7, 1941 it was several days before Herbert knew about it. When he went into town after his few groceries Herbert could not understand the flurry of activity he saw in Okeechobee. He bought his supplies and listened to excited conversations in the store. *Japan?* Herbert bought several newspapers and after reading the detailed accounts, he was angered over the death toll. He agreed the country had to declare war.

Karl Stello found Herbert and handed him a telegram the office had given him the morning of the 8th of December. Leo Brauer could see money slipping through his fingers without the Welderz Frend. His telegram to Herbert Irwin was short and to the point: he wanted his patents, land, factory, and machine shop. Brauer would meet his price.

Herbert immediately wired back to Brauer he would sell the whole package to him and demanded Brauer bring the money to Okeechobee, in cash. Herbert gave Brauer a week and told him to meet him in Karl Stello's office on the 16th of December to sign the agreements and deeds.

In Amarillo, Leo Brauer was annoyed he would have to go all the way to Florida to complete a transaction that could easily be done without such a trip. Brauer was surprised when his banker told him there currently wasn't a bank in Okeechobee. It took several days to arrange the money transfer to a bank in Ft. Pierce. Brauer knew when Irwin said cash, he meant cash. Brauer had his bank draft in hand and left for Florida.

Locked securely behind his gate under the Indian White Hammock Herbert pondered how the war would interfere with his activities. He had stockpiled supplies and fuel. He had buried enough metal to last him for years. There was little he needed he did not already have.

Herbert thought about all his uncompleted Welderz Frend generators he had brought with him from Amarillo. He could possibly have an outlet for them and sell them to the Army.

On the 16th of October, Leo Brauer claimed his cash at the Ft. Pierce bank and came to Karl Stello's office in Okeechobee. Stello and Leo Brauer discussed Herbert Irwin's brilliance and eccentricity. Stello admitted he still liked and respected the man.

When Herbert arrived at the office Karl Stello told Herbert Germany had declared war on the US on the 11th of December. A sale of such value would normally be handled by attorneys but Herbert insisted he do the paperwork. He had typed a lengthy agreement reassigning his eight patents on the Welderz Frend to Leo Brauer. Herbert included a clause exempting his partially constructed welders in Florida. Brauer was concerned about the Welderz Frend trademark name but Herbert assured him he had never registered it. He could draft his own instrument because there was no trademark registry on it.

Suspicious as always, Herbert asked Stello to count the cash Brauer had in his briefcase. The hundred dollar bills were stacked in neat piles of thousands, and then thousands more – and then more. For Herbert's benefit, Stello insisted on counting it several times.

Leo Brauer read over the deeds and agreements and was amazed Irwin did them himself. As experienced a businessman as Brauer was, even he would have hired an attorney. Brauer returned to Oklahoma ready to start up the Amarillo factory immediately and produce welders for the war effort. Brauer's Tulsa attorney, Charles McKnight, registered the Welderz Frend trademark name and dated their registration the same day of the sale. Leo Brauer was convinced the Welderz Frend was a lucrative venture.

Karl Stello watched Herbert Irwin drive out of town with his cash knowing full well Irwin would never take his money to a bank thirty-five miles away. Stello wondered at anyone holding that much cash.

In a country at war Herbert's oasis was untouched when other cities felt the change of activity at once. McDill Air Force Base near Tampa began flying training missions over the Gulf of Mexico and the coast. Plans were quickly implemented placing dozens of training bases in Florida. Whereas Herbert only occasionally bought a newspaper now he bought one every time he went to town to find out any new developments.

Herbert was a bit uneasy about living so close to the ocean. He considered the vulnerability of the Hawaiian territory, and the thought of the Florida peninsula being attacked concerned him. Herbert packed his lunch one morning and drove to Fort Pierce. He knew there was no harbor like Tampa Bay that would support ships of any size, but he still wanted to see for himself.

Herbert turned down side streets until he found himself staring at the Atlantic Ocean. He saw other cars and trucks on the beach and drove onto the white sand and parked his truck. Herbert watched fishermen casting into the surf and wondered what kind of fish they were catching. He stayed for hours listening to the soothing sound of the waves and the seagulls. Herbert returned to his sanctuary under the oaks thinking he would return to fish and experiment with trawling. Little did Herbert know his innocent trips to the beach would cause alarm in his neighbors.

Even though the war began in Europe US involvement brought the conflict to coastal waters. From Maine to Florida German U-boats would eventually sink 171 ships: 62 in the Gulf of Mexico and 141 in the Caribbean. Okeechobee began blackouts in January and signaled the town with a loud whistle from the cannery. Oddly, coastal towns resisted blackouts and only submitted to "dim outs." Vessels were outlined against a lit coastline and it was not "loose lips sink ships," it was lights.

The boardwalk of Jacksonville, Florida was shocked one evening in the spring of 1942 to see a monstrous explosion as the cargo ship, *Gulfamerica,* was torpedoed within US shipping lanes. People could not believe their eyes as a submarine surfaced a mile off shore and began firing to finish off the vessel. Private boats and yacht owners became a volunteer civil defense flotilla. The governor of Florida enforced a much stricter blackout but the heavy loss of US ships continued.

As Herbert read about these incidents he became suspicious of everyone around him. Dozier Smith came to see Herbert and was alarmed when Herbert threatened him and shot his pistol past him. As an explanation Herbert yelled he was making generators for the Army. Smith thought the man was impossible and left.

Civil Defense volunteers were mobilized to watch the beaches of Florida but in June four saboteurs were successfully dropped off the German submarine U-584. Four more were let off at Long Island, New York. One of the eight reneged from their mission to destroy factories and bridges and went to the FBI with the plan. All were captured and six were executed.

Coastal residents were anxious as repeated sinkings of US ships were reported. It was not uncommon to stand on the beach and see black smoke rising on the horizon from several ships that had been torpedoed. The public was not told of the extent of loss as U-boats operated with impunity. Rumors flew about bread wrappers from the local Bell Bakery washed ashore with the debris from a German U-boat sinking. In fact, the first U-boat sunk was off the North Carolina coast, not Florida.

Suspicion was irrational. This meant only one thing: there must be a local collaborator. Who would do such a thing? Who among them was different and maybe a sympathizer? Some of the bootleggers in the Bimini Community were fiercely dedicated to their country and looked to the only person they considered a possible suspect, Herbert Irwin. Didn't he look like a German officer? Always so spotlessly uniformed in those khakis he wore? What was he doing sitting for hours at a time on the beach at Ft. Pierce? Hadn't they heard stories from seaman who were rescued by a German officer who spoke perfect English and wore khakis? What about all those machines Irwin had in his workshop? What if he made radios and signaled those submarines? We don't know who he is. The good citizens of the Bimini Community who winked at liquor and import laws went to the FBI.

When Herbert came to the gate of his property to confront two men in suits he was enraged someone reported him as a possible collaborator. Herbert let the two FBI agents on his property but stopped them at his workshop. Refusing to open his locked door, Herbert told them he was producing generators for the Army and he belligerently questioned their authority to see his operation. If they wanted to see inside his workshop he insisted on proper authority from the Army. If Irwin really was supporting the war effort as a contractor they weren't informed about it. They probed Herbert as to his activities and trips to the beach.

Herbert brought them to his house and produced his typed field notes about trawling with fish baits. Herbert showed them his discharge papers from the first war and angrily denied their suggestions. He was able to produce work orders from the Army. They looked at his truck and did not see any radios or anything for parts for one. This man didn't even have a radio to listen to. They did not see any mirrors or beacon lights, neither did they see any antennas either on the man's house, workshop, or his truck. The FBI agents glanced toward Herbert's huge garden but didn't see the three-foot tall poppy pods beyond his corn. Herbert was more concerned about them seeing his stored fuel and metal in his workshop.

Amazingly, the agents backed down from a forceful man who insisted he was a government contractor. The FBI agents left, referring the investigation to the Army.

After the incident Herbert withdrew from people even more. He was convinced if the Germans or Japanese did not get him, "they" would. He did not know who reported him but he avoided people more than ever. Herbert stopped his weekly trips to town for months.

On those rare trips, the first time a merchant would not sell him sugar without a ration card Herbert turned away muttering. He refused to sign up for the ration cards. He simply would use his sugar cane.

By the end of 1943 Herbert had settled into a routine that kept him more unaffected by the war than most citizens. Completing his generators one at a time he eventually fulfilled his contract to the Army. Only a handful of people saw him and fewer still ever spoke to him. His trips to town were so infrequent only a small number of people knew there was a man living inside the metal fence of the Indian White Hammock.

Herbert had almost no contact with his family after their blowup of 1921. Carmon had seen Herbert once about his tax situation. Ruey saw him several times before he left Amarillo. But they were the only family members he had seen in years. His short note to Ruey was Herbert's only correspondence.

In Floydada, the three Irwin brothers sat down at a table together. Their mother, Martha, had passed away in Berkeley without a will. She had inherited some Copeland assets years before and it was necessary to have a legal succession and probate. They needed brother Herbert's signature. Delicate Alta Mae was being cared for in a New York institution. Gracie had family obligations in New

Mexico. It was out of the question for Ruey to go. Felix didn't think Herbert would even talk to him. Neither did he look forward to confronting his brother. Other than Ruey, the amiable Carmon was probably the one Herbert would least likely be angry with. Carmon was appointed to bring the legal document to Florida and have Herbert sign it. Leisure driving during the war was now prohibited so Carmon took the train.

The train to Florida was crowded with soldiers and WASPs and Carmon was one of the few men not in uniform. There were no berths available and Carmon slouched down and tried to sleep. Three days later in Okeechobee Carmon found a hotel and walked to the Okeechobee Hardware store. If anyone knew where Herbert was hiding out it would be the people here. The only address Ruey had for Herbert was a Post Office box. Ellis Meserve was out but the clerk knew of Herbert Irwin. He told Carmon it was eight miles out of town and if he would wait he could ride with his delivery truck driver.

When pressed for information, the driver could offer nothing about Herbert Irwin. He had never made a delivery to him but knew where he lived, at the Indian White Hammock. The driver dropped Carmon off at the dirt drive and told Carmon he would come back in one hour.

Carmon stood at the fence puzzled. He didn't see any gate although he saw a worn path a vehicle had seemingly driven right through the fence. The path extended into a thick grove of trees. All he saw was a continuous metal and barbed wire enclosure stretching into the underbrush to his right and to his left. Carmon yelled toward the trees, waited, then yelled again. He walked down the road but the underbrush was even denser. Surely Herbert wasn't squatting on this property living in the woods. Has he gotten this bad? Carmon walked back to the drive and whooped again. He was startled as a voice close to him spoke from the trees by the road.

"What do you want?"

Carmon wheeled and looked at his brother hid behind some thick trees and underbrush.

"Herbert, it's me, Carmon. I came to see you about some family business."

Herbert looked at the man but didn't recognize him. Herbert's memory of his brother was different than the man who stood before him.

Herbert said, "You're not my brother."

Carmon listened to the suspicion in Herbert's voice and saw a heavy bulge in his jacket pocket. Carmon was careful not to upset Herbert and spoke quietly to him.

"Herbert, it is me. I know it's been years since you've seen me but I'm Carmon, your brother. I have to talk to you. I'm not going to hurt you."

Herbert stood silently for some time unsure if this was really Carmon or not. Even if it was why would he come here? Ruey must have sent him.

"Why did you come here?"

"Because Ma died in California. You have to sign some papers."

"I don't want anything she has and I don't have to sign anything. Get out of here."

"We know you don't. Look Herbert, can't I come in? Ruey sent me. And the others. I just want to talk to you. And you can put that gun up. I've never done anything to hurt you."

Herbert debated and finally went to the gate. Fascinated, Carmon watched Herbert unlock the gate. It was totally hidden in the metal pipe post and he would never have noticed it had Herbert not opened it. Herbert was so smart. Why couldn't he be normal like everyone else? Why was he like this?

Carmon expected Herbert to guide him into the grove of trees but Herbert locked the gate again and returned to the trees to the side of the gate.

Herbert said, "You can't come any farther. What do you want?"

Carmon looked deeper into the grove of trees and could just see the bare outline of a shack through the dense vegetation. When Herbert had kept sheep his hired sheepherder stayed in the lean-to at the edge of the Hammock. Now Herbert kept his seed potatoes in it with some tools. Carmon could not see Herbert's house or monstrous workshop. Carmon thought, is *that* what Herbert is living in? For Herbert to be so brilliant Carmon was saddened his brother had come to this. Herbert's hands were out of his pockets and Carmon didn't feel as threatened. Now to convince Herbert to sign these papers.

"Herbert, Ma died and she didn't leave a will. We know how you feel so we drew up these papers for the succession. If you'll sign them we'll leave you alone. Ruey asked if you would do that for us."

Herbert unfolded the documents, annoyed Carmon was here and still harboring long held bitterness toward his parents. He stared at the papers for a long time.

Carmon said, "Your signature needs witnesses. We could either go to town or you could sign them later and mail them. Whatever you want. Ruey said you would."

Herbert folded the papers and placed them in his coat pocket. Carmon took that as reluctant agreement and tried to get what information from his brother he could. He asked the one question he knew would have an answer.

"What are you working on now?"

Herbert said, "I'm smoking meats. I invented a smoker."

"That's good. Are you doing okay?"

Well aware of the impression he was creating Herbert purposely avoided correcting Carmon and said, "I'm working on my smoker. You need to leave now." Herbert did not have any emotional sentiment whatsoever to his mother dying. It was only a fact to be digested. Carmon was keeping him from his work.

The meeting was awkward and Carmon glanced at his watch hoping his ride would come early. "Okay, Herbert. Let me out."

Even though they had not been thirty feet from the locked gate Herbert had to unlock it again to let Carmon out. Herbert locked the gate back and turned away as Carmon's attempted goodbye faded to silence. He had come half way across the United States for a twenty minute awkward conference. He watched Herbert walk toward the grove of trees.

The deliveryman picked up Carmon and they returned to town. Carmon took a train the next day. In Texas he told the family their brother Herbert was a pathetic fugitive from tax evasion. He was squatting on Indian property, broke, living like a hermit, still obsessed with tinkering. Their disgust for their brother was mutually shared. Ruey only listened.

Herbert signed the succession feeling justified in his hatred for his family. Being cut out of any inheritance of his mother's didn't surprise him and he did not care. Had they insisted Herbert accept his portion he would have cast it back in their face. The documents divided the assets among the other siblings. He mailed it to Ruey convinced he would not have to be bothered with his family anymore.

Eden Turns To Hell

While other cattlemen contracted with the Army Herbert quietly sold his cattle on a thriving beef black market. He never once thought about the legality of selling his cattle, only the profit. If the Army wanted his cattle they could pay what the black market was. To Herbert it wasn't a black market, it was a free market.

While even Hollywood celebrities felt the constrictions of a nation at war Herbert was almost untouched. The rest of the country dealt with shortages of fuel, sugar, beef, butter, and rationing of merchandise such as boots and clothing. Herbert's preparations had paid off. Those willing to operate outside the confines of rationing laws were a small but resourceful group. Neighbors bartered for their needs but Herbert was never part of it.

Herbert's concern in the early months of the war waned into apathy as the passing months stretched into four grueling years of global conflict. When German U-boat activity off the coast ceased with Navy escorts Herbert's paranoia lessoned. He followed the major battles of the war in the newspapers only as a curiosity. History was in the balance with soldiers dying every day but Herbert passed over the obituaries of Okeechobee's lost sons.

Herbert read about D-Day on June 6, 1944 well after the fact. He did not read of the atomic bombs dropped on Hiroshima or Nagasaki until the Japanese had announced their surrender on August 15, 1945. He read about this incredibly powerful bomb that had wiped out two whole cities but Herbert was only interested in the science of it. When the war was over and thankful Americans were wildly celebrating in major cities Herbert was quietly working. While parents, wives, and sweethearts mourned their loss with scars that would never heal, Herbert was indifferent to the national, battered sigh of relief.

Eden Turns To Hell

The country's consciousness gradually returned to domestic issues in 1946. Florida once again concentrated on its economy. The state began enforcing health restrictions in the cattle industry that had been in place for years. Whereas Herbert was able to avoid dipping requirements in previous years, inspectors made it increasingly difficult to ignore. Herbert angrily rejected the law and turned back to the black market, selling his cattle to those who did not care if his cattle had been dipped for ticks or not.

Herbert's life was marked in increments of time related to his garden, seasons, and his projects. He still worked on his smoker with his concentration completely focused on his food. He experimented with various traps and began work on a design for a crossbow. Herbert disliked the loud noise of a gun when he hunted or killed a trapped animal. He spent hours shooting his crossbow at targets.

Herbert had always enjoyed excellent health due to his lifestyle but he was fifty-three now. His teeth were bothering him and going to a dentist was not to be considered. He had two molars that ached and he frequently made a paste of heroin and tea leaves to relieve the pain. He decided he must pull them himself. Herbert used a mirror to cut his own hair and he fashioned a dental tool out of a mirror and metal. He positioned himself so the white light of his carbide lamps reflected into his mouth and dental tool into a mirror. He knew he could do it because pulling one's own teeth was not that uncommon to people unable to afford a dentist. Herbert had effectively used his heroin to tranquilize himself through storms for years now. He needed to medicate himself enough to pull a molar but still be coherent.

Herbert laid out his tools trying to anticipate any problems. He had several pliers. He tore up an old shirt for rags. He had some tongs. A bottle of water. Herbert injected his heroin, a heavier dose than usual. He made a paste of the bitter opium and packed the side of his gums knowing the residual from that would affect him, too. He reasoned he must pull the tooth quickly before the heroin overcame him. Before the euphoria escalated Herbert took a deep breath and clamped his pliers on the infected tooth. The grinding pain was still preferable to having anyone touch him. With a firm, hard pull he pulled the bloody tooth from his gum. Herbert felt dizzy and rinsed his mouth with water and packed his gums with opium tea leaves. He fell back on his bed with blood and water oozing from the side of his mouth. He drifted into a dreamy state of semi-consciousness.

Hours later Herbert roused with throbbing pain in his jaw. He pulled the bloody rag from his mouth and spat out blood clots. He rinsed his mouth several times and packed his gums again this time with a small amount of opium tea leaves. The day wore on as Herbert tended to his jaw easing in and out of a fog of awareness. He felt the familiar cramping in his stomach when he knew he had ingested too much heroin. By evening he was feeling much better and could distinguish the tender soreness from the extraction rather than the throbbing of an infected tooth. He was able to eat soup for dinner and the next day to work. Herbert waited a week and pulled the other infected tooth.

As 1947 brought heavy rains to southern Florida Herbert was more distressed with the weather this year since he had been in Florida. Summers always had a lot of rain but nothing like this. 1944 and 1945 had been drought years and it seemed the weather was making up for it. Herbert was often forced to spend a whole week inside his house and workshop and he took his heroin more often than he ever had. So heavy were the rains the state would eventually record 100 inches of rain in southern Florida that year, triple the amount of 1945. The whole southern portion of the state was waterlogged.

There were remarkably few people in Okeechobee who even knew of Herbert's existence. He wasn't active in industry anymore and did not socialize at all. Herbert had isolated himself from his neighbors in the Bimini Community. Those he did have contact with still held suspicion he was a German spy well after the war was over. They all left him alone.

By the 16th of September Herbert had been enjoying some rare clear days working in his garden. He was turning over the topsoil in preparation for a winter garden and paused to look at the cloud formations. These were very peculiar. He saw successive strings of clouds to the southeast curving and fading to the west. The clouds were wider to the east. He couldn't understand it. They almost resembled the ends of a pinwheel. By late afternoon Herbert felt the familiar agitation when the barometric pressure dropped that meant a storm was imminent. But it didn't make sense because the sky was clear except for those odd clouds. Herbert was puzzled. By late afternoon the eastern sky was overcast and dark with a brisk wind blowing. Herbert felt horrible and knew these were storm clouds. He locked his workshop and penned his mule. Herbert made sure he had enough water inside his house if the rain lasted a week.

All of southern Florida had been listening to their radios and reading their newspapers. They had been paying close attention to the hurricane that was bearing down on the Bahamas. Before it made landfall Floridians prepared for the worst. The residents of the Bimini community, bootleggers and farmers, orchard owners and cattlemen, all helped each other secure their livestock and supplies. They had been through this so many times before. As the wind picked up to gale force it began stripping leaves off the citrus trees. Everyone went home to ride out the storm. Birds flew deep into the trees as debris blew across the road. Cattle bawled from their barns and sheep nervously milled about in their shelters. Those few that drove past Herbert Irwin's place ignored him. Surely he knew.

Herbert took his heroin as soon as he locked himself inside his house. It had its usual calming affect on him but this time he seemed to be more agitated. Why was this storm any worse than the others? The wind blew harder and Herbert was alarmed as he heard the howling wind roar around his house. He listened to the limbs of the massive oaks groan with the wind. The wind wasn't gusting; it was hard, sustained, and was growing stronger and more powerful than he ever knew wind could blow. Herbert paced and paced in his house. The rhythm of his pacing did not calm him this time. The deafening noise was so intense Herbert held his hands to his ears. What was this? What could cause such a storm? What? *This had to be a hurricane.*

Herbert had heard Floridians talk of hurricanes but he had nothing in his experience to relate to this. As hour upon hour of 160 mile an hour wind pummeled his house Herbert's fragile equilibrium failed him. He felt his riveted metal home shake in the relentless wind. It shuddered and clanged as tree limbs slammed against it. Only the metal bars over his window prevented a limb from crashing through it. He covered his head and ears to make the noise stop, the noise, the intolerable noise. Several of the ancient oaks of the Hammock were uprooted from the saturated ground. The storm sounded like a freight train trying to mow him down with all the momentum and awful force of a great locomotive. The noise of rain so heavy it was like surf crashing against his metal asylum. Herbert's sobbing could not make the noise stop. He lost all sense of where he was and his frantic pacing gave way to exhaustion and he fell into his bed. He covered his head with his pillow but the awful noise would not stop. Herbert shrieked in his pain and fear. His mind skidded out of control until he had no comprehension of time or place.

The wind and rain battered the Indian White Hammock for hours. Herbert was numb with exhaustion but realized the wind had stopped. He lay in his bed wild-eyed and fighting for self-control. Shaking violently, trembling, Herbert sat up and listened. He could hear great noise but it was distant. The first thing he wanted was his heroin. Herbert staggered to his table and injected himself with a generous dose of the drug. Herbert tried to think. Momentarily, the heroin calmed him Herbert forced himself to remember what he had heard people say about hurricanes. He recalled them talking about the cyclones and how the eye of the storm passed over but the second half of the storm could be even worse. Herbert looked up through the slats of his shutters and could see stars in the black night. How much time did he have before it began to blow again? Herbert did not think he could survive another beating like that. He drank some water but couldn't bring himself to eat. Herbert thought he heard the wind lifting again. Yes, it was coming. In minutes the gale was upon him again.

The night of wind was one of incoherent nightmare. Herbert did not remember his screams or clutching his head in agonized delusion. He did not remember cowering in his bed wrapped tightly in his sleeping bag desperately seeking comfort when none was to be had. Even the heavy dose of heroin could not make the storm bearable. Herbert was consumed with terror for the first time in his life and he could not escape. This was hell.

Morning brought some measure of calm. The wind died and moved on. When Herbert finally gathered the courage to open his louvered vents and look out he was in shock. He saw the carcasses of his cattle stacked against his six-foot fence. His wind gauge was ripped off the fence post, and he had bolted the metal apparatus firmly. The top of the fence was only two feet above the lake of muddy water that surrounded him. There was water everywhere extending deep into the woods. The Hammock was the highest knoll on his property and yet the water was even with his doorsill. Another inch and it would have flooded his house. Herbert looked out the opposite window and saw two mighty oaks with their tangled roots poking upward like a muddy black hand. Downed trees were everywhere. One of them had flattened the pen where he kept his mule. Herbert didn't see the mule anywhere. He saw huge limbs everywhere snapped and twisted off the grand trees. The only time Herbert had ever seen trees damaged like this was from tornadoes. The Hammock looked like a battlefield.

It would be a week before Herbert regained enough emotional stability to leave his house. He was afraid his precious machines were flooded although the workshop was at the same level as his house. Herbert donned rubber boots and cautiously waded through the water toward his workshop. He stopped fifteen feet from it and recoiled in fear. The water had receded enough there was a narrow strip of muddy ground against the east side of his workshop. Hundreds of snakes were packed solidly against the wall in a roiling mass like the head of a giant Medusa. Herbert cried out and returned to his house filled with a new terror.

Eden Turns To Hell

A second storm came but was not quite as bad as the first. But no matter to Herbert, it terrified him all over again. By the time a tropical storm followed the second storm Herbert's fragile mental state was all but gone. The incessant rain very nearly destroyed him. Herbert stayed in his house on and off for five weeks waiting for the water to recede and the snakes to leave. He had no idea what happened to his mule or his remaining cattle. While other cattlemen and farmers braved their flooded property to try and feed them Herbert had no regard for his animals other than monetary value. If they survived the storms, fine. Herbert was only concerned about his paradise turning into a watery prison. Herbert had made a decision in among the wind, the rain, and floods. He would leave Florida. *He absolutely could not tolerate this.*

When Herbert was eventually able to get out he found his emaciated mule on a high knoll at the northwest side of his property with his surviving cattle. The only reason his mule had lived was the downed oak broke the fence and allowed it to get out and find higher ground. Herbert led the mule back to his pen at the hammock and found dry hay and grain for it.

The final report on the series of storms made history. It was two days before the first category-four hurricane passed completely over the state. It dumped so much rain it would be six months before the floods completely dissipated. The eastern part of the state from Orlando to the southern tip of Florida was flooded with a five million acre lake. Seventeen people were killed in Florida. The storm would eventually claim fifty-one lives when it crossed the Gulf of Mexico and hit Louisiana and Mississippi in a subsequent landfall. As if that weren't bad enough, a second hurricane slammed Florida from the southwest. It crossed Okeechobee on the opposite track of the first storm, right over the Indian White Hammock. After the second hurricane a tropical storm hit, all within a five-week period. Southern Florida was a battered fighter hanging off the ropes trying to recover from nature gone berserk. The first hurricane would eventually be classified as one of the worst in Florida's memory.

When the ground dried out enough Herbert could again drive out of his property he went straight to the Post Office in Okeechobee. He had a carefully composed letter addressed to International Paper Company asking them about property in Sabine Parish, in the far northwest corner of Louisiana.

Herbert was making plans to leave Florida. He would move far enough inland a hurricane could not reach him. He would be high enough in the hills floods could not drown him. He would find peace in a place called the Free State of Sabine.

1949 – 1981

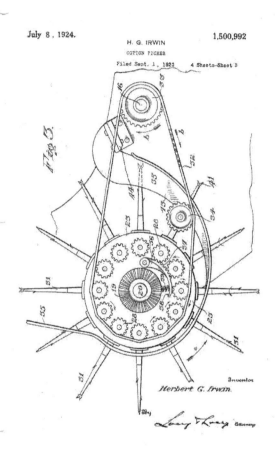

July 8 , 1924.

H. G. IRWIN

COTTON PICKER

Filed Sept. 1, 1920   4 Sheets-Sheet 3

1,500,992

Inventor

Herbert G. Irwin.

Chapter Eleven

Refuge in No Man's Land

Herbert never did anything out of whim. Every move was calculated and thought out with deliberate consideration. Years ago Herbert recalled hearing about Sabine Parish – No Man's Land. It immediately came to mind when he determined he must leave Florida. He had driven through Sabine Parish on one of his trips to and from Florida. Relocating to Louisiana appealed to him for many reasons. He needed to live far inland from the Gulf Coast, safe from the ravages of another hurricane. Even if one hit the Sabine River head on and tracked inland he wouldn't have to worry about flooding in the hills.

If Herbert ever decided to go into manufacturing again a place centrally located in the country would keep shipping costs down. Going back to Texas to open old wounds was not an option. He readily recalled why he left the first time. He still stung with resentment over his family and his tax problems. He had never let go of his emotional pain associated with his home state. Herbert needed to remain in the south with a warm climate because of his lifestyle. More than that he sought a place where he could comfortably live off the land by growing his own food.

In the same manner Herbert located his property in Florida from the Consolidated Naval Stores he communicated with International Paper Company about land in Louisiana. Herbert received correspondence from IP

169

stating there were several parcels of land available in northwest Louisiana, in Sabine Parish. Herbert made plans to drive to Louisiana as soon as the roads in Florida allowed passage after the storms.

Herbert wanted to produce smokers but there were changes developing in the welding industry as well. His Welderz Frend technology was fading and the industry was now looking at portable cylinders of compressed gas. Royalties from Herbert's agricultural patents had effectively run out although he had amassed a considerable fortune. He considered manufacturing tanks for welders as well as smokers. The particular tract Herbert was interested in was situated beside a railroad and would be an ideal location for a factory.

Sabine Parish possessed a climate Herbert could easily adapt to. There was an abundance of good water, unpolluted air, and sufficiently isolated. Louisiana's tax system was desirable with their liberal Homestead Exemption law.

Herbert sought a place that would afford him a comparable level of privacy as he had enjoyed in Florida. Herbert knew his reclusive lifestyle was peculiar from how most people lived but he was helpless to change. This was how he wanted to live and this was how he was comfortable.

Herbert was interested in those factors that would serve him and people were incidental to his decision. He had no intention of interacting with them any more than he ever did. Herbert did not consider how his presence or his habits affected people he came in contact with.

Herbert's reasons for choosing Sabine Parish were unrelated to its complex history. At one time both the French and Spanish claimed the land that would later be named Sabine Parish. Even though the area was in dispute since the 1700s it acquired the label "No Man's Land" with the

Louisiana Purchase in 1803. Its western boundary is the Sabine River, which separated Texas and Louisiana. The eastern boundary extended to Los Adaes (or, Arroyo Hondo) and the Calcasieu River. Los Adaes was one of many Spanish mission forts on that branch of the El Camino Real that stretched from Mexico City to Nacogdoches, Texas, then continued to Natchez, Mississippi. The mission was established in 1716, located a few miles east of Robeline, LA.

Los Adaes was the provincial capital of Texas for fifty years. The dispute lasted until 1806 when the Neutral Ground Treaty was ratified and the area was named the Sabine Free State. Consequently, No Man's Land became a neutral territory with no jurisdiction or law enforcement by either. The issue wasn't completely settled until 1819 when Spain abandoned all claim to land east of the Sabine River. No Man's Land could be applied in cultural as well as legal terms. Sabine Parish still proudly calls itself No Man's Land.

Folklore has long held pirates regularly made their way up the Sabine River from the Gulf of Mexico. There is some historical record to indicate that. The absence of any law enforcement in No Man's Land encouraged such activity. There are some who insist Murrell's Gold and Blackbeard's Treasure, among others, are buried on the former banks of the Sabine River. If there was any treasure it is lost underneath Toledo Bend Lake. Mention any pirate's name from history known to frequent the Gulf of Mexico, and there is usually a tale placing him in No Man's Land.

The Caddo Tribe who inhabited the area lived in general tolerance of the white man's encroachment. They were some of the last tribes to submit to moving Native Americans onto reservations. There are darker complexioned residents of

Sabine Parish who for generations were incorrectly identified as Mexicans. Recent academic study has identified them as descendents of the exiled Spanish official, Y'Barbo. He brought some Apaches with him into the region, resulting in a community named Ebarb. Another group of distinctive Spanish speaking residents has been traced to Castilian Spain.

The Sabine River that separates Texas and Louisiana is a topographical and geographic barrier for such a small river. Whereas southern Louisiana is marshy, flat, and pocked with bayous, the northwest is marked by rolling pine hills. Even though the Texas side of the Sabine River is similar the acidic soil on the Louisiana side is particularly hospitable for growing pine trees, hence, timber company dominance.

Small patches of privately owned timber in Sabine Parish existed but most property was owned by International Paper Company. Herbert knew the timber companies would never sell out their vast land holdings and he was almost guaranteed an isolated existence.

The rolling hills of thick forestland is well suited for someone to hide in who does not want to be found. No Man's Land has always attracted its share of people who are more comfortable residing in isolated forests.

There are several classes of people in Sabine Parish. There are the landed gentry; those families who managed over generations to accumulate power and wealth by controlling the land, banks, politics, business, schools, and therefore, people's lives. The class distinction is discernible, still entrenched today. Then there are the poverty stricken and poorly educated. They scrape out a daily living in one of the few places such an existence is possible. They would argue they are independent, free of property or responsibility. The demographic in between is mixed with those who managed to secure exceptional jobs, commuting outside the parish, off shore oil, or start businesses. Then, anyone who excelled had to leave to do so. A generation later, Noble has a higher medium income level than the rest of the parish.

Herbert had known of the Free State of Sabine before but it was his first visit to Noble. When Herbert arrived the tiny village was a poor logging town with gutted dirt roads and gravel. Noble is located off Highway 171, so poor in 1947 horseback and team and wagon were common transportation. The Noble Mercantile still had a hitching rail behind the store. Most people had trucks and only a few had cars. Certainly no one in the parish had a green panel truck. In a small town where residents could observe their neighbors in the normal course of their business Herbert attracted immediate notice.

As mayor of Noble at the time O.B. Knott had petitioned International Paper Company for years to release some of their land holdings in town to the residents. In discussions with IP District Manager, Sam Scott, O.B. was told, "I'm really sorry, O.B, but IP is just not in the real estate business. We grow pine trees." O.B. could not accept his answer and appealed to the Regional Office of International Paper Company in Mobile, Alabama. IP finally initiated the process to sell property within the city limits of Noble. One of the first petitioners was O.B. Knott for the land his family had been residing on for over a decade.

It is hard to describe the village Herbert drove into that first time. Content with what little they had, Noble was a hardscrabble town hopeful for better times. Political and cultural influences would hardly allow them to rise above leverage working against them. There never had been any landed gentry in Noble; only hard working people. Noble cared about its neighbors and looked out for each other. Children could wander all over town and unconcerned parents would not worry about their safety. Someone would offer them a drink of water or a snack and shoo them home before dark.

In this setting, Herbert Irwin was seen in Noble one bright fall afternoon in 1947, behind the Knott family house. Herbert had studied the plat IP sent him and stood on the property looking around. A north south dirt road divided the property into a two-acre tract across the road with four acres on the east side. The railroad paralleled the road a quarter mile away to the east. Herbert looked across the pasture to the south to view his nearest neighbor in a house some two hundred yards away. There were large pines across the road and on the north side of the four-acre tract. He noted there was ample space for his workshop and house. There was room for a garden although not as large as he had in Florida. The lot was level and would be easy to build on. Herbert would have preferred more acreage but with timber company ownership surrounding the area, it would suffice as an adequate buffer so people would not be too close to him.

O.B. was an imposing figure at six feet four with a resonant voice. When he saw a green panel truck parked on the parcel of land behind his pasture he summoned his twin boys, Roland and Ronald, to follow him to see what the man wanted.

O.B. sized up the man as he approached him. Herbert was dressed the same as he always was, pressed khaki pants and immaculate shirt, clean brogan shoes, and fedora hat. His appearance was striking with a military presence and bearing.

"I'm O.B. Knott. I was wondering if I could help you." He extended his hand but the stranger only nodded.

"I'm Herbert Irwin. International Paper Company told me this land is for sale."

Surprised, O.B. said, "Well, that's interesting. I have an offer to buy this property. There hasn't been any land for sale here in fifty years. Are you interested in buying land?"

"Yes. This land. I'm a manufacturer. I make smokers for meats. Spices. I'm hunting land for a factory."

"A factory? You would put in a factory here?"

Herbert nodded his agreement.

"How many men would work in your factory?"

Herbert sensed this man had information and was willing to share a little of his plans.

"I'd start with a dozen. Maybe more if I manufactured tanks for welders."

O.B. thought of what a dozen jobs would mean to Noble. There had been efforts to get jobs in Noble since the big mill closed in 1919. The only jobs in town were with a small sawmill that paid five men 75 cents an hour. Most everyone else worked contract labor cutting timber and pulpwood.

"We need jobs here. If you are going to put in a factory I'll help you any way I can. I can even recommend some good workers to you."

Herbert asked, "Do you know where the boundaries are on this plat?"

Familiar with the tract, O.B. showed Herbert the corners of the property. They walked across the road to look at the two acres. Herbert said, "This lot would be for parking."

O.B. thought if he was thinking of the cleared area across the road for parking Irwin must be considering a large facility in time. Herbert asked, "Will the town try to tell me what I can do here?"

"You can do anything you're big enough to do here. And legal."

Herbert asked the next question that was important to him. "Is this good soil?"

"No, this whole country is red clay. It isn't good for anything except growing pine trees. But this tract is where the old planer mill was back fifty years ago. This lot has good topsoil. That's why we have such good gardens."

"Did the mill dump any chemicals here?"

"No. That part of the mill was in my pasture. The only thing here is decomposed wood chips."

The conversation lasted almost an hour and the men walked back to Herbert's truck. O.B. admired the vehicle noting it was new and clean, something cars and trucks in Noble were not. The logging trucks on the roads kept everything dirty. Herbert wanted to do something for this man who helped him and reached into his truck. He handed a penny paper sack of spices to O.B.

Herbert said, "I make these spices for my smoker. I use some on meats. These are for beans."

O.B. thanked Mr. Irwin and called his boys and they parted. Excited about the prospect of a factory in Noble, O.B. left Herbert Irwin with, "If there is any way I can help you let me know."

Herbert Irwin impressed O.B. but at the same time, he had never had anyone refuse to shake his hand before. A factory in Noble was definitely news and O.B. told his family about it when he walked back to the house. They lived in a pieced-together large house that had been remodeled from an old sawmill office.

O.B. poured the contents of the sack of spices on a saucer and joked with his wife, Viola, and sister, Maggie, "Smokey's" spices would help their cooking. One thing O.B. stressed after meeting Herbert Irwin is that this was obviously an intelligent man and he should make them a good neighbor. Ten-year-old Roland had listened to the conversation, fascinated with Herbert Irwin's whole persona.

Herbert never knew about the nickname O.B. had bestowed on him. The name, "Smokey" was not given in derision. In an area rife with endearments, Noble had men with nicknames of "Mulcy, Dooch, Puss, Ace, and Lightening." Smokey was easy to remember and descriptive enough everyone thereafter knew whom you were referring to. The name stuck even though Smokey was always called Mr. Irwin in person.

Herbert made the long trip back to Okeechobee and made his offer to IP to buy the tract in Noble, Louisiana. Southern Florida still bore the scars of the September storms. There were so many trees downed it would be months before they could be removed, and years to repair the roads that were washed out from the floods. Herbert began making plans for his move to Louisiana immediately.

The Arnold family of the Bimini Community knew Irwin's land was for sale and asked to look over the three twenty-acre parcels across the road from the larger tract. Herbert showed William E. Arnold the corners of the property and an agreement was made.

No one had entered his gate since Irwin had sold his sheep soon after moving there. Dozier Smith was interested in the larger 1380 acre tract but had little idea of the pasture, creek, and trees beyond what he could see from the road. Herbert had removed the passenger seat from his truck years before, and Smith stood on the running board and held on as they bounced over the perimeter of the property.

When they were completing the deeds William E. Arnold was also surprised Irwin insisted on typing the deeds himself and did not consult an attorney. Herbert refused to have any interaction with the Arnold women and stopped all conversation when they came near him. His negotiation was strictly with the male members of the family. Herbert literally turned his back on them and stubbornly commented, "A woman and a smart lawyer almost broke me."

Herbert turned his attention to securing the property he wanted in Louisiana. When Herbert had dealt with the Consolidated Naval Stores the purchase of his Florida property progressed swiftly. Herbert was annoyed with how long it took International Paper Company to plod through their corporate bureaucracy. He did not know IP had to approve the sale at the company's headquarters in New York City. As the months dragged on he became increasingly agitated about spending more time in Florida. His mind was made up and he did not want to remain into the next hurricane season. Finally IP's regional office in Mobile, Alabama mailed the deed to him in April, 1948.

The move from Texas to Florida seven years ago was hard but this move troubled Herbert worse. At times he took his heroin just thinking about the monumental task he was about to undertake, again. As spring stretched into summer Herbert looked around his property with regret. He had everything he ever wanted here. The Indian White Hammock was a tropical paradise. He had his garden and orchard. He had his beautiful workshop and the house that saved his life. But when Herbert reflected on the hurricane his fear was enough to convince him he had made the right decision to leave.

Just as he had inventoried his vast collection of machines, generators, and lathes before leaving Amarillo, Herbert reevaluated his needs for the move to Louisiana. With another factory in mind, Herbert would keep all his equipment. He would leave the workshop and house. Herbert still had enough metal stockpiled to build a near identical workshop in Louisiana. He retrieved his workshop plans and labeled the galvanized, metal railroad panels to fit together as an elaborate puzzle. The only difference between this move and the previous one was he must bring his fruit trees, his berry bushes, his seed stock, and most importantly, his heroin poppies. Over the long wait on IP to complete the property transaction Herbert began packing his machines on pallets.

Okeechobee was spared any hurricanes that season. Herbert contracted two brothers who dealt with cattle and who owned an orchard to move his equipment from the Indian White Hammock to the railroad in town. It took two weeks. The men were incredulous when they saw Herbert Irwin shoveling dirt off of stacks of sheet metal that apparently had been buried throughout the war.

Herbert took one whole side of his north fence line and every scrap of metal. Herbert left nothing except the stump puller he had made. One of Herbert's neighbors commented "It looks like he took everything that wasn't bolted down." Even with five fully loaded rail cars there was some machinery and metal that would not fit. Herbert contracted the Paige brothers to drive their cattle trucks to Louisiana to bring the remainder with his fruit trees and berry bushes. Herbert negotiated the sale of his cattle in exchange for their moving his equipment. He left Florida for Louisiana in September, 1948.

Herbert had found his city of refuge away from floods and hurricanes. He found the climate he wanted, the state, and the particular locale he hoped would be his final move. Herbert was fifty-five years old. More than that he hoped he would be left alone.

The Building The Fence

Chapter Twelve

The Building; The Fence

The Kansas City Southern Railroad was the only freight line down the western corridor of Louisiana in 1948. The tracks divided Noble, and what little activity occurred in town was centered at the junction of the railroad and the gravel road that intersected it. Freight trains could be seen coming from their approach from the south. Locomotive horns were a familiar background noise in logging towns along the rail line.

There were plenty of observers that morning in September when five well loaded railcars rolled into the east spur that separated the Noble Depot and the Post Office. Spectators gathered while the railcars slowed to a stop.

Noble had few deliveries. They had outgoing freight of wood products several times a week off the west spur, but rarely incoming freight. This was a real event! This was the proposed factory that would soon provide much needed jobs. Anticipation was high.

The three stores that faced the railroad tracks, the Noble Mercantile, Youngblood's, Helm's, as well as the Post Office, were ideally situated for the bench warmers to report their observations. The postmistress and her daughter, Marilyn Edwards, glanced through the open door of the Post Office and Mrs. Helm looked on from her store. Mr. Youngblood watched from his store porch. The town was so poor few could afford a camera and photographs were scarce. Folks' memory was the only thing that recorded the occasion. Winnie Webb later commented, if they had known how notorious Smokey would prove to be they would have paid more careful attention to him.

Lots of people asked questions about Herbert Irwin but no one had any answers. A person's origin and reputation were only what they told you. People weren't saddled with the burden of proving their identity. This was a time when wage earners were still paid in cash or paychecks without Social Security numbers. Herbert Irwin never said where he came from although residents did notice the Florida license plate on his truck. All Noble knew or cared about was, this man was supposed to put in a factory.

From Herbert's perspective, it did not occur to him to give any explanation as to his activities or purpose. Manufacturing smokers and tanks for acetylene welders was his genuine intent, but it wasn't his sole reason for moving to Louisiana.

The railcars were stacked with panels of galvanized corrugated metal. Metal rods and steel pipe were piled up in large bundles. Spectators thought this must be the factory building itself. At least it looked like one. Who knew what equipment this factory was supposed to have? Large and small crates were shrouded in tarpaulins. No one could say with any conviction what was on the pallets. One had a monstrous propeller jutting out from the side of it. What was this man doing with an airplane propeller?

Captivated by the sheer volume of the shipment townspeople watched and speculated. This must indeed be a large factory. Marilyn Edwards saw a wheeled contraption protruding from one tarpaulin and wondered why the man had half a car. All manner of unrecognizable metal jutted upwards out of the one mill gondola car. It looked like scrap metal to her. She wasn't the only one puzzled by it.

Depot agent Glenn Hough managed all the freight at the Noble Depot. Hough took pleasure in his authority but even he deferred to Herbert Irwin. Irwin insisted on personally supervising the unloading of his freight.

Herbert hired a local timber contractor to unload and transport his freight to his property. The contractor assigned six men with two flat bed trucks and one winch truck to the project. Young "Top" Anderson and Huett Garcie were thrilled to be paid $1.50 an hour when most laborers were being paid just 75 cents an hour.

Across the road several men watched the unloading from underneath the red oak tree. Young Peyton Youngblood stood on the porch of the family store. Everyone agreed this was the most exciting thing to happen to Noble since the mill closed. The dozens of crates measured up to six feet wide, four feet tall, and some eight feet in length. Smaller pallets were rigged with cable and carriage bolts so they could be picked up or pulled by a winch. Larger pallets were pushed and pulled and then settled onto a truck bed.

When the trucks were loaded they passed in front of the Knott home and turned right down the dirt road beside their pasture, to Irwin's property. The distance from the rail cars to the proposed factory site was only a half-mile.

Irwin had the lot scraped by a tractor blade a few days earlier to provide a smooth dirt floor. The lot was fairly level and little site preparation was necessary. Zoning boards and planning commissions were still entities of the future and a state permit was unnecessary, certainly in a small town. A property owner had the freedom to build a structure of any quality he chose. He was not bothered with any construction criteria or regulations. That was left to the builder.

The Building The Fence

The large crates were moved into place and Irwin repositioned the pallets by inches until he was satisfied. They were arranged in a particular order and alignment.

Next, the galvanized metal panels were off loaded and were taken to the factory site. Irwin directed the placement of the panels in increments around the perimeter of his building grid. The long process of unloading the rail cars and moving the contents to the factory site took all of five days. Crews used to handling whole railcars of timber, telephone poles, and cross ties were duly impressed with the systematic precision of the whole operation. Top Anderson remarked how heavy the pallets were.

Herbert hired a local laborer to help him assemble the building. Some said it was Clifton Malmay, others insisted it was his brother, Herman. Regardless, it was one of Vic Malmay's sons. Pleased to have a job, he paid little attention to the contents of the crates. The young man resembled many laborers in Sabine Parish. With his facial structure and brown skin he was referred to as Mexican but he was really Native American. He lived with his parents a short walk up the dirt road from Irwin's property, on Highway 171.

Herbert slept in his panel truck while they built the workshop and rarely left the property. He worked alongside his hired hand rather than directing his labor. A two-man crew was all that was necessary to construct this almost prefabricated building long before "prefab" was a common construction technique. Holes were dug at measured intervals around the perimeter, 120 feet by 40 feet. Cement was mixed and each metal pole was set with a vertical bubble level. Every load bearing center pole, vertical strut, cross braces, panels, doors, windows, and sliding garage door were all numbered and coded to fit together in an elaborate large-scale puzzle. Herbert was again the architect of every structure he built to work in. He had taken his workshop from concept, to detailed drawing, to actual construction.

Herbert positioned his workshop so the clerestory windows faced the southern sun. Thirty feet from the building on the north side were thick woods with second growth pine trees. They were over sixty feet tall intermixed with hardwood trees. Herbert reasoned the woods would act as a natural windbreak for any thunderstorms, yet far enough away as not to endanger the structure.

Herbert built the same basic workshop design in Florida. His Louisiana workshop was also new construction made from stored metal he had shipped from Texas to Florida, and then to Louisiana. The volume of galvanized, corrugated railroad metal hoarded all these years to fabricate two very large workshops was staggering.

His helper remarked to several people the whole project was one of overkill. Irwin bought heart red cypress from the Sabine Sawmill in Zwolle for board braces between the pole supports. The cypress boards were fitted with metal plates that were bolted in a sleeve around the poles. Every juncture was bolted rather than nailed for maximum strength, eight bolts being preferred whereas four would have sufficed. Each of the galvanized and corrugated metal sheets fit together in tightly fitting overlapping panels. It would have been difficult to insert a knife blade under them. The only pallet Irwin uncovered besides his tools was an oxyacetylene welder to weld the three-inch diameter metal poles of the workshop. It grew upward to its thirty-five foot tall peaked roof with clerestory windows running the full length of the roof line. An elaborate system allowed for a person to turn a crank at ground level and raise or lower the clerestory windows for circulation.

The Building The Fence

Herbert set the windows in his workshop for as much air circulation as possible. The workshop didn't have glass windows. Instead, the openings in the panels were topped with hinged galvanized plates that lifted up and could be propped open to allow for air flow. There were four on each side and two more at both ends. The inside window opening was fitted for an angle iron cross piece. The window panel left space for a crossbar to be shoved behind metal bars to lock the windows at night.

Herbert installed a garage door into the building he could drive his truck inside the workshop. Most garages had "barn doors" that opened from the middle, outward. From the road one couldn't tell there was any opening at all. It blended into the side and was so perfectly aligned in the closed position it appeared as a seamless wall. The garage door glided into a locked position and looked no different than the panels down the expanse of the building. One had to look closely to see the fist-sized padlock on the outside, inset into a boxed pocket so deeply set, it would be impossible for anyone to cut it. The lock could only be opened with Herbert's key.

There were two entry doors centered on the north and east sides of the building. Heavy gauge flat, galvanized sheets were riveted over the heart cypress core. The door frames were metal angle iron with wide machined hinges. The doors had several large interior locks on the inside. It seemed to the laborer an excessive amount of security but after all, this was a factory.

Both door sills had a one-inch high, two-inch-wide lipped pan, which caught the rainwater as it sheeted down the outside of the doors. Rain fell to the pan and drained out a series of holes drilled in the underside of them.

Herbert added a wind stop to prevent the doors from slamming open and shut in the wind. He welded an "L" shaped piece of metal that attached to the sides of the door frames. He fastened a rectangular piece of hard rubber, one-quarter inch by one inch by three inches, which protruded edge-outward from the doors. As the doors shut the rubber lip caught on the L shaped metal and held it against the wind. The construction of the building was remarkably quick for its size and was finished in a few weeks.

Herbert Irwin's building grew into a building that dominated a village of small wooden houses. The only larger building in town was the Noble school. Old small-scale sawmills were abandoned in rusted tin while Smokey's building gleamed bright in the sunshine. It was a dramatic departure in every way to all other structures in town: the depot, the grocery stores, the Post Office, and the two-story Lodge Hall. The only comparable building in the region was a sprawling factory twenty-five miles away, Nabor's Trailers, in Mansfield.

The Post Office was the town center and people crossing the village from any direction could see Herbert Irwin's building. Most of the town had been clear-cut of timber decades earlier and there were only a few trees to lessen the glaring spectacle of the building. Even the forest ranger could see it from the fire tower east of town. Since no one had the resources to build such an impressive factory people wondered what type of house Irwin would build.

Shortly after the workshop was finished two cattle trucks appeared in Noble with Florida license plates. The drivers approached O.B. hunting for Herbert Irwin and he directed them to Irwin's building. He invited the two men to his house for coffee after they made their delivery. O.B. saw the trucks parked south of the building but could not see what they were unloading.

The Building The Fence

Late that day the brothers parked their empty trucks on the gravel road and came to the house. Bobby and Jack Paige introduced themselves as cattlemen and owners of fruit orchards from Florida. O.B. welcomed the chance to find out more about his mysterious new neighbor and asked them, "Are you friends of Herbert Irwin?"

The brothers looked at each other and one replied, "Well, no. Irwin showed up in our area before the War. No one knew him or where he came from. We think, Texas. We didn't really know exactly where he lived until he hired us to move him. We thought he lived somewhere close to the Indian reservation. We heard Irwin ran cattle in the woods. A man can make pretty good money doing that. He said he was leaving because the government was going to make him dip his cows and he wouldn't do it."

O.B. was still curious and asked, "Does he have any family there?"

The other brother answered, "Not that we know of. Irwin keeps to himself and never mixes with people. You know, a loner. Irwin lived by himself in the woods. He came by one day and asked if we would take his things to Louisiana. We took some of his cattle in exchange for hauling his stuff and here we are. We did well. We really don't know anything about him. He appeared in town every week or so and then disappeared down the road. Sometimes it might be months before anyone would see him again."

Knowing only a little more than he already did, O.B. pressed them for a few more comments. He thanked the Paige brothers for their information and they left.

Sabine Parish in 1948 was used to open rage with cattle and hogs roaming freely in the woods. Half-wild cattle bedded down for the night all over Noble. Brands and earmarks were the designation of ownership and fenced pasture land was rare. The only fences around Noble were to protect people's gardens. A few families had picket fences around their yards for aesthetic value.

After Herbert and his helper finished the building they started the fence around the property. If people had any fence at all they normally felled one of the plentiful white oak trees scattered around the parish. They would split the logs and make fence posts from them. Metal fence posts were unheard of in Sabine Parish except chain fences in towns. Herbert used U shaped angle iron for his fence posts. By double layering thirty-inch wide hog wire, the fence was five feet in height. The wire layers were secured with metal twist ties. That would have been adequate to have kept any bull or hog. Such a fence created enough discussion but then Herbert bolted metal risers on top of the angle iron posts, facing outward, and strung three strands of barbed wire across the top. He now had a barbed fence six feet tall totally surrounding the workshop and four of his six acres. His gate was inset from the property line so when Herbert drove onto his property he parked in front of his gate. It was necessary to unlock the gate, open it, drive through and park a second time, and return to lock the gate. Then, to drive to the garage door, get out and unlock it, then drive inside his building. The door was shut and locked from within.

The building and fence were an insult to most residents. There weren't any thieves in Noble. We don't even lock our doors. Does this man not trust the town he chose to live in, and put his factory in? People considered fences were constructed elsewhere to keep livestock in, not here to keep people out.

Herbert's compound was completed. He planned for his building to last him the remainder of his life. He lovingly uncrated the rest of his machinery after the hired hand left.

Herbert paid him for his labor and escorted him to the gate. Anticipating future employment and what would appear an innocent question his helper asked, "Mr. Irwin, when are you going to open the factory?"

Herbert answered, "I'm going to get every Mexican I can inside this building and electrocute them."

The young man was shocked at such a statement and left hurriedly. He repeated the statement to anyone who would listen. What began as excitement over a new business in town changed to wary suspicion. O. B. Knott was told of the comment and as mayor and Irwin's neighbor, was asked to speak to him. His acquaintance thus far with Irwin had been positive. He couldn't fathom why the man would say such a thing but could see no reason to do anything. He would wait unless Herbert Irwin proved himself other than a responsible citizen.

Local reaction to the fence was as disconcerting as it was to the building. It didn't look like a factory at all; it looked like a detention facility. Several veterans remarked it reminded them of some of the prison camps they had liberated in WWII. A few locals who knew what the inside of a cell looked like murmured the barbed wire reminded them of their incarceration, only the barbed wire faced outwards.

Coupled with Herbert Irwin's threatening statement, his appearance and demeanor raised more questions. So soon after WWII he resembled what many thought was a German officer. He was not in the least friendly. And now, Irwin was holed up in this forbidding facility that dominated their town. What did that comment about electrocuting Mexicans mean? In a small town with few secrets, rumors soared.

Oblivious to any controversy surrounding him Herbert shut and locked his gate. He had deliberately made that menacing comment to his hired hand knowing it would instill enough fear in people they would be afraid of trespassing. All the anxiety of relocating, all the upheaval of having to move and step outside his comfortable routine, it was all worth it. He had his machines. He had his secure workshop and fence. He had his poppies.

Herbert couldn't even think about a house and at this point he did not care. The Paige brothers had brought his prairie bed and it stood inside his east door. Herbert breathed a contented sigh of pleasure and turned to his beloved machines.

No one would enter his building the next thirty-three years except for one forty-five minute visit from an FBI agent.

Suspicion

Chapter Thirteen

Suspicion

While the factory was being assembled, Postmistress Adna Edwards noted a few minutes before she closed for the day, when no one was there, Smokey came daily to the Post Office. Upon completion of the building and after his gate was locked, no one saw him for weeks.

All eyes were on the galvanized building that shimmered in the sun – the factory. There was speculation Smokey had sneaked out of town at night and wasn't even there. If he did no one saw when he came back. No light, no activity, no presence. No sign of a new business opening or notice of employment opportunities. Where was he? Hope for jobs in Noble was fading with each day of silence from the factory.

Smokey was contentedly setting up his equipment inside his workshop unaware of the stir of expectation that had the town watching his building so closely. He was seriously exploring manufacturing smokers and tanks for acetylene welding but that could wait. In the process of packing and relocating Smokey had to store his precious machines for months. He had not been able to indulge in his compulsive tinkering and it was almost more than he could bear. Smokey uncrated his lathes, his generators, forge, band saws, tool presses and dies. He wanted, indeed he was compelled to hear the whine of his machines. He must smell the acrid odor of carbide again.

Suspicion

Smokey felt so deprived he nearly worked himself to exhaustion, often forgetting to eat. Smokey napped, rose and worked again, completely unconscious of time or anything outside the walls of his workshop.

Smokey began reinforcing the superstructure of his workshop, welding into all hours of the night. While Smokey worked citizens saw the tell tale, blue white throbbing of light flashing from the clerestory windows. Smokey was definitely in that locked building, but what was he welding in there?

Smokey vaguely thought he needed to think about building a house beside his workshop like he had in Florida. He had placed his prairie bed in the northeast corner of his building temporarily. He was able to rise at any hour and work. He thought how wonderful it was to live with his machines. He had camped in his truck traveling back and forth from Texas to Florida, and now to Louisiana. It worked very well. Maybe he really didn't need a house. After all, who was to dictate how he should live? There was a time he had to be concerned how his idiosyncrasies were perceived by business and his industry. But the older he became the less he cared about what anyone thought of him. He would try a couple seasons and if he were able to tolerate the climate he would not build one. Smokey had much to do inside his workshop. One could always sleep, but work must be done every day, all day.

Noble was well familiar with their residents, but one Friday afternoon began a rigorous schedule with Smokey the town would observe with rare exceptions. The only thing that would alter Smokey's Friday outings would be severe weather or something that needed immediate attention. This was Smokey's only venture into the town, once a week for what amounted to only minutes. He would drive his truck to the Noble Mercantile, buy a few items, sometimes with a visit to the Post Office, and then return to his building.

Precisely at two p.m. on Friday Smokey emerged from his building. He opened the sliding door and backed his panel truck out turning the wheels until the truck faced the gate. He got out of his truck, slid the garage door shut, and locked it with its large padlock. He got in his truck and drove it to the gate, got out, unlocked it and opened the gate. He got in the third time and drove forward through the gate. He got out and locked the gate behind him. Smokey climbed back in his truck, and left his compound. Locking his building first and then his gate required him to leave his truck four times but Smokey would never deviate from this pattern, ever. He refused to leave his building or gate unlocked even though they were within steps of each other.

While the village wondered what Smokey was doing inside his building his former neighbor in Florida, Dozier Smith, was negotiating to buy his remaining 1340 acres. It was prime property and they finally agreed on a price. Smokey made the trip to Okeechobee without anyone in Noble knowing where he was going, or when he was gone. Smokey wired Dozier Smith to have his cash in hand.

Smith wondered why Herbert Irwin would drive all the way back to Florida but wasn't surprised when he insisted he would come for his cash. He knew Irwin trusted no one and well remembered the two times he had pulled a gun on him. When Smith read the deed that Irwin typed he knew the man not only did not trust people, he was truly paranoid.

"And the Vendor doth covenant with the Vendees that the premises are lawfully seized free of all mortgages, liens, or other encumbrances, and that the Vendees have good right and lawful authority to sell the same; and the Vendor does

hereby fully warrant the title to said land and will defend the title against the lawful claims of all prior vendors or owners who are not acting for or in behalf of an armed force, political party, or different kind or form of government, or not acting with intention to use or repossess any right, title, interest or part of said premises under a different kind or form of government as of the date on which this instrument is executed."

Smith and his partner, James Leeper, had seen a lot of deeds but had never seen such an entry before. They weren't sure what Irwin was trying to say about a foreign government but they were satisfied with the conveyance of the deed. Herbert insisted on an OVC stipulation and they agreed with that as well. Herbert typed the deed stating $10,400 but Smith and Leeper counted out thousands more. Herbert made sure Karl Stello was on hand and asked him to verify the amount. Irwin shoved the pile of bills in his leather bag and lifted it into his truck. Without a handshake, without so much as a thank you, Herbert Irwin turned and left Florida for the final time a very wealthy man.

The Bimini Community would never forget the secretive man that had lived among them during the war years and would tell their children and grandchildren about him.

Herbert drove back to Louisiana with his leather suitcase packed with cash. He went over the transaction in his mind repeatedly. When he tried to rehearse the counting of his money it became a jumble of figures he did not think added up to what it should. Karl Stello had always dealt fairly with him but after all, Smith, Leeper, and Stello were all Okeechobee residents. Smokey was so afraid they collectively had cheated him he determined to find an objective third party, a banker, to verify the amount in his bag. Herbert drove to Many before he went back to Noble.

Shortly afterward, O.B. Knott was in Many at the Sabine State Bank. Melton Knott was president of the bank and saw his cousin in the lobby through his office door. Melton invited O.B. in and shut the door. He wanted to make O.B. aware of the type person he had living behind him. The banker didn't think he was compromising confidentiality and wanted to tell of the incident out of genuine concern.

Melton told him, "O.B., you've got a lunatic for a new neighbor. Last month Herbert Irwin came in to the bank and demanded to see the president. When he came into my office he shut the door and said he wanted a responsible officer from the bank to go to Florida and get his money. I didn't take him literally because he seemed like an intelligent businessman. I told him, fine, all he needed to do was sign some papers and we'd take care of it. I told him a draft on his account would allow us to deposit the money in his bank account here and that it would take about a week or ten days. Irwin became upset and began ranting about banks stealing from depositors, the Roosevelt's had destroyed America, and a whole lot that didn't make sense. He made me nervous. Then he stormed out of the bank saying he would go get his own money."

O.B. shrugged. "Lots of people don't trust banks. Not after the Depression."

"I know, but this man wasn't acting normal. He was in a rage for no reason. Up to that point I was really impressed with Irwin but what happened after that is even stranger. About two weeks later he came back and demanded to see me again. When he came in my office he was carrying a big leather suitcase. It was like a carpetbag only it was made of leather. He heaved it up on my desk and told me to count his money and give him a receipt. O.B., that one deposit was the largest single deposit ever made at Sabine State Bank. It was all cash. He never wrote a single check on it and then he withdrew it."

Amazed, O.B. said, "I don't suppose you can tell me how much he deposited?"

"No. No, I can't. It would keep several families well fed for a very long time, though."

O.B. left but pondered on their conversation. He assumed Smokey was affluent because of his truck and the investment he had placed in his new factory. Melton saying Smokey's was the largest deposit at the bank was saying a lot. International Paper Company and several large sawmills had significant company and payroll accounts at Sabine State Bank. There were no outward signs of wealth such as elaborate clothing or jewelry. Smokey didn't spend much and he sure wasn't extravagant. So why was Smokey living in a metal building with a dirt floor if he had such wealth? O.B. tried to remember if he had ever met anyone as intelligent as Smokey was and could think of no one.

From his first appearance Smokey seemingly had no past; or at least none he was willing to relate. He deliberately avoided people or mixing with them. He would never talk to people unless absolutely necessary. In a small town where everyone's personal business was common knowledge no one knew anything about Smokey. Only that he came from Florida and who knew if that was correct? To guard your privacy that zealously there must be something about him that needed hiding. Who was this man and why did he come here, to Noble? And what did he *do* all day inside that building?

Smokey settled into his beloved routine of tinkering while Noble waited. Was this it? They barely saw any presence inside his compound but as the months passed more questions mounted than were answered. People saw him at the Noble Mercantile or the Post Office but that was all. In a very short time he acquired the mystique of an unknown. Smokey was a mysterious presence beyond a fence, behind blank walls, partially hidden by vegetation and locked away.

The only thing Noble had to base their relationship upon with Smokey was events. There were few trees to block anyone's view of town and residents noted Smokey hardly ever left the city limits of town. He was seen a few times puttering up the road to Zwolle and at the feed store. Someone said they saw him in Mansfield once. One had to be poised to see him leave his compound and that only occurred once a week.

Noble watched Smokey go to the Noble Post Office twice a month. He had one of the largest boxes at the Post Office and he began receiving thick, official looking manila envelopes. Rumor soon circulated Smokey must work for the federal government. The postmistress, Adna Edwards, and her daughter Marilyn who helped out, observed Smokey mailing sealed galvanized boxes he had handmade. Only Mrs. Edwards knew the correspondence was to the US Patent Office and to her credit, never mentioned it.

Following WWII there was widespread fear of "the bomb." The only understanding in Noble was that it was responsible for destroying two Japanese cities, which led to the end of the War. The pictures circulated through newspapers showed images of utter destruction. That was the extent of their knowledge. There was no one in Noble, not even schoolteachers, who had the slightest idea what an atomic bomb should look like. Public schools in larger cities began having bomb drills instead of tornado drills. Such was the pervasive fear in the national consciousness. That fear filtered all the way down to tiny Noble.

Radio was the primary media that kept the public informed. Television reception was poor unless you had a very tall antenna. In depth news coverage was confined to periodicals and newspapers. Sabine Parish had a weekly newspaper but it included mostly local news. Some families subscribed to *The Shreveport Journal*. If students needed information concerning a given subject they were limited to local libraries. Exhaustive news coverage would not become common until twenty-four hour satellite television and the Internet. Today, the most insignificant news event is broadcast worldwide in minutes. Global information is available almost in any library in the world, in almost any language. News and information coverage today is excessive; in 1950 it was inadequate.

Neither did the generation that survived two World Wars enjoy the education level of modern times. It was not unusual for young men to quit school to support their families, as did O.B. Knott. A college education was confined to professionals or the very wealthy. College financing that is available to students today was nonexistent then. Consequently, in a largely uneducated populace more information was exchanged from personal sources than from ones of credibility. Too often that information was conjecture and unreliable.

Within this backdrop, Smokey entered. This man was so different, so mysterious, secretive, and was seemingly capable of terrible things. Even though he never harmed anyone whispered gossip became more absurd every month. After all, he does have that building. None of us know what he has in there. Maybe he does work for the federal government. He might even be a spy. Maybe he was a dismissed scientist who held a grudge against the government. Remember all that hatred spewed out about Roosevelt? What is he making in there, doing all that welding? What about those crazy spells he has? What if he's making an atomic bomb in that building? We wouldn't know. It could be the size of a truck or a golf ball we don't know. He might be planning on blowing us all up one day.

Farfetched maybe, but in 1952 such speculation about Smokey was very real. Noble talked about Smokey openly but particularly, busy Effie Helm. Her suspicions were passed on to every customer she had and were repeated and embellished. McCarthyism was rampant and even a reclusive man in a small southern village was not exempt from suspicion.

No one knew for sure who called the FBI and demanded an investigation but an agent appeared one day at the Sheriff's office in Many. The man identified himself as an FBI agent and said he wanted to see one Herbert Irwin residing in Noble, and he wanted a local person to escort him. Oliver Elliott was raised in Noble and was a Deputy Sheriff for Sabine Parish at the time. Yes, he knew where Irwin lived and he would take the agent to see him. Another Deputy, George Autrey, watched them leave together.

Oliver welcomed the opportunity to talk to an FBI agent. Oliver made several attempts at conversation but the agent would offer nothing in explanation of why he was there. Oliver stopped to see O.B. Knott because he had accompanied the Sheriff or deputies whenever they needed to serve a warrant in the area. Part of the reason was most of the local outlaws were rough loggers and worked for O.B. Many times he was the one to post their bail because he needed them on the job Monday. For the first time, O.B. recused himself and told them to honk their horn as a signal to Smokey. O.B. refused to be a part of any investigation of Smokey. He did not want his friend to think him in any way responsible.

Oliver and the FBI agent drove to Smokey's gate and honked repeatedly until Smokey came out of his building. Oliver accompanied the agent to Smokey's fence and the agent showed his badge over the gate. He had a warrant and wanted to come inside the building. Smokey asked him to wait fifteen minutes and the agent agreed. Smokey went inside and came back in a few minutes and literally ordered Oliver to stay out. Smokey and the FBI agent were inside for forty-five minutes. When the agent came out Smokey locked the gate behind him and returned to the safety of his building.

The FBI agent did not comment and told Oliver, "Take me back to town." The agent would say nothing else on the return trip regardless of Oliver's questions. When they arrived at the courthouse he thanked Oliver and left as abruptly as he came.

Oliver Elliott was quiet to a fault. O.B. was fond of saying "Oliver is so tight-lipped he counts breathing like he does change." But Oliver told several people the FBI had investigated Smokey. Afterwards, talk about any atomic bomb faded and Noble found other things to wonder about.

While Smokey was grudgingly accepted into quiet Noble, the Irwin family had their own problems. Samuel Irwin's other children moved their ailing father back to Texas to a nursing home. When Samuel passed away in March, 1949 they were faced with trying to settle their father's estate. Their father did not leave a will and left a substantial estate including prime cotton land, a house, farm equipment, war bonds, a car, and cash. The children could not settle the distribution of their father's assets without brother Herbert's signature.

The surviving children of Samuel and Martha Irwin met together in Floydada to discuss the division of their father's assets. Carmon had been successful in getting Herbert to cooperate after Martha's death and they again appointed Carmon to find Herbert. Ruey had a note Herbert was living in Noble, Louisiana. Ruey sat silently as Felix, Carmon, and Gracie tried to figure out how they could force Herbert to sign the legal papers. They knew it would be a battle because Herbert had sworn he would never speak to them again.

Whereas Herbert cooperated with their mother's estate, their father's was a different matter altogether. Alta Mae's attorney from New York had sent word he would abide by what they decided as long as she received an equal share. Over the course of the discussion it was decided they would file a lawsuit as leverage to force Herbert to sign the documents. It was a volatile meeting and Ruey refused to take part in the manipulation. He understood Herbert as none of them did and pleaded for them not to sue their brother and disinherit him. His appeals were dismissed and Ruey left.

Ruey remembered what Herbert had offered him years ago during his tax investigation. He had never claimed Herbert's offer but now thought he had a solution to avoid a family lawsuit and satisfy Herbert his siblings could not take advantage of him. Ruey hired his own attorney and had him prepare a simple document: he, Ruey was due Herbert's one-sixth interest of their father's estate. Ruey only said he and Herbert had an "agreement." The document was composed listing, "other considerations." Ruey would not say what the other considerations were, but the transfer of one-sixth interest of a sizable estate was conveyed to Ruey for ten dollars. Ruey mailed the letter to be in Herbert's possession before their brothers and sister could file the lawsuit. He explained to Herbert what they were doing in a cover letter with instructions what he needed to do.

Five days later Herbert read the letter from Ruey slowly. He smoldered as he read it, not at Ruey, but at his brothers and sister. It was obvious what his siblings were doing. He would be pleased to sign this document – anything to keep them from using him again. He had made a promise to Ruey years ago and would stand by that promise.

Herbert knew Arthur "Papa" Helm was a notary and went to his store that afternoon. O.B. Knott always thought a lot of Papa Helm and that was good enough for him. Herbert told Papa Helm what he needed, and also told him he didn't want Effie to know about it. Mr. Helm well understood why, and notarized his papers on the hood of Herbert Irwin's truck in front of the store. Herbert walked next door to the Post Office to mail his notarized papers to Ruey.

Shortly afterward, O.B. saw a car he didn't recognize turn the corner toward Smokey's and stop. The car sat there several minutes, backed up, turned around and pulled into the yard at the Knott home. The car had New Mexico license plates. The man came up to the porch and introduced himself as Carmon Irwin and asked O.B. if he would help him with his brother Herbert. Carmon had seen the characteristic metal building and fence that had Herbert's stamp all over it. He was sure that was Herbert. Carmon was the only real tie to Smokey's past and O.B. found this brother pleasant and easy to talk to. They sat on the porch for some time talking about Smokey. Carmon shared their frustration about a brother the Irwin family simply could not understand or tolerate. O.B. was able to fill in some blanks in Smokey's past.

204

Suspicion

Carmon said, "You know Herbert was friendly and outgoing as a youngster. Difficult with us, but he would help anyone who asked. Herbert was a mechanical genius from the time he was a child. I mean that. Everyone who ever watched him work on something called him that. He could fix or make anything. He just knew. No one taught him, he just knew."

O.B. asked him, "Was he always this way? A loner? Suspicious?"

Carmon shook his head. "No. Herbert's just different. He's had lots of things happen to him. We've had some family problems, of course. That ... well, it was pretty bad. Some people handle things differently than others. Herbert was a manufacturer. He had a factory and machine shop that employed a hundred men. A hundred! You wouldn't believe the business he had. Herbert had a disagreement with the government over taxes and those agents pleaded with us to talk some reason into him. He wouldn't listen to anyone. Herbert closed his factory rather than pay the taxes. You wouldn't believe what those agents told us about that. He didn't believe in taxes. He took off to Florida after that. We knew about where he was but he still wouldn't have anything to do with the family anymore. Not after .... well, we've tried. Really, we have. I went to Florida in '43 to see Herbert after our mother died and I could see how much he had changed. It took awhile but I finally convinced him to let me inside his fence. You should have seen that gate. Herbert is so smart. You know he didn't even recognize me? His own brother. It was a real short visit. Well, now our Pa has passed and I need to see him."

O.B. took Carmon to Smokey's gate and honked the horn. Smokey eventually came out and stared at Carmon; hardly a greeting for two brothers who had not seen each other in years. When Carmon asked to come in Smokey refused. He told Carmon to go to Zwolle and get a room at the Arlington Hotel and he would see him later. Smokey turned around and walked back into his building. O.B. was dumfounded, thinking there is far more to this family saga than he was told. Carmon was not surprised at Herbert's reaction and shared some more things with O.B. Carmon thanked O.B. for his help and left.

Carmon drove to the Arlington Hotel in Zwolle and got a room. Knowing Herbert would not come after dark Carmon waited on him. Soon there was a quiet knock on his door. Carmon opened the door to see Herbert standing in the hall warily.

Carmon opened the door wide and asked his brother in. Herbert hesitated several minutes. Carmon coaxed him inside with assurances he only wanted to talk to him. All of Herbert's body language told Carmon his brother did not trust him. He looked ill at ease in the unfamiliar room and ready to flee at any minute. Carmon knew he should come to the point of his trip quickly or Herbert would leave.

"Herbert, Pa died a couple weeks ago. We need to settle the estate. I've brought papers for you to sign."

"I'm not signing anything." Herbert stood within reach of the doorknob.

"I'm sorry but you have to. If you don't sign we will disinherit you for abandoning the family. We'll divide your portion of the inheritance. We're all agreed and we've already filed the lawsuit. That's what Pa wanted. He told us he didn't want you having anything of his. You know that and you know why."

Herbert knew it was coming but somehow thought they wouldn't follow through with it. He was trembling and started pacing. "Abandonment! Is that what you're calling it? You would sue your own brother? They stole from me! *I'm* the inventor! I should have all those patents and don't any of you forget it! Pa knew what he was doing when he took that money. He *knew!* You're too late, anyway. I gave my part to Ruey. I don't want any inheritance and now none of you will have it either! Don't you ever come here again, any of you!" Herbert was yelling, his voice cracking in rage. Carmon backed away from his brother not sure what he would do next. Herbert stopped pacing and jerked the door open.

Carmon stood in stunned silence as Herbert slammed the door behind him. Herbert's rages were terrible and he was truly uneasy. He had no doubt Herbert did give his one-sixth share to Ruey. No wonder Ruey had been avoiding them lately. Carmon thought he would spend the night and head back to Texas early in the morning. There was nothing else to be done.

Back in his building that night Smokey paced back and forth alternating between frustration and out of control rage. After hours of compulsive pacing he calmed down and seethed in his anger. The idea! His brothers and sisters suing him for his inheritance! He didn't want it nor did he need it. Smokey sat down at his typewriter and began a final letter to his family. After this letter he would be assured they would never bother him again. Sixteen pages later he had vented his rage and divorced himself completely from the Irwin clan. As he listed slight after slight by his family, the betrayals, the lack of understanding, his anger flared all over again. There would never be another reason for him to see or hear from his family again. Indeed, after this letter they wouldn't want to. He would mail the letter tomorrow.

Early the next morning Carmon passed through Noble. He spoke to O.B. and told him about their meeting and then went to the Post Office. He pulled a piece of paper from his pocket and handed it to postmistress, Adna Edwards.

"Good morning. My name is Carmon Irwin and Herbert Irwin is my brother. We've had a rather unpleasant visit and I know none of the family is going to hear from him again. I can see years from now someone will find him dead in that building over there. I want to leave my name and address so someone will contact me when it happens."

Mrs. Edwards took the paper and assured Carmon she would keep his address. Carmon left and she took the note and placed it in the back of a locked drawer.

A week later Carmon, Felix, Gracie, and Ruey passed Herbert's letter around. Some of it made sense and other parts did not. Herbert called himself a "social misfit" in his letter, which was an understatement. At times the narrative rambled and the brothers and sister in turn were perplexed. With other passages they fidgeted in guilty agreement. It was a scathing recount of all their parents and they had supposedly done to Herbert. Even Ruey agreed Herbert's account wasn't quite accurate. They filed the lawsuit according to their father's wishes and the final distribution of their parents' assets. They knew they would never hear from Herbert again.

Family squabbles in Noble were sometimes very public but the drama in the Irwin clan went unnoticed. A few people were aware Smokey's brother came to see him but that was soon forgotten. Noble went about their business still watchful of the reclusive man in the metal building.

In 1968 the Sabine River Authority was formed and the monstrous Toledo Bend Reservoir was built. It was the largest man-made lake in the South. It certainly was the biggest thing to ever hit Sabine Parish. The lake propelled an isolated and thinly populated region into modern times.

Suspicion

Toledo Bend took 197,000 acres of real estate eliminating roads and completely rerouted traffic patterns. The lake has an irregular shoreline of over 1250 miles and one arm of the lake is only a couple miles west of Noble.

The cultural and economic impact on Sabine Parish was extraordinary. Retirees moved to the lake from all over the US. Subdivisions were developed, new roads, new businesses, resorts, restaurants, hotels, fishing tournaments, bass clubs, and recreational facilities sprung up where nothing had occupied the area before except pine trees. Toledo Bend was a constant topic of conversation and the Knott family was involved with development as well.

Smokey went to see the lake but the activity and people around it caused him to back away. He drove thirty-five miles to see the Atlantic Ocean in Florida and trawled in it. Toledo Bend interested him enough he considered fishing in it but he couldn't contend with the people. Smokey had all the fish he wanted in the creek and pond close to his property. He felt vulnerable at the lake and returned to his pond to fish in total privacy.

When Smokey lived in Spur he was engaged in the growth of a small city as a young businessman. In Amarillo, he was heavily involved in industry and manufacturing. His business was the foundation for any relationships he had in local society. In Florida, Smokey was part of a rural landscape. Cattle and his garden were explanation enough for his activities. But this was the first time he lived in a small town. Even though he was personally a private man before moving to Noble, he became a recluse in every sense of the word.

Fear and suspicion can create fantastic speculation in a populace with little else to talk about. Gossip was a pastime and ridiculous hearsay circulated about Smokey.

Suspicion

Men walking home from the sawmill one night claimed they heard shrieks of agony from more than one woman as they passed Smokey's building. Others said they saw several men sneaking in and out of his building in all hours of the night. Or, a variation on that theme, Smokey was the public face to a team of sinister men holed up in the building. No tale was so outrageous it wasn't believed. Eerie lights, strange sounds, chickens refusing to lay, cows going dry when his truck passed, trees dying, blight in their gardens; any unexplained incidence was blamed on the quiet, private man in the darkened building who only wanted to be left alone.

Rural legends are an odd phenomenon. There was no concrete information to condemn or acquit Smokey – so rumor filled in the blanks. General knowledge of Smokey was confined to a few miles around town. Amazingly, many residents raised in Noble never actually saw him, but everyone heard of him. Only a handful had exchanged words with him. The rare occasions when his green panel truck was seen, children and adults alike quickly went to their houses.

Smokey's presence was more apparition than reality, fable rather than fact. He was a convenient scapegoat and the local bogeyman. If their children wouldn't come in at night parents would threaten them with, "You better come in this house! Smokey'll getcha!"

Suspicion

Noble Mercantile

Chapter Fourteen

Noble Mercantile

The one place Smokey frequented other than the Post Office was the Noble Mercantile. The Knott family's store was virtually Smokey's only social outlet, if it could even be called that. If residents ever happened upon Smokey it was normally there. In the micro environment he lived in the store was close and convenient. Smokey could shop for his bare necessities uninterrupted by noise and distractions. He considered the few people he encountered a necessary unpleasantness. The store was a vignette out of the past and Smokey was comfortable in its familiarity. It was a weekly appointment he kept without fail.

Typical of southern rural grocery stores, the Noble Mercantile was a solid old frame building left over from its early history as a bank. The store was across the road from Youngblood's store and faced the east railroad spur. The embankment was only sixty feet away and the store shook every time a freight train came through. The lot sloped downward toward the tracks, with the foundation of the east side of the store almost at level ground. The front porch on the west side was four feet up from the ground. It had a flat-faced front that glared white in the late afternoon sun.

Most of the floor was scuffed bare pine planks. The iron stove that heated the old building was positioned on the concrete slab where the bank safe used to be. The flue was

free standing and jutted upward eighteen feet through the
ceiling. The same dark beaded boards that covered the
ceiling lined the walls. A huge shop fan roared in the back
wall to relieve the summer heat.

As a customer entered the worn screen door a bread rack
was to the left. Behind it was a wooden counter with a
gallon cookie jar at one end. Down the left side of the store
dusty board shelves sagged with canned goods and staples.
Sacks of feed and fertilizer were stacked in the far left
corner. Immediately inside the front door to the right, were
three wooden display cases with a glass top and front. The
first one held a gallon-sized Tom's candy jar. Viola kept her
cash register on the middle one. The round black keys of the
cash register had to be depressed hard before they would
release the cash drawer. It was an antique even before it was
put into use. The cash drawer never would shut completely
and Viola kept about $20 in change in it. The zippered bank
bag that had most the store's cash was hidden behind the
counter in back of extra large packages of toilet paper.
Everyone knew it was there but politely went to the far side
of the store when she needed more change. The refrigerated
meat case stood beyond the display cases in the rear of the
store. On top of it was the meat slicer. None of the store
equipment was new. Potato and onion bins were in front of
the third wooden counter. The outdated nickel Coca Cola
cooler beside them was well oiled more from grime rather
than good maintenance.

Ladies would whisper quietly to Viola when they needed
feminine products and she would pull them out of discreet
paper bags set on a back shelf – as if that fact of nature did
not include women in Noble. The store carried minor
necessities besides groceries; handkerchiefs, combs, razor
blades, motor oil, antifreeze, batteries, sewing thread,

brooms, and yarn. Dry rotted fan belts hung forgotten on the back wall.

Smokey drove into the gravel lot in front of the store and parked in the exact same place every time. Noble had idle whittlers who would sit on a bench outside the door of the Noble Mercantile or Youngblood's depending on the time of year and the position of the sun. None of them dared try Mrs. Helm's disposition at her store. Most of these men did not work and lived off of hard working wives or family. Several were injured or shell-shocked veterans of two wars who were unable to hold jobs. Smokey never acknowledged these men and passed them by as if it were an empty bench. Smokey was courteous to most people and nodded a silent greeting. He tipped his hat if he happened to pass anyone, but not the whittlers that occupied the bench. These men seemed capable but were obviously unemployed. In open contempt he ignored them.

If this Friday was his regular Post Office visit Smokey would leave his truck and walk from the Noble Mercantile across the road. He avoided people at Youngblood's and Helm's by walking at the edge of the road directly to the Post Office. He always appeared anxious to return to his building. This chore of shopping kept him from his work and he must get back as soon as possible. Smokey did not dawdle, stop to chat, or even pause on his focused awkward walk.

Smokey always wore his starched khaki pants and a long-sleeved shirt buttoned at the neck. His brogan shoes were polished. Smokey was immaculately clean and shaved with his hair trimmed neatly. In a logging town with dirt roads his attire was in sharp comparison to laborers and even the casual dress of businessmen. Many men wore khakis but they were never laundered to the spotless perfection Smokey's were.

At times Smokey picked up an item and read the contents carefully, and then replaced the box or can on the shelf. The few items he did buy were staple items such as sugar, flour, cornmeal, cooking oil, or salt and pepper. Every time he examined the label as to content and locality. He bought few canned goods and rarely fruit in the off-season. He never bought any candy, snacks or soft drinks, or ice cream. He never bought frivolous or impulse items. He never bought prepared or packaged foods, or processed meats or bacon.

Troy Webb came to the store once and saw Smokey in front of the canned goods carefully studying the label on a can. Troy went about his business and picked up a few items. He chatted with Viola while he drank his Coke. He paid for his groceries and left. As Troy came to the door fully ten minutes later Smokey was still laboring over the same can hunting for information only he knew.

When Smokey first moved to Noble, O.B. worked locally. When he took a traveling job shortly afterward, daily management of the store was turned over to Viola. Smokey had one ritual when he bought his groceries O.B. could never understand. Every Friday afternoon Smokey pulled a crisp new $20 bill from his wallet. The "wallet" was made of cardboard from a Kleenex box. He had whipped the edges with cord. Smokey always paid with a $20 bill regardless of how little he bought. The practice irked O.B. He wondered why Smokey could not use smaller bills like everyone else, especially when his purchases never amounted to more than a few dollars. Smokey always had the one bill, never any ones, fives, or tens, and never any change. It was necessary to keep adequate change on hand or else it was a fifteen-mile drive to the nearest bank in Many.

Noble Mercantile

Knowing Smokey would take up his change O.B. made a habit on Fridays of keeping more cash on hand. Equally annoying was Smokey's practice of placing the bill on the counter and him keeping a good step away. O.B. was forced to count his change replacing it on the counter for him. Smokey would stare at the money and pick it up and put it in his right hand pocket.

The puzzling part was the bills themselves. This was 1949 and the bills were dated from the twenties and thirties. O.B. still was not sure about Smokey and felt compelled to take one of the $20 bills to the bank to verify they were genuine. They were. The bills were as crisp as if they came off the US Mint presses that day, even after twenty to thirty years. It was whispered Smokey was counterfeiting money because he always seemed to have new bills.

The store was something of a meeting place for Noble. This was where you caught up on who was getting married or expecting a baby, who was sick and who had died. Viola's prayer partners came and had many a prayer meeting around the iron stove. The population of Noble in 1950 was about 195 people. There were four churches in town: Baptist, Methodist, Pentecostal, and in the late 60s, Catholic. Each had a membership of thirty to forty people. Anyone who was inclined to attend church did so. Those that did not had probably refused more than one invitation to a service. It was understood they had no intention of coming.

Viola was a woman of extraordinary compassion. One day at the store she steeled up enough courage to invite Smokey to church. He shot her a look of don't-you-ever-ask-me-again. He replied, "I'm Baptist," with enough hardened rejection, she didn't. Whereas Smokey and O.B. deepened their friendship Smokey was wary of Viola after that innocent invitation. Viola was dedicated to helping those in need and she was convinced everyone's troubles would be cured with conversion. She had little in common with him and could not understand anyone so inwardly focused. Viola tried engaging Smokey in conversation but rarely got beyond exchanging pleasantries. All Smokey wanted was his groceries and then to return to his building.

Observations of Smokey were becoming more bizarre by the month. Two episodes at the Noble Mercantile triggered real fear and caution. One day Smokey picked up a can of corn and read the ingredients label. He began a rambling dissertation about additives to food. Smokey pronounced the chemicals enunciating each syllable with familiarity. He elaborated on the dangers of chemicals, becoming more excited as he spoke. He put the can back on the shelf and began pacing back and forth and was soon in a high state of anxiety. Some of the discernable comments he made were, "They're poisoning us, the government is poisoning us! It's all from California. It's those Roosevelts! They're trying to poison us." The tirade wasn't to anyone in particular but more like he was thinking out loud.

O.B. watched Smokey clasp his hands behind him, stride five steps, wheel around, and repeat the same amount of steps again. O.B. wondered if Smokey had spent time in a cell. His strides were so precise O.B. said he would spin almost on the same nail head in the floor. Smokey was in such an agitated state frothy saliva formed at the corners of his mouth. After five minutes of ranting he stopped as suddenly as it came over him. Smokey straightened up and seemed to come to himself and finished his shopping as if nothing had happened. The next time a similar episode occurred he calmly walked out.

Those that observed the outbursts stood back in stunned silence. They cautioned their neighbors to give Smokey plenty of space and never confront him. This was a man to be feared. If another customer was in the store when Smokey entered they quietly left and came back after they saw his green truck was gone.

Noble had its own violent history. The Post Office had bullet holes in the door from the not too distant past. The law in Sabine Parish then was more satisfied with an explanation instead of an investigation. More than one killer was living freely as a reformed citizen.

Children were warned never to ride their horses or wander close to Smokey's property. Used to walking at will around the village women made sure they had an escort or a friend accompany them past his building. Everyone avoided the road Smokey lived on after dark. Even though Smokey never genuinely threatened a soul or raised his voice in anger to any individual, the risk was silent and unspoken. He had proven himself capable of irrational action and who knew what else he would do?

O.B. watched his behavior and waited for Smokey to erupt in violence but he never did. Other than being obsessed with the purity of his food O.B. could not figure out why Smokey had such an intense hatred for Franklin Roosevelt, years after his Presidency. When residents would come to O.B. about their fear he would repeat his admonition, "That man has been really hurt to behave like that. He hasn't bothered anyone and hasn't done anything against the law. Just leave the man alone." Other than voicing his fear of contamination, O. B. did not hear Smokey say anything derogatory about his country, only FDR.

No one knew how hard these excursions into the public were for Smokey. His retreat inside his fence and building was his sole place of comfort and familiarity. Outside his fence was a strange place occupied by people, and he never could figure out why people behaved the way they did. On one level he wanted companionship and on another he genuinely feared it. Smokey's heroin use had escalated from his first experimentation with self-medication in Florida. He had come to depend on it regularly to cope with whatever it was that agitated him so badly. Now it was a necessary prerequisite to his Friday outings. It was a balm to quiet his anxiety attacks outside his gate. It soothed his troubled mind enough he could visit with O.B. His heroin was the only thing that made his entries into the outside world tolerable.

If O.B. was on his porch on Smokey's Friday trips to the store or Post Office he would stop. O.B. listened and watched Smokey seeing extreme differences in his demeanor. At times Smokey showed heightened awareness of whatever they talked about. He was engaged, more verbal than usual. Other times Smokey's comments made no sense whatever. O.B. would come in the house shaking his head, "Smokey is really on the weed today." O.B. was always convinced something caused Smokey's erratic behavior but he did not know what.

Every week Smokey bought eight gallons of kerosene from the store. Roe worked in his parents' store at the time and it was his responsibility to fill the empty cans and carry bags to customer's cars. Smokey was adamant about wanting only four gallons in each can even though they were five-gallon containers. Roe remembers everyone else's kerosene cans were rusted and dented. He had to contend with a rag or potato stuffed in the opening because the cap always seemed to be lost. Smokey's were in perfect condition, clean, and he insisted Roe place them on one particular spot on the porch of the store.

Smokey said, "Four gallons in each can. Not five. Put the cans here. Right here."

Roe was fascinated, yet half afraid of Smokey regardless of how much his Dad liked him. "Yes Sir, Mr. Irwin."

Smokey would not let Roe carry anything to his truck and would never open the doors to let anyone see inside. Smokey picked up his kerosene cans himself and loaded them in his truck.

Aunt Maggie Cross worked in the store in the afternoons. She greeted Smokey with the same respect she saw O.B. and Viola give him. Smokey had noticed Maggie working in the family garden and asked her questions, recognizing she must know more about raising a garden here than he did.

Smokey said, "I analyzed my soil. It's acid. That's not good. What do you do to your soil?"

Maggie was an accomplished gardener and knew exactly what he needed. "Now you know why pine trees grow so well in Sabine Parish, Mr. Irwin. You need to add lime to your soil. Our dirt here is really acidic. We have some in the back of the store. If you will read the directions you'll know how much you need for your garden."

Smokey retreated to the back and studied the instructions on the sack of lime for a very long time. He finally bought several sacks. He heaved them up on his shoulder easily and carried them to his truck.

Smokey did not feel threatened by Maggie like he did Viola and spoke to her often. Maggie was always impressed with the technical knowledge Smokey exhibited, not the way people usually discussed how their garden was producing. Smokey spoke at length of chemical differences and how a particular element would affect produce. Maggie was convinced only a chemist would have such knowledge.

Noble Mercantile

At times Smokey asked Maggie to find things for him for his experiments. It was a peculiar list of items. He asked for a curled feather from a specific duck's tail, a brown egg shell, a certain weight of string, a particular kind of cotton material, not synthetic and not dyed, but natural colored, and a length of hair. He never would tell Maggie what they were for, only that he needed them. In exchange for her finding these items he would bring her fruit from his bushes and trees. In particular, his plums were always oversized, firm, and sweet. Maggie called them "picture perfect" when everyone else's plums were much smaller and did not taste as good.

Smokey was powerful and strong even as a middle-aged man. But as he aged he became more a source of amusement than fear. He emerged from his building one Friday afternoon with a four-inch metal pyramid affixed to his hat. The people who saw him at the Noble Mercantile gawked in disbelief. No one spoke to Smokey and no one dared snicker. The rumors concerning him were at two ends of the spectrum. There were sinister accusations, and then they had this. Most laughed after he left and the fear associated with Smokey gradually changed to head-shaking entertainment. Maggie's son, Onnie Cross, was a civil engineer and asked him about it one day at the store.

Onnie was polite to everyone and greeted him. "Hello, Mr. Irwin. How are you today?"

Smokey paused and nodded.

Onnie asked, "Mr. Irwin, would you mind telling me why you are wearing that pyramid on your hat?"

Smokey answered him, "I'm trying to communicate with outer space."

Onnie didn't miss a beat and asked again, "Well, are you having any luck?"

Noble Mercantile

Smokey said, "I think so."

Onnie nodded and said, "That's good."

Smokey's truck was seen on rare occasions in Zwolle in front of Levkovits Hardware and Drygoods, or Maxey's Feed and Seed. He bought his gas at Mabel Elliott's Grocery on the highway but his only consistent outing was to the Noble Mercantile. The store was reminiscent of ones he had frequented as a child and a young man. Country stores really didn't change that much. They carried the same products and with minor variations as to layout and construction were almost the same store. The Noble Mercantile was Smokey's familiar and regular destination.

After O.B. passed away Roe helped his mother close the store in the latter 70s. Roe had no idea what severe anxiety this caused Smokey. He had to adjust a routine he had established over decades. Change was always hard but altering this habit was more difficult than ever. When Smokey bought his gas at Elliott's Grocery on Hwy 171 on his Friday outings he now added his few groceries.

Without O.B. and without the Noble Mercantile, it was never the same for him.

Neighbors

Chapter Fifteen

Neighbors

Smokey had long recognized he was emotionally incapable of giving of himself. He was helpless to change that part of his personality and accepted it. Neither did he feel the need to. A person living the life he did was naturally egocentric. Smokey was, even more so. There were human emotions he simply could not relate to: familial love, compassion, empathy. Certainly, never sharing in the love of a woman. In that respect his thoughts still sometimes recalled Amarillo, with pain. He did not understand people in the least and expected the worse from them. His passion was machines and inventing, and if people were unpredictable the physics of his work was something he at least could count on. Machines did exactly what you designed them to do.

Smokey had business relationships as a teenager, in Spur, and in Amarillo but he did not maintain lasting relationships with any of his early acquaintances. He knew Karl Stello in Florida but when Smokey left, with one exception, contact with Stello ended with his departure. He used several patent attorneys in Washington DC but he had never met any of them. Smokey was dependent on their legal and ethical performance, but he was barely comfortable using them. He eventually fired a couple during two prolonged patent claims. Suspicion was an ingrained part of his nature. Smokey was sure his family had exploited him and he dismissed them from his life completely. Smokey was convinced he had ample justification for not trusting people.

Smokey's reputation in Amarillo was based on respect for his professional expertise. His industry contacts knew Herbert Irwin as a brilliant and successful businessman. He knew a district judge and most of the city leaders in Amarillo. Even with a large work force at his factory and machine shop none could call Herbert Irwin a friend. When he called on Willborn Brothers to submit statements for his patent appeal they were more than willing to defend his claims. When Smokey was finished with whatever need he had at the time, people did not hear from him again.

Friendship can be a peculiar relationship to analyze. In contrast to Smokey's personality, O.B. Knott had a large extended family and maintained business relationships and close friendships that spanned decades. The Sunday dinner ritual common with many southern families included the Knott household. The house was filled with laughing relatives. The only noise at Smokey's compound was machinery and never any visitors. Smokey had found a measure of contentment in his life and not having a family or friends did not trouble him in the least. This is what he preferred.

With just a basic education, O.B. was a well read and well-traveled businessman. He had lived in St. Louis and south Texas, and later contracted timber over three states as a regional timber buyer. He was the first person Smokey went to with any problem. Noble residents were mindful of his tolerance for Smokey, and O.B. was the main reason they left him alone.

Over years, the friendship that developed between these two diverse men was built one conversation upon another, one positive incident leading to the next. They shared similar

Neighbors

experiences in both were self made men, employing their natural abilities. O.B. never took advantage of him but it took years before Smokey would trust him.

Usually travelling weekdays, O.B.'s favorite spot on weekends was the swing on his front porch. The Knott house did not have air conditioning until the 1970s and the porch made the summer heat tolerable. People would wave or honk as they passed or stopped to visit.

Smokey chose this neutral ground for any conversations they had. O.B. was never invited to his building in return. Smokey's visits were usually several times a month and he normally had specific questions he wanted answered. If Viola or Maggie were outside they went inside to leave the men alone. As a child, Roe would watch the men talking and listen from a respectful distance. O.B. noted Smokey never gossiped, largely because he had no interaction with people. He rarely discussed politics or national business, and never sports, religion, or international affairs. Smokey only spoke of those immediate things that directly affected him or were important to him.

Used to meaningful conversation, O.B. would often come in the house after Smokey left and mutter, "I have no idea what that man wanted." Smokey's conversations were disjointed and he would jump from one subject to another. O.B. thought Smokey was the most difficult person to carry on a conversation with he had ever met, and he had never met a stranger. He recognized these were clumsy attempts on Smokey's part to have a friendship with him. O.B. offered coffee and pie repeatedly but Smokey refused both until he stopped offering. Neither would Smokey come inside the Knott home or anyone's house. Smokey's narrow comfort zone was the front porch, but no farther.

Neighbors

There were two swings on the porch of the Knott house, one to the right and one to the left of the front door. O.B. sat sideways in the left swing with his back to the wall facing the road. It was a vantage point that gave him a clear view of town, beyond the railroad and stores to the fire tower at the top of the hill. O.B. could look the opposite direction and see the west side of town. In a village used to friendly interaction, visitors would stop, pull up the rocking chair and sit so both faced the road while they talked of the week's events. But not Smokey.

Smokey pulled the rocking chair away from the wall on the porch and with his right shoulder to the wall, faced squarely in front of O.B. By the time he came to Noble, Smokey had already had a lifetime exposure to loud machines and factory noise. The machinery that dominated his world had left him with a severe hearing impairment that progressively became worse as he aged. With his booming voice, few people had trouble hearing O.B. but Smokey often depended on reading lips.

Smokey had to be focused on the person in front of him to understand and absorb the spoken word. O.B. did not relate the slight tilt of Smokey's head and soft monotone to a hearing impairment, only to social awkwardness. Whenever Smokey was standing beside someone he usually faced the individual or stood so his right ear was inclined toward them. Smokey would never admit he was almost deaf and submitting to an exam to get a hearing aid was out of the question.

Soon after Smokey moved to Noble, O.B. took a traveling job as a regional manager for Manassas Timber Company, based in St. Louis, Missouri. He consistently drove a thousand miles a week over several states before returning home on weekends. At the same time, Smokey had never left his building. O.B. met and talked with dozens of people conducting business while Smokey had not seen a soul or uttered a word. The first man was personable and entertaining; the other reclusive and socially awkward. O.B. could number countless people as close friends and hundreds as acquaintances. Smokey could do neither. The two men were polar opposites but somehow found a common ground.

When O.B. rebuilt some of his fences, he chose the most inexpensive means to build it, using white oak fence posts. Smokey asked his neighbor why he used wood since it would only last about fifteen years and metal would last at least fifty. O.B. couldn't believe a middle-aged man would be concerned about his fence lasting that long. To Smokey the fence was inadequate because metal was always his material of choice.

In the fall of 1949, International Paper Company began building a pulp wood yard in Noble along the west spur of the railroad. Logs were loaded from pulpwood trucks directly onto railcars. It was sometimes necessary to store logs for a period of time in the pulpwood yard until shipment. This particular spot was centered between Smokey's property and the railroad. It was the same tract he had wanted for his railroad spur for his factory. During construction the yard had two entrances; the main one on the gravel road through town with an alternate entrance on the north dirt road beside Smokey's property. Smokey was upset over the project and came to O.B. waving a letter in his hand about it. He had written KCS requesting a railroad spur and had even offered to pay for it himself.

Such a large project would have been planned for some time and as mayor at the time, O.B. was unhappy he wasn't informed about it. This was undoubtedly the reason the KCS Railroad refused Smokey's request for a spur to his property.

Neighbors

The site of the wood yard was a low spot beside the railroad tracks and required hundreds of yards of fill dirt. From fall through spring heavy equipment dumped load after load of dirt to raise the large rectangular six-acre tract to a level elevation with the railroad spur.

Smokey was as distressed over losing the railroad spur as he was with the activity around his property. With every dump truck that rumbled past his property Smokey knew "they" were going to do him harm. He was convinced there was some other reason trucks were being routed past his property line. O.B. knew Smokey was upset but there was nothing he could do for him. O.B. tried to reassure Smokey a wood yard was the only reason for the construction. The project that disturbed Smokey disappointed O.B., because this meant a factory in Noble was no longer a consideration.

O.B. was not a patient man by nature but he extended himself repeatedly to allow for Smokey's paranoia. Smokey's psychological makeup didn't allow for logic when it came to outside influences. He knew O.B. was telling him the truth as he knew it but he still had trouble accepting his explanations. He asked for reassurance about the wood yard for months.

In a local economy based on need, Noble bartered, borrowed, and lent tools as a matter of course. They exchanged smoked meats and garden produce trying to make life easier for all concerned. But not Smokey. He would occasionally loan his tools to the Knott family but no one else. Because of his apparent selfishness, Smokey was looked on as being anything but neighborly. O.B. wanted to be the best friend he could be to Smokey and repeated himself, "Just leave the man alone. He's not hurting anyone." The contradictions in Smokey's personality were perplexing but O.B. respected his desire for privacy and accepted him as he was.

When a single mother in town passed away the townspeople purposed to give her a decent burial. This was a destitute woman whose husband had abandoned her during the Depression She had a difficult life raising three children but she was well thought of. People were asked for donations for her burial and twelve-year old Roe was talked into seeing Smokey.

Smokey saw the child from his garden and came toward Roe at the road. The boy blurted out his request from over the gate. Wide-eyed, Roe watched Smokey launch into a furious tirade about Roosevelt. Roe caught only a few of Smokey's incoherent statements but most centered on his philosophy people should work. Smokey said people were being ruined expecting handouts from the government. Smokey paced back and forth with his hands clasped behind his back. White saliva collected around his mouth and his face was red with anger. It was a terrible scene to behold. Smokey finally stopped and looked at Roe, wheeled, and went into his building without any explanation. Roe rode his bicycle away from there as fast as a twelve-year old boy can ride a bike on a dirt road. He told his father about Smokey's fit of temper. O.B. thought Smokey's reaction was completely inappropriate for asking for a simple donation. His only comment was "Someone has really hurt that man."

Smokey wasn't consistently mean-spirited. If he had been, people would have called him a crabby old man and would have been satisfied. He was distant but on rare occasions Smokey could be almost pleasant.

When the boys were thirteen Roe and Ron were riding their bicycles down the road past Smokey's. They saw him outside shooting what looked like a crossbow. The boys had never seen one and watched while Smokey took aim and hit four empty tin cans without a miss. When he walked forward to remove the arrows and turned, Smokey saw them.

They were about to run away when Smokey motioned for them to come in the gate. They paused at first but came toward him remaining at a comfortable distance. Smokey asked if they would like to shoot the crossbow. At first they hesitated but then agreed. Smokey unlocked the gate and motioned for them to follow him. With a few words he demonstrated how to shoot the crossbow and the boys each shot the bow several times. Smokey had a quiver attached to his belt. The arrows were a sleek lightweight metal, not commercially produced arrows, but some Smokey had made. Smokey told them he wanted to show them something and told them to wait. He walked into his building taking his bow, arrows, and quiver with him. In a few minutes he returned with a box and opened it for them. The box contained a .22 single shot rifle. He let them look at the rifle, turning it and holding it but would not let them touch it. Smokey returned the rifle to the box saying nothing, and walked back into the building without any explanation. The boys ran to their bicycles and went home.

Roe's fascination with Smokey grew. He was enthralled with this man who was so impressive, so exact in everything he did, and so mysterious. Smokey's intelligence was obvious, his penetrating gaze, mesmerizing. Roe wasn't sure if Smokey wanted to befriend them or if he was trying to instill fear in them to protect his privacy. Regardless, the man was riveting.

When Smokey fenced his property free-range cattle and hogs could no longer graze on it and the weeds and seedling pines grew up quickly around him. O.B. suggested to

Neighbors

Smokey he buy some goats to keep the vegetation under control. Smokey responded he wanted it "to grow up so no one can see me." In a few short years the vegetation was head high except for his garden and Smokey's activities were further hid from the town. They occasionally saw Smokey's straw hat above the weeds when they drove by but they had no idea what he was growing in his garden or doing around his building.

Smokey spent as much time in his garden in Noble as he did in Florida, only on a smaller scale. The Paige brothers had brought the remainder of his odd tools and many of his fruit trees, seedlings, and berry bushes. They brought his seed potatoes and garden tools. The only thing Smokey did not have them bring was his opium poppies. Smokey brought a goodly supply of dried pods and seed with him in his truck. Back in Florida, there were a few scattered opium poppies that came up years after he sold the property. The Arnolds' plowed them under and planted an orchard of orange trees. In Noble, Smokey planted his opium poppies with care behind his garden. He made sure they were hidden by the high underbrush. Smokey used to consider his heroin his "storm medicine" but he consistently needed it to combat his anxiety to simply leave his property.

As trucking is the major means of commerce today, when Smokey moved to Noble railroads were the leading means of transport. The daily roar of steam locomotives passing through Noble was part of the landscape. Steam locomotives were being phased out in late 1963 and in early 1964 Smokey mounted the steps of the Knott house with a pressing question on his mind. He pulled the rocker over to face O.B. and without any greeting he asked simply, "Where did the steam locomotives go?" It was an innocent question from a soul so engrossed in himself he did not notice when diesel locomotives replaced steam. O.B. was well tuned to the world he lived in and was dumbfounded Smokey missed the transition. He explained the evolution of steam to diesel and Smokey seemed satisfied.

Smokey was a source of amusement to some people. One day when his truck pulled onto the road they saw a monstrous three-foot long propeller protruding from the grill of his truck. As he accelerated, the propeller speed increased. People left their houses and stood on their porches to watch the spectacle. Mixed with laughter and arm slapping were comments of, "Poor old thing! Smokey's really lost it this time. Surely he's not so crazy he thinks that truck will fly?"

Smokey thought nothing of the kind. His wind power machines provided an easy remedy for an ongoing problem he had. Smokey's weekly trips to the Noble Mercantile and on rare occasions, to Zwolle, were not enough to recharge his truck battery. What better way to solve the problem than to use a device he designed to charge batteries? One of his patents (Inventions, #20) was an improvement to his previous two wind power machines. This model had a belt tightener, which compensated for variable wind speed. The attachment was also useful to recharge twelve-volt batteries. Smokey considered the internal combustion engine for multiple uses, not just to power a vehicle. Smokey mounted his propeller to his van to recharge his truck battery.

Smokey's health was generally good and the only problems he really had were with his teeth. Having pulled several teeth in Florida he had a means to deal with his deteriorating dental health. Over the course of several years Smokey pulled one after another and eventually pulled all of them and made himself dentures. His opium poppies grew just as well in Louisiana as they did in Florida and he had no lack of heroin to complete the job.

When his gums were healed enough and would not shrink anymore he made a plaster mold of his upper and lower jaw as if he were replacing a casing in a motor. His material of choice was always metal and he made his dentures out of metal alloy and fitted them. Smokey ground and shaped and polished them until they fit. Finally, he had a well-fitted set of dentures.

Smokey stopped to speak to O.B. afterward and O.B. couldn't help but notice the metallic gleam in Smokey's mouth. He had to ask.

"What have you done to your teeth?"

"I pulled my teeth and made dentures."

"You pulled your own teeth? What did you make your dentures out of?"

"Metal. Works good."

O.B. was flabbergasted but he couldn't deny what he was looking at. O.B. wondered what he used to dull the pain enough he could pull his own teeth. O.B. came inside the house and joked with his wife and sister.

"Don't let Smokey get a hold of you. If he clamps down on you with those metal teeth you'll never get loose."

O.B. and Smokey's friendship was amiable with one notable exception. Smokey was 77 years old in 1970 and O.B. asked him if he was a WWI veteran. With little elaboration, Smokey told him he was. Assuming he lived on limited income, O.B. talked Smokey into coming to Fort Polk in Leesville with him to apply for a pension. O.B. was not a veteran although he worked for the Department of the Army in 1956-57. He was misinformed exactly what benefits would be available to a veteran. His intent was to establish Smokey's veteran status should he ever need medical care. His interest was only to help his somewhat detached neighbor who appeared to need assistance.

Their conversations were never that lengthy but O.B. took the 75-minute ride to Leesville as an opportunity to try and gain answers to his questions about Smokey. O.B. first spoke of the Depression thinking he and Smokey had some common experiences to talk about. He was wrong. O.B. talked of bad times and how difficult it was for him as a teenager to find work when he had to support his widowed mother. He spoke of desperate people in St. Louis and how he had to leave and come to Noble with only a Model A, his wife, his mother, and few belongings.

Smokey listened but was unable to grasp the weight of what O.B. was talking about. They did not have the same experience at all. While most the country was in total collapse Amarillo was still surviving off the oil and gas industry. Smokey had a decline in his business but was never without work. If he ever considered telling his neighbor about his manufacturing and inventions, this would be the time. After listening to O.B., Smokey changed his mind and sat in silence.

When they arrived at Fort Polk, O.B. drove to the post hospital. Anyone familiar with plodding bureaucracy knows what an ordeal this must have been for two elderly men. O.B. took command of the process and helped Smokey complete some forms. Smokey's eyesight was so poor he answered questions for the administrative clerk. Given his personality, it is surprising he complied with such requests. O.B. wondered later why he submitted to them. He wasn't sure Smokey completely understood the reason for the trip.

When Smokey was ushered into an exam room for evaluation by an Army doctor Smokey insisted O.B. accompany him. The doctor asked Smokey to remove his shirt and he refused with a vigorous shake of his head. The doctor asked again and Smokey spoke emphatically, "I am not removing my shirt for you or anybody." In Smokey's mind he was able to avoid this invasion of his bodily privacy before, and saw no reason why he should submit to such a demand now. Besides, he needed to hide the scars and needle marks on his arm, the most recent injection, just a few hours earlier. He would not let the doctor touch him.

The doctor pleaded with O.B. "Can't you talk him into at least taking his shirt off? I have to examine him."

O.B. was annoyed by now and said, "No, I can't. If he won't take his shirt off I am not going to talk that man into anything."

They left the hospital and walked to the car, punctuated by O.B. snapping his hat against his thigh in irritation at the wasted trip. O.B. was thoroughly angry with Smokey and made no attempt at conversation on the return trip. It was a silent ride home.

A month later O.B. was on his porch swing when Smokey drove up. He was hardly out of his truck when he began waving an envelope in the air. Smokey was in a high state of anxiety. "I told you I don't want this! I never asked for it. I don't want any government handouts. You send this back to them. *Now!*"

The good Army Captain had submitted Herbert Glen Irwin for a pension without a complete physical. Part of that processing included a Social Security number. Up to this point Smokey had never had one although he had his Army service number memorized. The Army, in its quest for trouble-free record keeping, chose to give him a Social Security number along with his veteran status. As bad as his eyesight was, Smokey did not read what he was signing and simply answered questions when he completed the paperwork. Smokey had never applied for or paid into Social Security because he did not believe in the system. Smokey had a long held hatred of anything that hinted of socialism. It was reminiscent of Roosevelt's legacy and he slapped the envelope down on the rocker beside O.B. He was livid.

O.B. did as he was asked and went inside with the letter. He addressed an envelope and included a note about a bull-headed old man and apologized for the trouble. Satisfied, Smokey left with O.B. shaking his head, mystified.

Smokey's 1941 panel truck was still running smoothly in the spring of 1975 but Smokey was having trouble cranking the engine due to his waning strength. He was 82 then. Smokey had to crank it almost every time he drove it because the battery would not hold a charge. He asked O.B. to help him buy another vehicle. O.B. took him to a dealership in Many and after looking at several cars settled on a used Ranchero.

Smokey walked around the car several times and asked one question, "Where's the crank?" So totally isolated, he honestly did not know cars had long been manufactured without cranks. The salesman was baffled and didn't know whether the old man was serious or not. O.B. knew Smokey was a talented mechanic and given his interests was surprised he did not keep up with such advances. Smokey was comfortable with his familiar surroundings and his rigid routine including living with a decades old lifestyle. They agreed on a price and Smokey followed O.B. and the salesman inside the dealership. Smokey wore a loose cotton jacket over his khakis that day and reached in both pockets and pulled out from each one two rolls of money held together with rubber bands and placed them on the desk.

Smokey told the salesman, "You count it." He turned to O.B. and said, "You watch him."

Neighbors

The salesman peeled off the rubber bands and counted out $1400 in new $20 bills. There was another six hundred left on the table, and the salesman pushed the roll back toward the edge of the desk. When Smokey was assured everything was correct he put the roll of $20s back in his pocket. O.B. glanced at the bills and noted the issue dates on the bills were from the thirties and forties – and this was *1975*.

Smokey was adamant he sell his old truck to Roe and his Dad arranged the sale. O.B. thought Smokey considered him a friend after thirty-plus years. Surely, by this time he trusted him. Roe drove to Noble that weekend and the truck was parked in front of the Knott house. The agreed on price was $300 and O.B. had already given Smokey the cash. He sat down with Roe and the bill of sale and Roe gave his Dad a check.

O.B. was never one to mince words and was capable of irritation, especially over a point of integrity. He slapped the bill of sale in front of Roe pointing to it. Smokey had taken a typewriter and "X'd" out every white spot on the entire page that wasn't covered by text, completely to the cut edge of the paper. O.B. couldn't believe Smokey would go to such lengths and express that much distrust over an inexpensive transaction. Even after a thirty-year friendship Smokey could not lay down his suspicion.

One afternoon Smokey came to O.B. and told him people were trying to poison his food supply. O.B. listened to him patiently and asked Smokey how he came to this conclusion. Smokey said people were parking across the road and trying to get into his food containers at night. O.B. finally decided Smokey was referring to the couples that occasionally parked on the dirt road at the edge of the woods, which had always been a local lovers' lane. O.B. had a hard time convincing Smokey this was the case and that his food was the last thing they were interested in. Regardless of the subject O.B. had to repeat himself often to ease his friend's mind.

O.B. never intruded into Smokey's safe environment but made sure he knew if he ever needed anything he could call on him. When Smokey came to see him O.B. gave Smokey his undivided attention. He would not take a phone call and stopped whatever he was doing to listen to Smokey. For all his eccentric behavior, O.B. still had great respect for him.

It is a grand thing when friendship develops in spite of reason people should never have a relationship in the first place. Common interest is not necessarily a factor. Similarities in age, comparable experiences, or political and religious affiliation are not benchmarks. They simply like each other. Mutual respect and consideration were the primary basis for Smokey and O.B.'s friendship that grew from the first day they met. Through all his ramblings, Smokey found a man who appreciated him and didn't judge him. With all his troubles Smokey found someone who respected his privacy and would not exploit him. The contrast between these two men was remarkable, and it was a one-sided friendship in some respects. But it took a quantum leap on Smokey's part to seek O.B.'s companionship in the first place.

O.B. was in good health for most his life but became sick quickly in August, 1976. He died after a brief hospital stay. The front yard of the Knott house was a virtual parking lot with people paying their respects to Viola and their sons. We don't know who told Smokey, maybe the postmaster, but an hour before the funeral Roe glanced toward the rear of the Pentecostal Church and saw Smokey sitting alone at the far side in the fifth row. Roe was stunned to see him and immediately went to greet him. Smokey sat leaning forward grasping the back of the pew in front of him with both hands. There was a pained expression on his face as he stared toward the front of the church at the casket of the man he had known for so long.

Roe said, "Mr. Irwin, thank you for coming."

Smokey nodded toward O.B.'s casket and said with great emotion, "He was my friend."

Roe could see genuine grief in Smokey's face and of all the people who came to mourn O.B. Knott, Smokey's presence sincerely touched him. Smokey rose and shuffled out the door of the church on the verge of crying.

This was the first and only time Smokey ever attended a public function in the thirty-three years he was in Noble, and that was to pay his respects to his neighbor and friend, O.B. Knott.

Smokey was never seen to enter a church, attend a political rally, a restaurant, a mall, a festival, or any social function, except his friend's funeral.

The Gift

Chapter Sixteen

The Gift

Smokey had observed Roe from the time he was a young boy. Roe always spoke to him with respect and Smokey appreciated that. Most of the interaction they had was positive. In his conversations with Smokey O.B. told him where the twins were and what they were doing. Smokey didn't really follow their diverse careers but noted it was Roe who came home regularly. Smokey had no children, no close nephews to dote on, and no one to pass on his knowledge or values to the next generation. But he did have Roe. They talked often but Smokey wanted to develop a deeper relationship with the son of the only friend he ever had.

One afternoon in 1975 Smokey came to the Knott house and opened the rear doors of his truck. O.B. came down the steps and stood a polite distance from Smokey. He watched while Smokey reached in and pulled out three cages; one large, one medium-sized, and one small. Smokey told O.B. he wanted him to have them. Since Smokey had never given anything to him before O.B. wondered if the old man needed money. He thought maybe this was his way of expressing a desire to sell them. O.B. offered him cash and Smokey refused. O.B. knew how full of pride Smokey was and insisted he take it. Smokey did, although reluctantly. Smokey then said he needed to show O.B. how the traps worked. Both men carried the traps to the back yard under

243

the oak tree. O.B. had worked in the woods most his life, and thought he knew well enough how to operate a trap but listened patiently while Smokey demonstrated them.

When he was finished Smokey wanted to know when Roe would be in. It happened that Roe would be in the next day and Smokey said he wanted time with Roe alone so he could show him the mechanism of the traps. O.B. had given up trying to figure Smokey out and wondered why he couldn't show Roe how they operated just as well as Smokey. O.B. told Smokey to come back the next day.

When Smokey drove up the next morning O.B. stayed in the porch swing while Roe greeted Smokey in the yard. Smokey motioned for Roe to follow him and the old man shuffled around the back of the house under the large oak tree. Prior to this Roe and Smokey had talked regularly for years but not at length. You never did get into any real long discussions with Smokey and even then it tended to be pretty one-sided.

All three traps were lined up the smallest to the largest. Roe thought the traps were wonderfully constructed. They were made out of galvanized mesh wire. They were more or less the same trap but different sizes. They had perfectly straight lines and the spring mechanism was more complex than any trap Roe had seen before. Each trap door was machined from galvanized sheet metal. Roe thought they were beautiful and, he had not seen a commercially produced trap as well made as these. Roe absently thought this should take ten minutes at the most.

Smokey started with the smallest trap telling him to use this one for squirrel or rabbit. He went into great detail on different baits to use. He then went into positioning the trap, which direction it should face, camouflage, and how to anchor it securely with the metal stakes he brought. Smokey spoke of adjusting the tension of the spring door to allow for some animals being quicker than others and what angle to set it for maximum torque.

Roe was more enthralled listening to Smokey than he was interested in the traps. This was so out of character for him to talk this much. Roe wondered how many hours of experimentation it took Smokey to arrive at these conclusions. Plus, how many alterations he must have worked through to come to his final design.

When Smokey finished with the first trap he stepped over to the next largest one. He began all over again. This size was for turkey, possum, and raccoon with a whole new list of baits and how effective one was over another. The spring mechanism on the trap door was almost identical but Smokey thought he had to demonstrate it all over again. He set and released the trap repeatedly at different settings. Listening to him and watching, Roe realized this man had instructed people before. He recognized the repetition and thoroughness of military instruction techniques that had changed little with generations of soldiers.

Smokey then went to the last and largest trap. Roe thought what on earth in Sabine Parish would he be trapping with it? Smokey talked about wild boars and wild dogs, neither of which was that much of a problem anymore. The sheer size of the trap demanded a different mechanism. Smokey began as if this trap needed more detailed explanation. Roe listened to him thrilled to have this one-on-one meeting with Smokey. Roe paid closer attention to Smokey's mannerisms: his distinctive soft monotone voice, the inclining of his right ear, his substitution of gesture for the spoken word. Roe didn't attach any particular significance to any of it and concentrated on Smokey's instruction. While he spoke, Smokey looked at him with that piercing gaze that unnerved people who did not know him. Oddly enough, he would then turn his face away from him.

Smokey was studying Roe making sure he understood him and finally finished his training session. In a rare display of humor Smokey told him he would more than likely encounter a skunk and chuckled. He told Roe to throw a raincoat over the cage. Roe was so surprised at Smokey laughing he didn't know if he was serious or not.

Roe asked him, "Then what do you do with it?

Smokey turned and waved his finger in the air with a smile. The old man shuffled off to his truck with Roe following him. Roe thanked him and as Smokey drove away Roe looked at his watch. That quick ten minutes took every bit of an hour and a half, just to show him how to set a trap.

Roe sat down next to his Dad on the porch shaking his head. Roe had never spent that much time with him before. Smokey always asked for O.B. but this time it was Roe he wanted. How hard was it to operate a trap he needed that extensive of instruction? Roe had the distinct feeling Smokey was seeking his company and evaluating him but he didn't know for what.

Later that year Smokey came to O.B. and told him he wanted to buy another vehicle. Smokey was adamant he wanted Roe to buy his truck. Roe didn't dare try to bargain with Smokey, and was thrilled to own this jewel, his 1941 panel truck. Roe made plans to come to Noble for the second time that month.

When Roe arrived that Saturday Smokey's 1941 Ford ¾ ton, 110 in. wheelbase, 85 hp, Lochaven Green panel truck was parked in front of the Knott house. Smokey drove into the yard a few hours later in his used Ranchero. Smokey would have it no other way than to instruct Roe in the idiosyncrasies of his old truck. They started at the front bumper and raised the hood. Smokey showed him the notorious crank and how difficult it was to use. Roe gave it several turns and was surprised Smokey could turn the crank this long. Roe knew a whole lot more about electronics and radar than he did mechanics, but tried to be a good student nonetheless.

Roe could see Smokey had made some major modifications on the engine and wiring. He needed to pass on this information to a mechanic friend who had committed to work on the truck for him. Roe noticed the cleanliness of the motor and marveled how quiet and rhythmic the thirty-four year old engine idled.

After Smokey went over the alterations in the motor they moved to the cab of the truck. The lone seat was worn with a slight tear in it but the dash gauges and switches were all functional. Amazingly, the truck had just 58,000 actual miles on it. The pedals were worn smooth from use but were the original rubber. They walked around to the back of the truck and Smokey opened the doors wide. Smokey showed him the braces he added inside his truck panels to haul metal rods and lumber. He didn't mention why he had added interior lock boxes to the walls of the truck and at the time Roe didn't think why he had them. This was strictly a utilitarian vehicle and it made no pretense to be other than what it was. Other than some serious dents on the right side fenders it was a beautiful old truck. There was no rust on it whatsoever. Smokey was satisfied Roe knew enough about the truck and left. He had spent well over an hour explaining why this truck was different than any other he had experience with. Roe recognized Smokey as a master mechanic to keep the truck running so perfectly. He towed the truck home that weekend.

The Gift

After O.B. passed away in 1976 Roe did not hear from Smokey for several months. Smokey came by and asked Viola when Roe would be in town. She told him he would be coming in two weeks and he asked if Roe could meet him at the house. An appointment was made and precisely at ten o'clock on Saturday morning Smokey appeared in the yard and began taking things out of his Ranchero.

Not knowing what Smokey wanted Roe greeted him, "Hello, Mr. Irwin." He watched as Smokey removed some tools from his car and placed them on the ground. Roe did not ask why but waited on him.

In his flat voice Smokey said, "I'm going to show you how to kill fire ants."

Roe had other things to do that afternoon but welcomed another chance to be with Smokey. He said, "Okay. Thank you, Mr. Irwin." He waited for Smokey's instructions.

An explanation is in order why this was so important to Smokey. Fire ants were in rampant infestation in several southern states by the 1970s and the USDA sponsored a program to help eliminate fire ants, including in Louisiana. The state hired private contractors to spread the insecticide poison with crop dusters.

The first time Smokey saw a yellow powder on his building he immediately came to O.B. saying the government was poisoning him. O.B. explained the program to him and gave Smokey the same assurance the USDA gave to the general public, that the poison was harmless to humans and it would stop the progression of fire ants. Smokey was not convinced and left. In a few months the program was halted due to many people who handled the poison becoming violently ill. A less toxic and less effective poison was developed a few years later and it was left to the individual landowner to manage the fire ant problem. By

The Gift

1976 fire ant infestation was a common problem throughout northwest Louisiana including the Knott pasture adjoining Smokey's property.

Smokey told Roe even though he had his under control the fire ants would return if the Knott pasture were left untreated. He wanted to show Roe how to eliminate the fire ants. The pasture was indeed infested with over a hundred foot-high mounds scattered around the pasture, some within a dozen feet of Smokey's fence. As invasive as fire ants were, he had every reason to be concerned.

Smokey was dressed to work with his overalls and long sleeved cotton shirt, straw hat, and rubber boots. He unloaded his Ranchero with what was essentially a fire ant removal kit. Smokey had a two-gallon gasoline can two thirds full of gasoline. He had a handmade wooden box with a hole through the handle for a grip. The box was divided into four compartments. It held a handmade metal funnel and a cup, sized to contain a half pint of liquid. There was a Coke bottle with a cork and aluminum sprinkler head containing gas, plus a huge wooden mallet with a large square head. The last item of his kit was a five foot long metal rod, a half-inch in diameter, with one end sharpened into a dull point.

Roe did as he was instructed and carried Smokey's tools through the fence into the pasture. They stopped a short distance from a large anthill. Smokey explained his procedure in short simple sentences and told Roe to observe him.

Smokey strode up to the ant hill quickly and sprinkled gas from the Coke bottle over the ant hill. He took the metal rod and pushed it deep into the center of the anthill. He moved the top of the rod slightly in a circular motion to form an inverted cone-shaped hole. He then removed the rod. He placed the funnel in the hole and poured the cup of fuel into the funnel. When the fuel drained Smokey removed the funnel and rod. He took the mallet and pounded the anthill until it was almost level with the ground. Roe was surprised Smokey was still vigorous enough to do this at his age.

They moved on to the next ant hill, only this time Smokey motioned for Roe to perform the same routine. Roe thought he was following his example, although a bit casually. Smokey stopped him several times to correct him. Roe was reminded of his Air Force training instructors in the manner Smokey drilled him; repetition and thoroughness. Roe noted the similarities in how Smokey coached him with the traps, and now with the ants. It may have been a simple little exercise in property upkeep but Smokey approached it with the exactness of an important problem. Roe thought again this man has definitely instructed others before and was far more interested in what that might have been than fire ants.

They continued working for several hours going from one ant hill to another over the course of the afternoon. Smokey hardly spoke the whole time gesturing whenever he wanted Roe to do something. Every time Roe looked up from his task Smokey was watching him intently. Age had certainly not diminished Smokey's penetrating look. When he spoke it was with a few words at best. Smokey announced it was time to quit and they returned to the first ant hill.

Together they dissected the anthill with a small shovel and Roe saw that every ant in the anthill was dead. Smokey explained it was the fumes that killed the ants and that most people make a mistake in trying to fire the anthill or pouring gas over it. Most the ants escaped to build another mound. The queen must be killed with the whole colony. Using

The Gift

Smokey's method the queen was deep in the anthill and the fumes killed her along with the rest of the mound.

Smokey insisted on leaving the kit of tools with Roe for him to complete the job and left. Roe knew he needed to continue working on the pasture. He didn't want Smokey disappointed in him because the ants were a real concern to him. As much as Roe had to do he determined to finish the job that weekend. It took him all the next day but the fire ants were eliminated. It was twenty years before fire ants returned to the pasture.

Roe understood there was far more to the project than just an old man wanting to carry out some preventive maintenance with fire ants. Smokey wanted this time together with him and studied Roe the entire afternoon. This was the longest uninterrupted time they had spent together and Roe felt he was again being evaluated but he didn't know for what.

When Smokey talked to Roe he would often drop confusing comments that did not seem to relate to anything. Roe had always been puzzled at so many of the things Smokey said over the years. One remark did not necessarily correlate to the next one. A statement could easily refer to several different topics, none of which was about the subject at hand. Roe considered some of Smokey's conversations parables. The only problem was, Roe couldn't figure out the lesson Smokey was trying to communicate. He never knew if Smokey was speaking in the present tense or referencing something in the past. And sometimes he was convinced Smokey was referring to both. Piecing together the facts he did know, Roe picked up tidbits and obscure hints about Smokey's life. Roe would ask Smokey direct questions and frequently he would get a straight answer but other times

The Gift

Smokey would ignore him completely. Some things he simply would not discuss.

After a visit Roe would ponder for hours on Smokey's comments trying to reconstruct his meaning. Sometimes it was productive and other times it just raised more questions.

Their unspoken communication was another matter altogether. Roe became attuned to Smokey's gestures and mumbling, aware he could communicate so much without actually speaking. Sometimes Roe would offer a positive statement and Smokey would only nod agreement.

Roe did not see Smokey every time he came home to Noble. Their encounters were often enough Roe was convinced Smokey was deliberately seeking him out. Smokey was purposely interjecting himself into Roe's life and he clearly wanted a relationship with him. Roe never sought Smokey – he found Roe. Their conversations were never that lengthy but Smokey always seemed pleased to have seen him. Roe was reminded of the times his Dad said, "I have no idea what that man wanted." The same relationship Smokey had with O.B. was being established with Roe. Above all, Roe was positive Smokey had a reason for nurturing their relationship although he still did not know why.

The last time Roe saw Smokey their unspoken communication was far more important than the words that were actually spoken. Roe later felt the meeting they had was comparable to an assignment given by a mentor to his student. This definitely was not a casual visit. Smokey was determined he must tell Roe. It turned out to be a culmination of a man's lifetime.

Likewise, Smokey's last conversation with him held more significance than one would think on the surface, at least it did to Roe.

The Gift

In our research, we asked one of the docents of the Floyd County Museum in Floydada, Texas if the phrase, "yours truly" had any specific meaning other than the obvious. She told us in the Panhandle it is given as a term of endearment between friends. Or sometimes, "that's all there is, that's the end of it." Only friends used it.

****

We were coming to Noble every few months in 1977. Prior to one particular visit Smokey asked Viola when Roe was coming next. Normally, if Smokey wanted to see Roe he simply came over when he saw our car parked at the Knott house. This time he made an appointment.

Smokey had thought this visit over thoroughly. He was now 84 years old and he thought it was time for him to tell Roe who he really was. Smokey had intended to tell O.B. but his friend became sick and died so quickly Smokey missed the opportunity. He wasn't going to miss out on this one, and sought out Roe purposely to tell him. And he had another pressing reason as well.

Smokey considered Roe the only person he thought he could trust. Roe was the son of his friend, O.B. Smokey knew of Roe's professional background in electronics in the Air Force and engineering in industry. Who else except someone with the appropriate professional expertise would appreciate his inventions?

Smokey's disjointed statements over thirty years were definite hints of a past. But there was no point of reference, no context in which to construct a straightforward chronicle of Smokey's life. Roe had yet to compile all that information with facts to understand who Smokey really was. Even though Roe knew more about Smokey than anyone there were still unanswered questions.

Roe was at the Noble Mercantile only mildly curious why Smokey wanted to see him here instead of at the house. When he saw Smokey's Ranchero pull up he went outside to meet him. He was struck how frail Smokey had become in recent years. From his childhood, Roe remembered Smokey as a robust man with that intense gaze of his. Now Smokey was a feeble old man with clouded milky eyes. Roe wondered how Smokey could see to drive.

Roe stepped down from the store steps and stood a respectful distance from Smokey. He nodded. You didn't approach Smokey lightly, even though he was elderly and frail he still commanded respect.

Viola was inside the store and the only other person around was a local man standing on the porch of the store. He spoke gruffly, "What are you doin,' old man?" Smokey glanced at him but said nothing. There were some people Smokey did not think worthy of even acknowledging.

This was the first time Roe had actually heard anyone speak disrespectfully to Smokey and it irritated him. Roe answered him firmly, "I need to speak with Mr. Irwin." The man took the hint and went inside.

Smokey motioned for Roe to come with him. He rarely spoke when gestures served the same purpose but he had become almost mute. Smokey was dressed in his immaculate khaki pants and shirt buttoned to the neck. He wore rubber boots and shuffled several steps in front of Roe as they walked to the south side of the store in the open lot. Smokey looked all around to insure no one was watching and pulled a folded piece of paper from his shirt pocket and handed it to Roe.

The Gift

Roe opened the paper and looked at a drawing of three identical figures; it was a child-like rendering of what a simple robot might look like. The drawing consisted of two round eyes in a circular head placed on top of a cylinder. Roe was convinced Smokey was trying him. Roe knew if he did not take the drawing seriously the meeting would be over. His rapport with Smokey would unravel and would not be repaired. The implication of the drawing would have made most people smile and patronize an old man. Instead, Roe had enough respect for Smokey he asked him the only logical question.

"Mr. Irwin, are these aliens?"

Smokey nodded.

"Have you seen them?"

Again, Smokey nodded.

"Where?"

This time Smokey spoke in his characteristic monotone, "I see them on the dark of the moon. They are always thirty-two paces from my window. They're coming back after me one day."

How on earth do you respond to that? Knowing of the UFO scares of the fifties Roe did not think this was an unlikely wandering of the mind for Smokey's generation. The safer response was nothing so Roe folded up the paper and handed it back to him without comment. Roe kept a poker face and did not react one way or another.

Smokey paused but then did something quite peculiar. With lucid purpose he took the heel of his boot and repeatedly cut into the dirt until he made a small indentation in the dirt.

Smokey said, "Soil is interesting. You can hide a lot of things under dirt."

Carefully, he smoothed the tiny mound of dirt back over and patted his foot on it.

"See? Now you don't see it do you?" Then Smokey smiled. His grin was completely unexpected but held so much intrigue in his expression Roe knew without any doubt, Smokey was telling him something of value was hidden and buried. As always, it wasn't so much what Smokey said but his demeanor and what was left unsaid.

He motioned for Roe to follow him and they walked back around the side of the store to Smokey's Ranchero.

Smokey opened the door on the passenger side and pulled the bench seat forward. He lifted out a cardboard cylinder used for storing plats and mechanical drawings. He handed it to Roe.

Roe opened the cylinder and pulled out a roll of drawings and together they laid the drawings on the hood of his car. Roe had seen many engineering drawings and schematics in his career and immediately recognized them. They were masterfully executed mechanical drawings. Roe thought they were beautiful. He saw the seal of the US Patent Office and the name of Herbert G. Irwin at the bottom of each page. Roe was stunned on one level but not surprised at all knowing Smokey.

"Mr. Irwin, who drew these?"

In an uncommon display of pride Smokey smiled again and thumped his chest with his fingers.

Roe was still lifting the pages and saw more drawings with the text that accompanied each patent.

"Who typed them?"

Smokey had turned slightly to look around and did not hear Roe. He did not answer. Roe wanted to study the drawings but was concerned someone would intrude so he

The Gift

rolled the drawings back up. He placed them back in the cylinder and Smokey put them behind his seat again.

Roe was standing in front of the Ranchero and had the overwhelming feeling he would never see Smokey again. This was goodbye. He felt honored Smokey trusted him enough to confide in him. He also knew Smokey had never let anyone else inside his curtain of privacy, not even his Dad. Smokey wanted Roe to know he was an inventor and not the crazy old man the community thought he was.

Smokey's vague comments and parables over the years began to make clear sense. These drawings were the key that opened the door and Roe was filled with a wave of comprehension. It was not only acknowledgement of their relationship it was a moment where their friendship would never be closer. This was trust, in action.

Beyond that, Roe understood Smokey was giving something physical to him even though he had no idea what "it" was. The feeling was as tangible as if Smokey had handed him a chest of rare coins and clearly told him, "This is yours. Do with it what you wish."

Smokey's visual recollection never quite correlated into the same spoken description. Smokey was convinced he told Roe exactly where his fortune was buried. Roe knew full well that was his intent. In these simple statements Smokey had effectively bequeathed his legacy, his personal history, and everything he possessed to Roe. Smokey *thought* he had communicated to Roe all he needed; the rest was now up to him.

Roe wondered did he really mean paces or did he mean feet? Which window in a building full of windows? Thirty-two or twenty-three from a dyslexic thinker?

Smokey had a pleased look on his face and walked around his Ranchero to the driver side door. Roe was still caught off guard, his mind scrambling to assemble a true portrayal of this extraordinary man he had known all his life. Not knowing what else to do, he said, "Mr. Irwin, thank you."

Smokey turned and with his right hand pointed upward and traced a circle in the air with his index finger. With a broad smile he replied, "Yours truly."

Roe stood for a long time and watched Smokey drive away.

The Gift

Epilogue

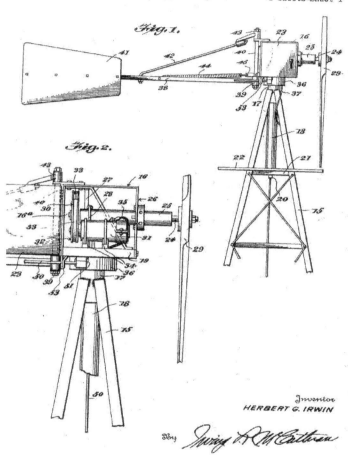

Inventor
HERBERT G. IRWIN

Chapter Seventeen

Survival Living

Environment

Twenty-two years was a long time to wait before entering Smokey's building. One reason was out of respect to a man's obsessive desire for privacy. We were told the property had been pilfered and ransacked years before and restraint seemed pointless after that. We knew property ownership would eventually be settled with Smokey's many heirs. It was common knowledge Smokey had not left a will. Louisiana law would give equal, undivided ownership to his surviving siblings and upon their death, the siblings' children. When Smokey died in 1981 there were fifteen heirs, and the legal entanglement would take years to settle, which it eventually did. A family member gave us verbal permission to enter the property. And last, we finally had the time to give our full efforts to this project.

We thought it prudent to inform the Sabine Parish District Attorney, Don Burkett, about what we hoped to find; field notes, possibly his original patents, or any significant documents. There was a real possibility of finding a cache of money. Since no word suggested any had been found, we assumed it was still there. We were told people had probed the property with metal detectors. Still, we wanted to be aware of procedure should we find any. We felt Herbert Glen Irwin was an inventor of significance in his field. Since the family had no knowledge or interest, we knew if we didn't secure those discoveries they would be lost to looters.

When we entered the building April 1, 2003 the building itself was unbelievably trashed. Knowing Smokey's exacting nature we knew he hadn't lived like this. We later rethought that premise understanding the extremes of OCD. Smokey probably began and abandoned an experiment simply walking from one area to another, dropping one object and picking up another. We sorely wished his building had been evaluated how an inventor lived and worked in his era, rather than casual removal of anything salvageable.

We interviewed Smokey's nephew, Sherman Irwin, in October, 2000. As the family representative, he was allowed to remove items from Smokey's building. We were pleased at least some of Smokey's belongings were redeemed. Sherman mentioned a few items: a lathe, welder, typewriter, a .22 rifle, a large vise, and "odds and ends."

After Smokey died residents told us trucks with Texas license plates backed up to the sliding garage door of the building and it took them all day to load two large trucks. Any equipment or items of significance were removed. We wish we had an exact record of what tools and machines Smokey did use but we probably will never know for sure. He was always vague about that.

Smokey's building was locked after that but when we came in April there was a gaping hole cut into the east side of the building. Someone had used a crowbar (and left it) to force the door and pry it open. The same thieves had used a bulldozer to gain entry onto the property. They cut a ten-foot swath through the timber and underbrush to the back of Smokey's building. The downed trees had long dried out and lost their bark, which would indicate that happened at least a decade before, probably after Sherman Irwin removed the first items.

We know there was at least one drill press, a forge, generators, an engine, many of his inventions, and miscellaneous tools enough to fill several workshops. We know his header machine (Invention #17) was off loaded when he arrived in Noble. We saw his powder sprayer (Invention #12) in the building, left it, and the next visit it was missing. We regret leaving so much we knew was important.

Please keep in mind this narrative relates to found objects twenty-two years after Smokey's death. Walk with us over the dirt floor in his darkened building, the clerestory windows above stained by time. One's first impression is oppressive austerity, coldness, a lack of any human warmth. It is hard to comprehend anyone living in this.

Step over trash and discarded items. Pick up, examine, and wonder. Disregarding thirty-nine patents, Smokey's everyday life was one of constant innovation and invention. If he needed something he made or tooled it with materials he kept on hand. One ponders about his recycling being positive and his extreme hoarding becoming debilitating. Regardless, of the strewn items intermixed with trash and gadgets it was still possible to see how Smokey assigned designated work areas.

We entered the building with friends and Noble residents, Helen and Troy Webb. We individually walked around the debris of a man's lifetime picking up objects and asking the others, "Look at this. What do you think he used this for? What is this?" Sometimes it took group interaction and several attempts to figure out the purpose of things we found. Troy's knowledge of construction, farming, and welding were enormously helpful. Others, we still couldn't solve. We marveled over Smokey making almost everything he needed for his daily life and work. There were few commercially produced items in the building.

We saw four canister type wheels in the dirt where he parked his truck. We know someone has an extremely well made toolbox filled with fine tools. Noble had enough respect, possibly, more fear of Smokey few locals entered his building. We are well aware the looting was confined to individuals.

Smokey had made a large galvanized metal table with a huge roller on one end. Circular wood pieces of a roller were numbered right to left, twelve through one, instead of left to right, one through twelve. We already knew Smokey had dyslexia and had a lifelong problem with numbers. There were cranks on both ends of the roller and slats on top of the table. At the opposite end was a galvanized vat. What on earth was he doing with this thing?

Against the north wall was a large snow white roll of paper, ten inches in diameter, perfectly sized to fit the roller. We knew this paper had been there almost a quarter century and yet it was so pristine it could have come off the store shelves that day. What did Smokey treat that thick paper with? Possibly, with the chemicals sandbagged in the corner of his building? One of them resembled the texture of the roll of paper. Smokey may have been working on a method to preserve paper, perhaps to protect his documents. If he was, it worked extremely well.

Toward the north end of the building were stacks of soldering rods. We could see tracks in the dirt where flat boards acted as levels for whatever equipment was placed on them. We found larger welded pieces of angle iron in the northwest corner and a small pile of coal. Smokey was a master at recycling and used the southwest corner as a staging area for recycled pieces. We found neat stacks of corrugated tin, small sticks of wood up to large posts, plus odd discarded metal pieces. All waited for their second or third life as a new tool or part.

One window on the east side was sooted all around it with a cord over head to lift the panel. We assumed to allow for the
smoke and fumes from forging to escape.

We took samples from the pile of sandbagged chemicals but were never able to get them analyzed. The various powders were in several shades of white and gray, brilliant turquoise, some powdery, others lightly clumped like blown insulation. None of us were familiar with any of the substances, even after reading the faded sandbag labels. We still wish we had followed through with that.

Next to his sliding garage door we found two of Smokey's old cotton shirts bundled by a wire hanging from a cypress brace. They were pieces cut out for shop rags. We also found two discarded brogan boots, size 9 ½. One was beside his bed the other tossed outside his building. The boots had been resoled several times, not by a shoe cobbler but by Smokey. These were the only personal items left. I was touched by seeing those, absently thinking at the time there are no mementos, no favorite or personal things except Smokey's machines. Hopefully, the family has them, if any.

We puzzled over two pieces we never could decide what their function was. We can only guess they were left over from an experiment Smokey was conducting or one he had abandoned. One was as large as the motor and tub of a wash machine. The other slightly smaller, both mounted on galvanized tabled stands. Parts of both pulled, turned, moved, or spun in some manner but didn't perform a function we were familiar with.

We found five washtubs and a galvanized tank. Smokey did not drink well water, only rainwater. He did not have a well or city water in Florida or in Noble.

Smokey had houses in Texas and Florida, as "normal" as he ever came close to. Smokey was wealthy enough he could easily have lived by society's standards when he came to Louisiana. Instead, he chose to live in a metal workshop with a dirt floor with no running water and no electricity. When he first arrived in Noble his equipment was so valuable to him his first concern was a proper and secure workshop to house them. A house for himself wasn't a concern after that.

Temperature Extremes

Even so, how was it possible for Smokey to live in a metal building with no insulation in scorching summers and icy winters? How could a young person exist in that environment much less an elderly one?

At one time we were convinced Smokey had an underground room to escape the summer heat and protect himself from the cold. After observing what clues he left we concluded Smokey did indeed live in his workshop.

Anyone who lives in the south can testify to suffocating heat that must be endured in the summers. Temperatures consistently in the high 90s and in the 100s for weeks are common. Air conditioning is one of the life-altering inventions of modern times and those of us who remember not having it appreciate its comfort. However, Smokey being born in 1893 lived his entire life without air-conditioning even though most his generation gladly adapted to it.

How did Smokey cope with the humidity and heat? Without electricity or air-conditioning how did he heat and cool his building? One can look back to the design of early southern houses to see the same principles he applied on a much larger scale. He just never left his generation.

Because heat rises it is desirable to have high ceilings with an opening at the top for hot air to escape. The temperature at floor level was measurable degrees cooler than at ceiling level. There was no dropped ceiling in Smokey's building or insulated attic space to trap heat. The roof above and ceiling below was the same 29 gauge galvanized panel of railroad metal.

Employing cross circulation, his building had large open windows facing every orientation to allow airflow regardless of wind direction.

Smokey exploited the properties of insulation and convection. A primitive dirt floor cooled the airspace in Smokey's building until the heat of the day overrode it. Smokey rarely opened his windows before mid-afternoon in the peak of summer and did not open his windows until the inside ceased to be comfortable.

Smokey's building was not in the shade but on open acreage. His building would have suffered the baking sun of a southern summer. On an August day of 98 degrees the inside of such a metal building can easily reach 120 degrees. The circulation of air inhibited the inside temperature from being hotter than the outside, certainly tolerable to a person unaccustomed to air conditioning. Not having an insulated building allowed the heat to escape quickly as the night cooled.

We know Smokey slept in his panel truck on freezing nights in a sleeping bag. He used his panel truck as a camper in his trips back and forth from Texas to Florida, and to

Louisiana. When he came to Noble he lived in his truck while his workshop was being completed. We found an old fashioned bed warmer filled with coal to heat the mattress in his truck. He had used a sleeping bag since his stint in the Army and replaced it as needed. It would be simple to heat the small space of his panel truck rather than the whole building. He used his prairie bed for naps and hot summer nights. After he sold his panel truck in 1976 he had only his bed. As uncomfortable as it had to have been for a frail old man this is what Smokey preferred.

We found two sets of perfectly cut cardboard blades for fans with ruler straight lines. The dual-angled single blades were about fourteen inches long and three inches wide at the outside. The center was pierced with a bolt and washers, which then attached to a small motor. It seemed a perfect size for a personal van when there was a particularly hot night. This was typical of Smokey making whatever he needed for his daily needs. We regret not removing these items but we had no authority or right. We could see Smokey's inventive mind within so many objects we saw and held in our hands.

Smokey relieved the heat in his building with an invention left over from years before; the propeller from his wind-powered generator. On particularly humid nights Smokey directed his propeller into one giant fan similar to shop fans utilized today. Smokey applied unorthodox uses of his resources and operating a monstrous-sized fan to relieve the heat in his building was just one more. He employed what was readily at hand.

Centered in Smokey's building is a sunken area with glass bottles in it. Apparently others thought something was buried there and tried digging under them. They succeeded only in breaking bottles and disturbing them. We dug deeper, trying to figure out why an obsessively neat man would have a pile of glass bottles in his building. This definitely was not a trash pit. The deeper bottles were in perfect alignment touching each other horizontally and vertically in precise layers as one would stack cordwood. The glass bottles were small dark blue Squibb bottles, Milk of Magnesia, or lemon juice bottles, approximately six inches tall. The perimeter was about three feet deep by three feet in a circular pit. Why would Smokey stack bottles like this? He recycled virtually everything and we can only offer one possibility.

This is pure speculation, but Smokey may have heated the bottles to the point the glass pit became a thermal radiator to heat his building in the winter. Instead of a fire he may have constructed a glass and water-fueled radiator. Depending on the composition of the particular glass, the lowest heat glass will melt is at 900 degrees Fahrenheit and some up to 3180 degrees Fahrenheit.

One comment on the lemon juice bottles; as we estimated the number of bottles in the glass pit we absently wondered what Smokey used all that lemon juice for. When we finally determined his heroin use much later, we found out lemon juice is used to process raw opium milk into heroin. At the same time we found out a common complaint of heroin users is stomach cramping and constipation. There were hundreds of lemon juice bottles, Milk of Magnesia, and Squibb over the counter medicine for stomach aches.

Electrical

Smokey lived with electricity as an adult only for a short time. Most of Amarillo had electricity including the Willborn Brothers. But Smokey worked out on the pipelines.

Most boarding houses had electricity, but the relative hours he stayed in one were negligible. Smokey's intent at Noble may not have been a quest for pure independence but that is essentially what he had. His Amarillo factory, nor his Florida or Louisiana properties had electricity. Generators and storage batteries were his preferred means of electrical power, not commercial electricity.

After his building and fence were completed the residents of Noble were poised in anticipation of seeing a utility pole installed as the precursor to his factory opening. It never did. Seeing electrical utility poles at rural houses is part of the landscape. When Smokey moved to Noble in 1948 the only telephone in town was at Helm's store. Depending on Mrs. Helm's mood that day she might or might not let you use her phone or relay any messages. Smokey had no friends or close family ties, and no business acquaintances to ever have the need of a telephone. Any business he conducted was through the US Postal Service and wire service.

When Noble saw light emanating from the clerestory windows in Smokey's roof at night most assumed it was from carbide lights and kerosene lamps. Smokey had generators and dozens of small motors if one of his experiments demanded electrical power. Smokey had serviced and used twelve-volt batteries as a young man. We found remnants of battery storage units of four, six, and eight batteries deep on bolted wood supports. Electricity wasn't necessarily a requirement for all his experiments. Between using kerosene, an internal combustion engine, and storage batteries in various combinations Smokey never missed electricity. If one wanted total independence rejecting public utilities was a means to accomplish that.

Weeks after Smokey finished his building, brilliant blue flashes lit up that side of town every night. Those strobe-like bursts from his clerestory window were the familiar signs of welding. This was Noble's only hint of the nature of Smokey's pursuits. Looking inside his building today you can see where Smokey added to the structural braces of his building after the initial construction. The roof is heavily reinforced with thick rods lacing across one side of the roof to the other.

Smokey purchased relatively large amounts of kerosene. He used kerosene generators to run his metal lathes, a drill press, band saws, fans, a welder, a kerosene refrigerator, a kerosene wash machine, and others we only wish we knew of for sure.

We found a sandbag and a pile of coal on the ground on the far side of his building next to where he welded and soldered. We believe there was an iron stove of some kind from the impressions left in the dirt and the piles of coal dust surrounding the spot. He may have used this as an incinerator as well. We did not find any indication of a trash incinerator outside. While the rest of Noble added a log to their cast iron stoves and dug out more quilts for warmth in the winter, Smokey was tolerably comfortable with extra clothes. We did find a Sears package for an electric blanket. We assume he had to use it in later years when he slept in his bed and not in his panel truck.

Smokey's freestanding bed was positioned approximately fifteen feet from the north wall and twenty feet from the east wall. Fifteen inches off the dirt floor, it was the kind of bed one sees in many Texas museums referred to as a "prairie bed." It had wood slats, eight-inch high sides with vertical struts protruding above the sides, specifically designed to support mosquito netting, a sheet, or a blanket. This would allow a person to turn over easily in their sleep. Upon rising, a man simply threw off the mosquito netting and swung his legs to the floor through the space cut into the side. His bed was pointed north south with the opening in the side facing the open building.

Smokey did not prepare for bed and retire to a bedroom. He was one of those people who needed little sleep and was used to taking short naps and then rising to work on his experiments at any hour. He developed the habit early in life, particularly after WWI when he returned to his parents' farm in Floydada. Watches and clocks were generally for people with families, appointments, and public jobs. Sleeping close to or with his machines allowed him to pursue his work with little interruption. The practice was so agreeable he slept with his work for the rest of his life.

When describing Smokey's environment sadness is often the first impression. Smokey lived with the machines he dearly loved and he ignored societal standards. He chose this lifestyle and who is to say his was less than acceptable?

.

Food

Smokey's living area was confined to the northeast corner of the building. He lived in a twenty-foot square "room" without walls. A long planked table more resembling a counter where he prepared and ate his food. We found a burner plate from an iron stove. The only container we found to prepare food in was a cake pan and a frying pan resembling his gaseous condiment generator (Invention #39). We found remnants of his smoker (Invention #33). We found handmade racks for drying fruit and produce. There were two nine-inch stainless steel cake pans with holes drilled through the center, obviously not purchased to cook with. We found an aluminum ice cube divider left from his kerosene refrigerator. The refrigerator itself was removed. Other than one lone fork and a spoon all other cooking utensils were gone.

Smokey was fanatic in his quest for pure food untainted by fertilizers, insecticides, or chemicals. His diet was obsessively importance to him. Curiously, he refused to buy any canned goods from California. He was convinced of prolific chemical use there and any number of threats to his health. Why Smokey thought California's agricultural practices were any more hazardous than any other state is a mystery. He may have been aware of some particular chemical use in California even though widespread use of pesticides and fertilizers in agriculture was already commonplace in the fifties.

Smokey's immersion into botany and gardening in Florida was part of his obsession with food. He didn't just garden, he experimented with the genetics of different strains of produce. Raising his fruit and vegetables was the only way to guarantee the purity of his food supply. He bought seed at Maxey's Feed Store in Zwolle. He grew several different kinds of beans, potatoes, onions, carrots, tomatoes, cucumbers, rutabagas, turnip and collard greens, and cabbage. His fruit trees included plum, pear, peach, fig, and persimmon. Dewberry, boysenberry, strawberries, blackberries, blueberry, and muscadine grapes all thrive in north Louisiana. Smokey brought his opium poppies with him and continued to use the drug the rest of his life.

Smokey spoke with Aunt Maggie Cross about gardening and brought produce to her in appreciation of her finding various items for his experiments. Maggie repeatedly praised the unspoiled beauty of Smokey's produce when the rest of Noble's vegetables were afflicted with blight or insects. Smokey's never were. When asked he would only smile and not say why his produce was so pristine or what he used. We are absolutely sure he rejected all artificial pesticides or fertilizers. Unfortunately, those practices, natural prevention, and field notes that described them are lost. In this day of organic farming such information would be valuable.

Smokey was never seen to drink or eat anyone's food or beverages but his own or eat in anyone's presence. To our knowledge Smokey never ate in a restaurant his adult life. He couldn't tolerate the food or the people.

When the pulpwood yard was put in dozens of diesel trucks were routed past Smokey's property for months dumping loads of dirt. One afternoon at the store Smokey asked Maggie if she had turnip greens yet this year. When she said no, Smokey said he could taste the diesel in his turnip greens and that had never happened before. He attributed the taste to the trucks. Smokey had an extremely sensitive palette.

Smokey was familiar with the variances in Texas' many climate regions but had to adapt to the subtropics of southern Florida. He studied vegetables and fruit that flourished there and brought his fruit trees with him to Louisiana. Smokey relocated to three diverse climates: arid northwest Texas, southern Florida, and the piney woods of northwest Louisiana. For most people these moves only involved a change of address. For someone finely tuned to growing his own food as Smokey did, the climate differences were dramatic changes he had to adapt to.

Smokey never purchased any processed meats from the Noble Mercantile. The store carried fresh chicken, sausage, bacon, ham, pork, and some beef but he did not buy them. The little meat he did buy came from Lefkovits meat market in Zwolle, four miles from Noble. They had a wide reputation as having the best meat available in the parish.

Lefkovits had dry goods as well and Smokey replaced his few clothes from this store.

One of Smokey's patents while living in Noble was a humble fishhook, the least sophisticated of his patents. Actually, not the fishhook itself but the ingredients of a pouch he used as bait on the hook. The exhaustive description within the patent text, suggest months of experimentation as to what combinations would attract different species of fish. Given the complexity of his industrial and agricultural inventions this is surprising if it were not for his obsession with food.

We found three fishing poles in his building cut from slender tree branches, one with the string still attached, the other two worn smooth from use. The pole and string were only long enough to fish immediately in front of him off the bank of a stream. The fishing poles were still there the first visit but gone the second.

Smokey's two acres across the road from his building were left undeveloped. One-half mile from those two acres was a ten-acre pond hidden in the woods with deep pools of fresh water. The pond was known to have a fine stock of bream, perch, catfish, with some bass. Road construction spoiled the pond in late years, but a spring fed stream flowed from the west side of the pond for several miles. This was a remote patch of woods visited or known by few people. Smokey often walked from his workshop across the road under the cover of heavy woods and fished undisturbed. Surprisingly, a few sardine cans were the only remnants we found of him eating any canned meat or fish. We assume because he was too frail to walk to the pond to fish anymore.

In the mid-70s Smokey offered O.B. some animal traps. Smokey had several rolls of heavy gauge galvanized mesh wire leftover from his construction projects in Florida. He had trapped panthers and bobcats in Florida to protect his livestock. The wire traps are works of art. Forty years later they are functional and sturdy with no weak or broken pieces. Smokey used them in Louisiana to trap rabbit and turkey. Wild turkey did not move into the region until the 1970s. Consuming organically raised livestock, or wild meat is often the only means to avoid antibiotics and growth hormone in commercially produced meats today.

Thirty yards from his building is an odd basin apparatus Smokey washed his produce in. Basically, it is a washing station. It is made out of galvanized sheets of metal, thirty inches high, seven inches deep, four feet by six feet, with one side partitioned into a narrow seven-inch wide rectangular basin. Within the larger rectangle is a square-shaped bowl. All four sides resemble the lip of a wide jar to allow for run-off. There is a drain in the center emptying into a pipe set into the ground. It seems excessive just to wash produce or fish.

Smokey canned his own vegetables and fruit. His pressure cooker was removed from his building but broken pint and quart jars were found in his small trash pile. Metal rims and tops were on a hook beside one of his worktables. Smokey had a large garden and there came a time he became too feeble to raise his own food. His stored canned food would have lasted him years after he quit gardening.

We found a water heater-sized apparatus to the side his garden area. Made of iron and extremely heavy, black, with valves, pipe, odd fittings and gauges, we had no idea what its function was.

Clothing

Smokey never attended social functions, not a church service, public meeting, club or lodge, dance, dinner, or political rally. He never dined in a restaurant or frequented any other gathering of people. Because Smokey did not attend social events his clothing was naturally limited. He either worked in his shop or in his garden. His "dress" clothes were the khaki pants and long sleeved shirts he wore when he left his property.

Smokey wore a straw hat and denim overalls with a long-sleeved blue cotton shirt when he worked in his garden. Smokey had two pairs of khaki outfits and possibly four overalls and shirts. As durable as these clothing items are they would have lasted him years and the khakis probably decades. Roe remembers him wearing a coat in the winter but he doesn't recall the type. Smokey brought all his clothing with him to Noble and if he did buy any it was only a few replacement items during his life in Louisiana.

He had a kerosene wash machine to wash his few clothes and starched and pressed them himself. These items were also removed from his building.

Smokey wore brogan shoes common to his generation. Assuming he was wearing his rubber boots when he died Smokey probably had only two or three pair the whole thirty-three years he lived in Noble. In late years Smokey was in the habit of wearing rubber boots out of concern for snakes, and the difficulty of lacing his brogans. He wore a leather belt with his khakis and one belt would have lasted him while he lived in Noble.

Smokey was never seen in public without his fedora style hat or, when gardening, his straw hat. When you look at 19th and 20th century photographs most men and many adolescent boys wore hats. We doubt he ever replaced his fedora while in Louisiana. He could have gotten years of wear out of his straw hat but more than likely replaced it with a couple. These straw hats can still be purchased at any feed store for a few dollars. Smokey's only other garments would be underwear, socks, and handkerchiefs. He had the bare minimum of these items and replaced them only as needed. Smokey may have rejected pajamas except in the winter or he may have slept in his clothes. He adopted the Army's policy of sleeping bags on his mattress. It was more practical for him than sheets, blankets, and a pillowcase.

Serviceability was his only consideration for clothing and Smokey never entered a mall in his life. He was not subject to the whims of fashion and kept his clothing selection to functional use only. Smokey spent less on clothes in his lifetime than some people do today in one shopping trip. He was never observed scruffy or dirty in public. I don't think we can stress enough how immaculately clean Smokey attired himself.

Smokey was always clean-shaven with his hair neatly trimmed. A twelve-inch square mirror was found close to a table in his building but his scissors and razor were gone. In Smokey's mind going to a barber was far too personal an invasion of his personal space and was a task he did himself. He bathed in a large washtub.

Medical

The prospect of living one's latter years without medical attention is a huge consideration for the elderly. Smokey saw a doctor only three times as an adult; his enlistment and discharge physicals, and when O.B. took him to Fort Polk in 1971. Smokey was blessed with good genes and to further maintain his good health he did not smoke or chew tobacco. He did not drink any alcohol and ate only fresh fruit or vegetables. He rarely ate commercially canned foods and was careful they were free of preservatives or chemicals. Even with such deliberate attention to his health Smokey still suffered an occasional health crisis. Most of this was from stomach cramping from his heroin use.

Although Aunt Maggie went to a doctor on occasion, she understood Smokey's reluctance to see one. She frequently shared her home and herbal remedies with him. Maggie was wise in folk medicine and such knowledge was common to a generation used to living without Medicare. To further insure his good health Smokey did not expose himself to the general public. Smokey did not need to worry about viruses or an influenza epidemic sweeping through a populace.

One extraordinary way Smokey dealt with the problems of aging was to extract his own teeth. Although it was not all that uncommon for his generation, making his own dentures out of metal certainly was. Smokey began his heroin use as a tranquilizer but used it as a narcotic painkiller to pull his teeth. O.B. was sure Smokey was "on something" because of his irrational conversations. It was not until much later we confirmed his heroin use.

Some of Smokey's last patents dealt with drying spices, preserving, seasoning, and tenderizing meat (see Inventions, #33, 38 & 39). It was essentially a pressure cooker that infused seasoning into meat while tenderizing it. Smokey's metal dentures may have served him well but in his later years he had difficulty chewing his food. His dental health appears to have been his worse physical ailment. Other than his lifelong heroin habit Smokey never used anything except over the counter medicine.

Refuse

Survival Living

Most rural homesteads have a fifty-five gallon rusted drum in the back yard as a burning barrel. Smokey used his iron stove inside his building as an incinerator. Smokey had only small handfuls of decomposable trash to add to his compost pile. He did not buy disposable items and most of what he made was from metal. We found several plastic containers that would have held commercially grown berries. Unable to garden in his later years he bought what he could not grow anymore.

One issue of urban living today is the economical and ecological disposal of garbage. A single person today will generate at least a bag or two of trash twice weekly. Municipal landfills are tremendous undertakings and even with recycling efforts, trash is a formidable modern problem.

Smokey's workshop held the scattered remnants of his profession but it would be hard to classify the contents as refuse. Stepping through the scattered debris a machinist could still walk through his workshop today and find some use for the scrap metal pieces. The only waste we found on Smokey's property after him living there for thirty-three years were two minor trash piles, thirty yards from his building. One was of metal cans, the other of glass jars and bottles. Other than a few bread wrappers there was no plastic, Styrofoam, or scrap paper. Both piles heaped upon each other would barely total the cubic space occupied by an upholstered armchair.

About twenty feet from the corner workbench along the north wall we found the porcelain top of a "slop jar." This was one of the few commercial objects we found. There was no outhouse or any facility to deal with human waste other than remote woods.

The only thing one could categorize as trash was some discarded storage batteries mounted in tandem, in a wooden frame. We were surprised to see them but then reflected Smokey was used to working with batteries and comfortable handling acid. Smokey considered the carbide he worked with an acceptable risk. We're not sure if his heroin use or carbide exposure explains the deterioration of his mental facilities late in life.

Transportation

One of Smokey's concessions to modern living was to own an automobile, disregard he kept one over thirty years. He only owned three, possibly four in his lifetime. Smokey was completely unaffected by ad campaigns and felt no compulsion to buy a new one every few years when his old one ran perfectly well. When Roe bought Smokey's 1941 Ford panel truck in 1976 the bill of sale was still in the glove box. Having a car note was as foreign an ideology to him as commuting. Smokey was unaffected by a whole industry that is a major component of American culture today.

When Roe bought Smokey's truck it ran extremely well but we were unsure if we could get it licensed. We entertained the thought of refurbishing it and wanted to see if the truck was mechanically sound. It had one fender crushed but no rust. We brought the car to Natalbany, Louisiana and left it with master mechanic, George Malnar, and asked him to evaluate it. After a few hours he called Roe in a state of excitement and said, "I want to meet this man. I have never seen any car so perfectly maintained. He is a genius. He replaced some parts he machined himself. He completely retooled some and rewired it differently and better. His design is far superior to the manufacturers. It's beautiful. This man is a genius!"

We sold the truck to friend, Von Champion, but the truck was later stolen when he was off shore working. Smokey's truck is undoubtedly a prized antique somewhere today. We still hold the registration for him, license, complete with VIN number. We hope Smokey's truck turns up one day and can be returned to its rightful owner.

Cultural Awareness

Smokey was socially engaged in his world as a young man but later withdrew completely. Other than buying an occasional *Shreveport Journal* for a nickel from Roe once or twice a week in 1949 Smokey never subscribed to a newspaper or periodical while in Noble. We found two scrap pages in his workshop of a 1952 *The Pathfinder*, which was a subsidiary of the *Farm Journal*. The pages listed some legislation before Congress that affected agriculture but we were unable to locate the complete journal through the publisher's archives. We found a December 26, 1940 *Amarillo Globe* newspaper. One would think a self-educated man would keep some books but beyond scraps, that was the only written text found in his workshop. We found a nickel postcard from a Book-of-the-Month Club. If Smokey had a personal library, which we believe he did, it was removed. Sherman Irwin will only admit to having "a few" of Smokey's patents. We believe Smokey's field notes from a lifetime of inventing and observation exist. Either they are still hidden or they were removed.

Noble has a tiny library that hardly appeals to an avid reader much less to an inventive mind like Smokey's. In 1948 Noble's library consisted of eight shelves of donated books in a room of Mrs. Youngblood's store, and later only a tiny one-room library. Smokey was never known to have checked out any book from the Noble, Zwolle, or Sabine Parish libraries.

None of the stores in Noble sold newspapers while he lived there but Smokey glanced at the headlines of newspapers in stores in Zwolle to get news the few times he ventured out of Noble. He never owned a television set or owned a radio. His old truck didn't have one and we doubt he ever turned on the one in his Ranchero, or if it had one. On rare occasions Smokey overheard topical conversations from people, but in general he was in a cultural and current affairs vacuum. By the time Smokey came to Noble he was so emotionally scarred he simple did not care. He purposely insulated himself from the outside world because it upset him. That, plus the less he was involved in industry the less current affairs mattered. News did not affect the way he lived anyway so why bother?

It is interesting those events in our American consciousness that are our country's milestones he was oblivious to; the Korean War, The Cold War, Sputnik, Watergate and Nixon's resignation, the Kennedy Assassination, Civil Rights, Viet Nam, or Roe v. Wade. World events ticked by him without a nod. Consequently, Smokey was free of any anxiety associated with them. He was untroubled by fluctuations in the economy or presidential elections. Stock prices did not affect him. He did not care about foreign policy, bond packages, who won the World Series, or how many times Liz Taylor married. American culture literally was not on his radarscope. Weather was the only event that affected Smokey because his garden was his main food source, and how weather affected him.

Death and Taxes

Taxation funds our nation, states, municipalities, and schools through property tax assessment and sales tax. Louisiana has a liberal Homestead Exemption passed into law under Huey Long in the 1930s. A residence valued at up to $75,000 is not taxed. The law allowed Smokey to live in Noble over thirty years and not pay a cent in school or property taxes. Governor Long believed large corporations and oil companies should pay the majority of taxes, not the poor. Smokey was able to avoid property taxes except the minor city tax by the village of Noble, which amounted to less than ten dollars a year. When most homeowners today pay thousands annually just to live in a house, Smokey was able to evade the whole taxation system. Even the amount of sales tax he paid was minimal, simply because he bought very little. He paid income tax but we have no doubt it was far less than he should have by utilizing every tax exemption available to him.

Because Smokey had no liabilities and no responsibilities other than himself life insurance wasn't a matter of consideration. His lifestyle was his insurance policy. He was even able to avoid the cost of burial, which was laid upon his family. He expected to be taken away by his aliens. A responsible person will usually make provision for this life event if they are financially able so as not to burden surviving family members. Smokey did not buy a pre-need burial policy or leave any money in safekeeping for that purpose. Ruey ended up paying for transport and his brother's burial in the family plot on their father's farm in Texas. When Ruey was notified of Smokey's death he said, "Let's bring the boy home."

A generation earlier, when Samuel Irwin bought his 482-acre farm outside Floydada, a small portion of that land was dedicated to a church and cemetery. At that time it was referred to as Center but became the Rushing Chapel Cemetery. As of this writing, it is the final resting place of five members of the Irwin family, including Herbert Glen Irwin.

Smokey was able to avoid taxes all his life, even in death. We have no doubt this gave him extreme pleasure.

A Question Of Money

Chapter Eighteen

A Question of Money

Broke old man. Of all the negative references to Smokey by Noble and his family this particular one tries to cement his reputation as a failure. Smokey was many things but he was definitely not a failure. His financial management skills were exceptional. Neither did he squander his income with reckless living. Despite tremendous professional setbacks he was a shrewd businessman with insight into the needs of his particular industry. To suggest he "wasted his life" and died destitute is a terrible affront to a man who was self-supporting and affluent up until his death. We cannot provide a net worth figure to dispute peoples' perception but we can give some observations to ponder.

We often hear of reclusive people who pass quietly from this life and leave a fortune. Sometimes a personal banker is the only one aware of the individual's assets. Or, cash is found under floorboards, behind bricks in fireplaces, mattresses, coffee cans, or buried in flowerbeds. Over a lifetime of inventing, licensing, and manufacturing Smokey had accumulated impressive wealth. The nagging question is, how much? Whereas some people boast of their accomplishments and how much money they have made Smokey was the opposite. No one knew, including his family. He went to great lengths to hide his income. Some of what follows is speculation but we want to entertain the possibilities of how much that fortune could be.

A Question Of Money

As a teenager doing paid labor and independent contracting Smokey contributed a portion of his income to his family. It was not unusual for his generation to begin their working careers in their teens. The Irwins taught their children the benefits of thrifty living and were able to accumulate wealth and property in one generation. The concept was overkill with Smokey.

As a young man in Spur he was initially a wage earner working a forty-hour work week with overtime. Smokey was well compensated for his labor but he did not produce significant income until he opened his own repair shop in Spur. With the vigor of youth and a mind incapable of rest he worked ridiculous hours. Smokey was a lifelong workaholic. He regularly worked sixteen hours a day, seven days a week. This man never once took a vacation in his life. It is important to remember Smokey did not produce the accumulation of his individual career earnings, but two to three men's lifetime wages and investments.

Smokey not only worked twice as many hours as most men but was on the higher end of the pay scale. He was a master machinist and welder and earned two and a half times the pay of the average wage earner. He had no family to support and lived in boarding houses early in his life, which cost him only a few dollars per week. Smokey spent so much time in his workshop he almost always ate sandwiches or cooked for himself. Neither did he waste time or money by leaving the workplace, eating lunch elsewhere, and return to his shop. Smokey never took a coffee or smoke break. He never paid anyone to feed him. Neither did he pay anyone to launder his clothes or buy entertainment. No evenings out, no radios, televisions, games, no golf, new cars, no boat or expensive sports gear. It was necessities or nothing. He never bought one item that did not produce income or support his work.

Smokey's short stint in the Army did not produce more than a serviceman's pay but with government housing and wearing uniforms he pocketed almost all his paycheck.

Patenting his inventions took Smokey to a whole different income producing level. Instead of being limited to how much work he could perform, the question was now how much money royalties could produce for him. Not on one invention but dozens. Inventing itself does not produce income; selling or licensing the patented invention does. Many of Smokey's inventions were not income producers. But others definitely were, especially his early patents and his oxyacetylene generator. Although Smokey sold some of his inventions outright he was a sharp enough businessman he knew licensing was not only the best way to generate long term income but it allowed him control of his inventions. He also manufactured some himself.

When a patented invention is sold it is voluntary whether the inventor or assignee notifies the US Patent Office of that sale. Researching assignment indexes is no more than an incomplete picture of how successful a particular invention was. Too often it does not appear at all. This was the case with most of Smokey's inventions. Without an accurate listing of just which patents were licensed and sold it is difficult to measure Smokey's overall success as an inventor.

His acetylene welding patents are the only ones documented as having been sold. The buyer documented that sale rather than Smokey. The legal instrument selling the Welderz Frend patents is listed in the assignment index, but after months of searching and enlisting the help of researchers, we concluded they were misplaced.

A Question Of Money

Although documentation assigning a patent to a company or individual is fairly easy to research, licensing is nearly impossible to trace. Few companies will cooperate in researching their own archives for a record of specific patents. Our inquiries were ignored after several efforts to verify licensing. Some of the companies Smokey sold and licensed his patents with dissolved long ago, in particular, International Harvester Company. Those records were retired to the University of Wisconsin, but not in enough detail to pinpoint Smokey's licensing.

Still, we tried to find evidence to indicate revenue. We have reason to suggest licensing some inventions and have purposely excluded others. Smokey dropped maddening hints concerning them but would never admit to anything concerning his money.

We want to specifically note the three variations on Smokey's spark plugs in the early days of automotive development. They could easily have produced thousands of dollars of royalties for the life of the patent or the technology. Even a few cents royalties on these three patents would have accumulated significantly over the lifetime of the patent.

Although they may have had only regional acceptance Smokey found a ready market for his cotton bur separators and suction fan at the numerous cotton gins surrounding him. These were not incidental inventions in a time when "Cotton was king," in a major agricultural industry. We saw near exact devices in several cotton gin museums from the Panhandle to south central Texas. Without dismantling one we simply do not know for sure. These produced more income for Samuel Irwin than Smokey, possibly with S.E. Johnson Jr.

A Question Of Money

We cannot find any record of Smokey licensing or manufacturing his cotton picker. There were hundreds of "mechanical" cotton pickers of various levels of sophistication but none were commercially successful until the mid-forties. Even though Smokey invented his in 1920 (patented in 1924) labor was cheap enough it was less expensive than manufacturing and trying to market a mechanical picker. Timing plays a crucial role in marketing a product. International Harvester may have bought the patent and sat on it until the cost of labor could justify manufacturing the picker. By the time the Depression, the great Dust Bowl of the thirties, and WWII had come and gone technology had bypassed his cotton picker. Regardless, Smokey's 1920 cotton picker was truly a mechanical picker whether commercially successful or not.

We know Smokey sold his heading machine to International Harvester. We were thrilled to find one in the yard of the Dickens County Museum in Dickens, Texas. The rusted old header machine bears the International Harvester logo and was produced from 1923 to at least 1945. Smokey had to have been well compensated for this long-producing model. Retired corporate records (McCormick-Deering) call this farm implement a Vertical Corn Binder. As was common, this particular model was adapted by the manufacturer, in this instance, to harvest corn rather than Maize.

After arriving in Noble, Smokey seems to have hit a mellow stride, if not semi-retirement. He played with those things that intrigued him rather than pursuing industry improvements.

His spark plugs, the vaporizing attachment for an internal combustion engines, the device for cleaning electrodes, cultivator, heating primer, the push bar for tractors, and for a short time, his wind power machines, all had royalty potential. Some had minor promise, others we simply do not know.

The first nine months Smokey manufactured the Welderz Frend he sold twenty-five with just one of his vendors. We do not know how many vendors he had but do know there were several. They initially sold for $150 for the smaller unit and $200 for the larger model. If we establish an estimate of him eventually producing fifty of each or a hundred Welderz Frend generators a year with eventual price increases, Smokey probably grossed over $20,000 annually. One must remember this was 1924 to 1940. He produced the Welderz Frend for sixteen years, which would total over $320,000. This was only a small portion of his income during that time frame. His licensing from his other patents is unknown but such a desirable invention as an easily operated acetylene generator was in high demand, enough for Irwin Improvements to employ one hundred men. He was manufacturing it in the midst of the largest oil field discovery in the US at the time, the Borger Oil Field north of Amarillo. After manufacturing the Welderz Frend for so long, it still had value when Smokey sold it days after Pearl Harbor was attacked. We were told his assignee sold it yet again to Ingersoll Rand, but we were not able to confirm that.

The Irwin family has long believed Smokey's patents on his welder were stolen by "California people." We researched that possibility through old court records in every conceivable jurisdiction such a lawsuit would have been filed. It simply does not exist and had us on a false trail for months. Had such a civil suit occurred Smokey would not have been able to sell the Welderz Frend. To quote a legal researcher, "It didn't happen."

A Question Of Money

Smokey had accumulated enough resources by the time he left Texas in December, 1940 he was able to buy 1400 acres in Florida, in cash. He had settled with the Treasury Department and had enough reserves to not only buy a large tract of land and fence it but also to move six rail cars of metal and equipment halfway across the United States. Together this was a huge investment of capital akin to a small corporation relocating, moving assets, and reestablishing another base of operations. His token settlement certainly did not break him. When questioned, Smokey would just smile and refuse to answer.

Smokey's Florida property was not swampland. It had six miles of road and highway frontage on three sides and when we visited, there was a dairy with rich pastureland occupying the same acreage. Citrus orchards surrounded the dairy. At the same time he bought the 1400-acre tract he bought three industrial city lots in Okeechobee on a railroad spur. He sold his welding patents and his manufacturing facility in Amarillo a year later.

Smokey moved to Florida and built his metal house and large workshop before selling his welding patents. In addition, he fenced his property without the cash generated by selling his patents and factory. Our point in recounting these events is each of these moves and investments was individually funded without the revenue of a previous sale. Smokey was a wealthy man.

Smokey made a profit each time he relocated and sold any of his properties. He was well versed in the legal term "other valuable considerations." This phrase is used on deeds to make up the difference in the listed cost and to keep taxes on the transaction reasonable. It was also useful to mask the selling price to protect one's privacy. Generally speaking, the OVC on a deed is always more than the listed selling price. Virtually every deed where Smokey sold land this term is quoted and makes it impossible to figure his capital gain. We can only estimate what he sold his land for by looking at comparables; sales of neighboring property. We can say with absolute conviction Smokey at least tripled his money with his Amarillo property and again when he sold his Florida property.

When Smokey moved to Noble it involved the same coordination and cash outlay as his move to Florida, only on a smaller scale. He constructed his building and fence in Noble long before he sold his Florida property. That event did not occur until eight months later and illustrates only a portion of his cash reserves.

The banker who counted Smokey's large deposit for him would be the only one who could have told us how much Smokey sold his Florida property for. Smokey had a business relationship with Karl Stello and had him present to count and verify the thousands he sold his property for. But Smokey's nagging paranoia compelled him to have a banker in Louisiana count his cash again just to be sure. However much the whole exercise puzzled Melton Knott the only reason for it was because Smokey wanted the amount of money verified.

Smokey did not trust banks and only used one by necessity in Amarillo. We know he did not use any in Florida. Smokey came to Noble with enough cash reserves to support himself the rest of his life regardless if he worked or sold an invention again.

Smokey's New Mexico heirs were told he died "destitute and was buried by the state." This is simply not true. Ruey was contacted by Sabine Parish officials and his nephew came to Louisiana to arrange for Smokey's body to be shipped back to Texas. Smokey was buried in the family plot at Rushing Chapel Cemetery close to Floydada, Texas. His burial was paid for by Ruey.

We know how inexpensively Smokey lived in Noble. His weekly grocery bill including kerosene was scarcely $12. Most his food was generated by his own garden. His gasoline purchases averaged $4 a week plus sporadic miscellaneous expenses, probably another $3 a week. If you extrapolate up to a round figure of $20 a week his annual living expenses were $1,000 - $1,100, maximum. Smokey was a single man who lived for a thirty-three year interim for a *total* of about $36,000.

Operating expenses for Smokey's truck and later his Ranchero were minimal. He was the only mechanic that ever touched his vehicles. If he needed a part he made it. Whereas transportation is a major consideration for most of us Smokey had this element of his budget well under control. He almost always bought his gasoline at Elliott's Grocery. Based on an average monthly mileage of fifty to eighty miles he used little gasoline in his motor vehicle. Smokey used fuel for experimentation and a good guess would be another three to ten gallons depending on what he was working on. He used several small generators and an engine (besides his auto) for a power source. Most those generators used kerosene. Other than some notable gas wars the price of fuel from 1948 to 1981 generally ranged from 20-75 cents a gallon. Smokey's weekly gas bill was rarely more than $3 a week. The variation had more to do with his experiments than with mileage because that rarely deviated. He used a modest amount of coal for his forge and stove but that was not a normal monthly expense.

Smokey bought and renewed his driver's license for $3 every three years. We doubt he ever bought a fishing license and we know he did not hunt, at least not in the conventional sense. He trapped turkey and rabbit but he never bothered with a hunting license. Mandatory auto liability insurance was introduced in Louisiana in the early 1970s and we would be surprised if Smokey bought any kind of insurance, or if he even was aware it was a legal requirement.

A successful businessman once gave us his business philosophy. He said income thresholds in our lives dictate our lifestyle. His example at the time was a person's standard of living does not change a whole lot from $30,000 to $50,000. It takes a leap from $50,000 to $100,000, and again to $200,000. Up to $250,000 it changes only slightly. He was in the $500,000 to $1,000,000 bracket and remarked he could afford to be generous because his lifestyle would not change regardless of how much more he made. He had worked hard to achieve a particular standard of living and was indifferent to increasing it. He only sought to maintain it.

Smokey apparently had the same philosophy and did the equivalent, only in reverse. We want to stress whether Smokey was affluent or destitute his lifestyle was virtually unchanged since he was a young man. His life's work and dedication were all consuming and having money to Smokey only meant freedom to pursue his work. Smokey took steps to insure adequate income for his life but thereafter was indifferent to any financial excesses. It didn't matter. He was an inventor in its purest form and not a one-hit wonder who had to return to his day job.

How much we spend of our earnings will affect our accumulation of lifetime saved income. If our budget figures are anywhere close to being accurate Smokey certainly did not spend his.

After Smokey moved to Noble he signed an affidavit giving up his one-sixth inheritance of his father's estate to

A Question Of Money

Ruey, which amounted to over $50,000. Few people would give up a substantial inheritance if they were in need. Besides a token amount the document stated "for other considerations." One reason Smokey did this is because his other brothers and sister had filed suit to disinherit Smokey per their parents' wishes.

Smokey absolutely did not want his one-sixth interest to be divided among his other siblings. Ruey refused to take part in disowning his closest brother and understood Smokey better than any other family member. Troubled Alta Mae was not part of the lawsuit. Ruey had willingly offered to help his brother and never asked for repayment. Smokey thought he owed Ruey in some manner for safekeeping his cash and assets for him while he was under investigation by the Treasury Department. The "other consideration'" mentioned in the document was for hiding Smokey's cash for him. Smokey's cash assets were sheltered through all his legal problems and this is why he relinquished his inheritance, to repay Ruey per his verbal offer made years before. If Smokey's reserves were dwindling and the inheritance was necessary for his solvency, Ruey would never have asked Smokey to sign it over to him. Smokey simply did not need it.

Smokey had five sources of income beyond his wages as a young man: almost lifelong royalties from licensing, patent sales, machine shop contracting, sixteen years of manufacturing, property sales, liquidation of his businesses, and for a short time, raising cattle. Smokey was still receiving royalties in Noble from his patents even though his earlier ones had long since expired. From his youth to an advanced age, 1917 through 1964, the only time Smokey was not submitting patents was a seven-year gap when he lived in Florida during WWII.

A Question Of Money

Smokey did not live totally on saved income while he was in Florida. He was still receiving royalties from other licensing agreements. He sold his factory, machine shop, property, and the Welderz Frend patents on December 16, 1941. When Smokey shut down his factory in Amarillo he brought his partially completed generators to Florida with him. These production units were excluded from that sale to fulfill a government contract.

Smokey ran cattle on his property and only a rich old cattleman can tell you how much money can be made raising cattle on good range, especially dealing in cash. Smokey had a small herd of sheep in addition to his cattle for a short time. Raising livestock would normally have been out of character for Smokey but owning 1400 acres would have resulted in high property tax. As we would employ a standard tax exemption Smokey kept livestock on his land to avoid taxes. His agricultural exemption turned into an income producer on the black market.

What about Smokey's $20 bills? The issue dates on the bills and the time Smokey exchanged them is a telling account of how much he accumulated and how much he still had in reserve. Another perplexing question is what Smokey did with all his change. Anyone who has emptied his or her pockets and change purse into a plastic jug knows how coins can accumulate. Since Smokey purposely traded with bills because of his difficulty in counting he amassed a terrific amount of coins. How about for thirty-three plus years of weekly trips to the store?

This problem of counting did not surface when Smokey arrived in Noble. The change he accumulated prior to moving to Noble was exchanged for bills at a bank before he relocated. Bills are easier to transport and keep. Smokey had a particular affinity for burying things. He buried little of his coins on his property and hid most of it in his equipment. Whoever found that money thinks that is all there is.

We know metal detectors have scanned Smokey's property in Noble more than once but no one has found his treasure yet. To say Smokey was clever is an understatement. Trying to get an accurate response panning with a metal detector near his metal building would be difficult without a sophisticated unit. Maybe he deliberately buried it close enough to, or inside the building as to insure it would not be found.

We feel Smokey hid his cash in more than one place. We have reason to think there are three caches of money. Probably the larger amounts are deeply buried and camouflaged and a lesser amount was easily accessible whenever he wanted it. As Smokey aged and became feeble he recognized there would soon come a time when he would be unable to dig for it anymore. We think he removed a considerable amount the last time and hid it in his machinery, or possibly in his building. If so, that was discovered and removed from the building when Smokey died. Such a discovery would be difficult to keep quiet in a small village like Noble and we believe his greater fortune is still intact.

If Smokey's cash is ever found the value would be far more than its currency denomination. Consider the early bills, Silver Certificates instead of Federal Reserve Notes, and solid silver. Plus, coins and bills out of circulation for well over a half-century, possibly gold pieces or Gold Certificates. The prospects are enough to make a coin collector salivate. Can we put any kind of reasonable figure on how much Smokey left? Our broad guess is between $150,000 and $350,000, face value. And that is after living 88 years. We have specific reason to suggest that range.

A Question Of Money

With a numismatist appraisal that figure could easily quadruple.

Our one great regret is no one has come forward with any of Smokey's field notes. He kept lengthy and meticulously typed records of his experiments. These notes would be of great benefit to historians and botanists. Equally valuable would be an explanation of how Smokey was able to use heroin his whole life and still be functional. We are convinced he kept notes of his dosage and how it affected him.

We found two chemistry formulas in Smokey's building, one for preserving paper and one for fireproofing. Preserving his notes was extremely important to this inventor. We know Smokey kept all his inventions in his building and they are also gone. There are several Texas museums that would be pleased to have these as part of their collection.

Die hard money hunters should leave your metal detectors at home. One must first understand a truly paranoid soul who went to great lengths to hide his money. Smokey believed he told Roe where his field notes and money were hidden so he could have them upon his death. Or as Smokey believed, his departure. But the abbreviated parables Smokey spoke in did not give enough or exact information. His mind pictures never did correlate into lucid conversation. Puzzles, symbols, codes, parables, distances, directions, all compounded by dyslexia and an inability to communicate. Smokey was so pleased after passing this information on to Roe we know his intent but it will never come to pass. It would have been much easier had he made a will. If Smokey did leave one it was probably burned.

With verbal permission from an heir and knowledge by a public authority we made a couple token efforts to find what

A Question Of Money

Smokey left Roe. Other than finding a wonderful amount of information for this project we were unsuccessful in finding anything else. The few hours we devoted to it answered some questions but that is all.

As of this writing none of Smokey's final wishes have been carried out. His property was frozen in a legal battle for years, now settled. Once the legal maneuvering was eventually resolved his property was sold. We wonder how a family that once disinherited a brother could claim to be his heirs upon his death. Or, how a legal instrument can state, "We are well and personally acquainted with the late Herbert G. Irwin," when no remaining heirs ever met him. When that document was recorded in 1981 those who did know Herbert Glen Irwin had not seen him since 1949. They have since passed. Given the ill will in this family that has carried over the grave Smokey would be irate to know who has his notes and equipment, certainly any money that was found. Moreover, how they maneuvered to gain possession of it.

We're not sure with whom Smokey's fortune will likely end up. Our personal thought is, whole lives will be wasted searching for a hoard of money that may never be found. It is not our intent to create a "lost treasure" legend. But we know with absolute conviction there is one. We wish we could pass on some useful clues. We can't other than to note Smokey was fond of particular numbers. That may have something to do with Masonry. He was not a Mason but he had family members who were. Masonic lodges are dotted throughout west Texas and he was familiar with Masonry. O.B. Knott was a Mason and that might be one reason Smokey developed that friendship.

None of that is really helpful if you do not have a point of beginning or if you cannot count accurately. If you thought in images rather than in abstracts those figures would be useless in trying to communicate the image. It is a riddle without a solution.

We note the ground surrounding Smokey's building has been scraped bare. After much reflection and twenty-eight years, we have decided they missed it. That gives us a measure of amusement. All these years later we know it is still there. We just do not know where.

When Smokey was alive there were cleared areas for his garden distant from his building. When we last were on the property it was a forest thick with impenetrable underbrush. The pine timber has since been stripped and cleared, now a barren lot. Any remaining roots may totally envelop whatever he left. Or, in the process of removing stumps any containers were pushed deeper into the soil by a bulldozer. Finding "it" will not be easy.

If Smokey's fortune is discovered you can be sure it is elaborately concealed and possibly booby-trapped. If one is still persistent one may want to ponder how pitch and sealed Plexiglas, such as we found in Smokcy's building, can preserve paper. Formulas that will preserve paper will undoubtedly preserve money as well.

Another clue is the tubes Smokey kept his patents in. No, not the cardboard ones, plastic ones. Too often money hunters imagine the romance of a large chest, or even Mason jars. Smokey left far more than could be contained in a few Mason jars. Maybe you should be looking for a dozen vertically buried four-inch Plexiglas tubes. Or, rectangular flat boxes buried on end over six acres. If you ever do find Smokey's treasure we can guarantee the containers will be superbly designed. They will be ingenious and a marvel of engineering. Neither will it be where you would expect.

Be careful. And good luck.

A Question Of Money

A Social Misfit

Chapter Nineteen

A Social Misfit

Smokey was called crazy, eccentric, nuts, and every other negative one can think of. Eccentric is the only valid one we can agree with and after all these years we can offer a reason why. There is ample evidence to suggest the cause of Smokey's idiosyncrasies. Smokey overcame severe obstacles to live a successful life and we hope others can find his courage in coping with them. We pray reading of Smokey's troubles and triumphs encourage those who struggle, whatever the reason.

We are convinced Smokey had Asperger's Syndrome. This includes a range of symptoms within the Autism spectrum, also called high functioning Autism. Some refer to both as one in the same and it is only a matter of degrees where one disorder stops and the other begins. Some believe there is no difference, which may be closer to a real understanding of the disorder.

Austrian pediatrician Hans Asperger identified this neurological disorder in 1944. By then Smokey had lived over half his life never having been examined for this condition or any health or neurological affliction as an adult. Reading a comprehensive description of Asperger's Syndrome and comparing Smokey is like reading a personality profile of someone you are very close to.

A Social Misfit

Autism is at an almost epidemic level in the US. The Center for Disease Control has released figures stating 1 in 150 to possibly 1 in 100 children born in the US have Autism. More dialogue and research needs to be done to educate and help Autistic and AS individuals live productive lives. Public awareness has increased since we first began this project but treatment and education are depressingly absent. Parents are awash trying to figure out how to raise an Autistic child so he or she can be a self sufficient adult. Not being a professional in the field we can only offer what we as laymen know of the disorder.

This is not a diagnostic account, but more a chronicle of how Smokey's idiosyncrasies reflect Autism spectrum symptoms. Smokey's family referred to him as "different" and Smokey himself declared he was a "social misfit." Sadly, maybe what he really needed was a proper diagnosis. He would have to have been born a half century later to have that evaluation. One feels deep sympathy for a family unable to understand such behavior. His condition undoubtedly contributed to his estrangement from his family.

Smokey found his particular niche and thrived in it. He used his disorder and capitalized on its uniquely positive traits instead of being buried by the negative ones. There are some positive qualities of Asperger's Syndrome. Some researchers in the field have stated AS individuals are an untapped resource of knowledge and ability, "hardwired" in a way others are not.

Smokey developed his own coping skills and did not apologize in the least for his personality. He well knew he was different but did not have the benefit of knowing there were others like him. Smokey had plenty of excuses to succumb to his condition but he refused to. Regardless of his neurological or psychological disorder Smokey dealt with his condition as best he could. And for that we have the utmost respect for him.

The range of symptoms of Asperger's Syndrome varies from mild to severe and usually intensifies with age. Autism is sometimes described as an individual under sensory overload. It tends to run in families. What is symptomatic to one individual is not necessarily to another. Often of superior intelligence they become preoccupied with a particular subject of interest and become highly successful in their career fields. Some are savants. Some are never able to surface from the fog of neurological overload and need help with the simplest of tasks and must have lifelong care.

They are hypersensitive to taste, smell, touch, and sound. Most are preoccupied with routine and ritual. Obsessive compulsive disorder is usually a companion to the condition. Individuals often lack in social and communication skills and will react inappropriately. Many AS people are fanatic about proper body space. Smokey usually maintained a three to four feet distance from everyone and cultivated a persona that was intentionally intimidating. He refused to enter anyone's house. He felt threatened anywhere except his own personal environment. Proportionately, far more boys have Autism than girls.

Smokey's generation lived in an era if a child was different or perceived to be less than normal it was rarely talked about. Families did the best they could and hoped their child could learn a trade to support him or herself. If not, the child was kept home or in severe cases, institutionalized.

We wonder how the Irwins coped with their firstborn not knowing why this child was so different from other children. They must have been dedicated to their child's success because Smokey functioned well in society for years. They should be applauded for working with a condition in a child they had no doctor's encouraging help or support group to guide them. They were literally flying blind raising a child that defied all logic of parenting. They had no idea what they were dealing with.

The estrangement in this family could be equally attributed to Smokey's perception as much as any deceit. Self-absorption is a symptom so extreme in an AS individual it is impossible for them to be objective. We recognized deep frustration with the Irwin family in their efforts to reconcile with Smokey.

We cannot know for sure but the experience of Samuel and Martha Irwin was probably no different from other parents of children with AS. Most infants will snuggle in response to a maternal act of love but a baby with AS often will not. A common touch is tolerated and even the simple act of changing a diaper can be a battleground. Bathing, changing clothes, wiping a runny nose or any form of personal contact is violently shunned. A visit to the doctor can result in a screaming protest over being probed and touched. We are not suggesting such behavior is conclusive by any means. Early diagnosis is crucial but some babies may simply be contrary.

Toddlers are commonly afraid of thunderstorms but a child with AS can be so agitated as to reject any reassurance. Others will withdraw in fear and depression. Depending on the severity of the disorder, wind, rain, or even an overcast day is cause for alarm in an AS child. Some parents report allergy extremes.

Barometric pressure (as Smokey associated) may or may not have anything to do with it but such children react well in advance of a weather event. Caretakers of AS children know a weather change is imminent simply by the behavior of the children in their care. The 1947 Florida hurricanes plunged Smokey into such severe angst he was never the same thereafter. He may have had what some would term a nervous breakdown.

Smokey's reactions to weather caused him such extreme anxiety he sought a herbal medicine to cope with it. He used heroin from his middle age almost to his death. His periodic self-medicating increased over time but was not usually daily therapy. Of course, he was clinically addicted. We sincerely wish we had Smokey's field notes. He would have approached his heroin use with the cold objectivity of a scientist. There may be some benefit to reading how he dealt with heroin dependence. Smokey was often "high" when he visited O.B. although Roe spoke with him regularly for thirty years and observed consistent behavior. Surely there is some medication, maybe yet to be developed, an Autistic individual can use other than narcotics or tranquilizers to be functional in modern society.

Many AS children have highly sensitive taste preferences. This is far beyond simply not liking green beans. Not eating at all is preferable to eating something they cannot tolerate. Being coerced into eating some foods can cause an AS child to fly into a rage disproportionate to the issue. Some parents and doctors report hyper-food allergies, many directly associated with food additives, such as sugars, dyes, and preservatives. While Smokey was a child at home Martha complied with her son's demands as to food preparation to keep family peace. As an independent adult Smokey prepared and cooked his own food and never ate anyone's food but his own. The purity of his food was not an obsession for its own sake. Smokey truly could tell the difference in taste if his food was contaminated in the slightest. Reading his description of spice combinations for his gaseous condiment generator is excessive. One realizes how very important the taste of his food was to him.

AS people are sometimes described as awkward or clumsy. Smokey had an ungainly, distinctive gait. It was deliberate and focused as if he had to concentrate on lifting each foot and placing his steps. He tended to look down a few steps ahead of him instead of looking up and forward as most people do. Generally people swing their arms in a relaxed manner when they walk. Smokey held his stiffly to his side with his hands closed in a loose fist. He never paused to glance around him or became distracted. His head hardly veered to the right or left. As an elderly man he shuffled along in short steps, far more pronounced than older people with limited mobility.

Smokey's anti-social tendencies compounded over time. Up to his teens he was described as friendly and outgoing, at least outside his family. We see genuine effort on Smokey's part to fit into a society he increasingly had trouble dealing with. There came a point when Smokey's daily struggle for "normalcy" was too difficult to cope with. He surrendered to his condition instead of fighting it. He accepted his needs on an intellectual level and decided to live life as he was compelled to, not how society thought he should. Events in Smokey's life had a profound effect on his sensitive nature and contributed to his personality quirks.

Obsessive-compulsive disorder will manifest itself early in AS children. Smokey was praised as a mechanical genius and distinguished himself early in childhood. OCD can range from mild repetition to such an extreme it is disruptive to a daily routine. Some people with OCD will put the same books in shelves over and over. They may repetitively open and shut drawers or cabinets, rearrange silverware, or engage in a particular order in dressing. It can manifest itself in hand washing or eating habits. Some insert keys repeatedly in locks or any number of simple rituals that must be performed exactly. The slightest deviation requires the individual to start over, "correctly." Not all people with OCD have AS but most AS people have a measure of OCD. Smokey's ritual opening and locking his doors and gates was only a mild example. Everything he did had some form of repetition to it including how he conducted his experiments. Whereas a function could be proven with fifty repetitions Smokey would repeat hundreds.

OCD can degrade into situations where an individual is powerless to control clutter, hoarding, and will fall into severe disorder of personal space. Instead of a house overwhelmed in trash, Smokey's building was just on a larger scale, littered with the objects of his pastime.

People with AS will exhibit a pronounced obsession within a narrow field of interest: in Smokey's case, with mechanical devices. He instinctively knew mechanics and scientific principle without being taught. Dr. Asperger referred to Autistic children as "little professors." Smokey may have been a savant. His tinkering was part of his obsessive compulsiveness. His was so pronounced it overshadowed everything else, eating, daily routine, personal relationships, even sleeping.

The learning process is different with AS children. Educating an Autistic or Asperger's Syndrome child can be daunting and is still cause for debate. Trying to break through barriers to communication and understanding is not a task for the fainthearted. Depending on where a child is on the Autism spectrum it sometimes is never bridged. With those fundamentals taught by his mother, Smokey's intellect took off. He read adult level books as a child. He knew physics, scientific principle, and chemistry without being taught.

Some parents report developmental problems early in life. Frustration on the part of the child and certainly with his or her parents is the unfortunate hallmark of Autism. Even now there is no definitive clinical direction for parents of Autistic children to follow that is recognized as the best and most effective method. In 1900 it was nonexistent.

Smokey's strengths compensated for his difficulties. He was able to function and excel by developing his own coping skills. If Smokey were in our public education system today he would quickly have been evaluated for a learning disability in grade school, placed on medication, and put in a special education class. One wonders if he would have been able to accomplish as much in this generation with intervention.

Our public education system tends to apply the same criteria for all students, regardless of their individual talents or weaknesses. The same yardstick may not always be the most worthwhile measuring device for everyone. Standardized tests can only demonstrate knowledge of a portion of the whole person. Not just AS individuals, but other students with learning disabilities have trouble displaying their talents effectively. Public schools have made great strides in special education but more can be done for Autistic children to reach their full potential. Private schools are too often the more expensive option for parents to educate their Autistic children today.

Smokey was truly a self-educated man and left school at a young age rather than suffer through instruction he could not grasp. His formal education was limited to the one-room schoolhouse he attended in Antelope. He did not return to school after the second grade. We looked at every college and technical school within Smokey's geographical range and did not find record of him attending any. We were initially excited about finding the Texas Agricultural Experimental Station in Spur thinking he may have attended there but Smokey knew scientific theory as an adolescent, long before he arrived in Spur. Compared to the current science at the TAES at the time Smokey was far ahead of their research, especially with his cotton picker and header machine.

Somewhere in his early experience, possibly from International Harvester owner manuals of his father's farm implements, Smokey was exposed to mechanical drawings and taught himself to draw. His draftsmanship was just a companion to his inventing. Some Autistics have written and spoken of their mental processes in images and color rather than in abstract thought. Observation is often the only key an Autistic needs to duplicate what they have seen and heard. Autistic artists and musicians are not unusual.

Smokey read a great deal to develop the vocabulary and accomplished writing we see as an adult. His twenty-five page typed defense of one of his oxyacetylene patents is a joy to read. He read books and periodicals to acquaint himself with current technology. He had an extensive knowledge of chemicals. We are amazed at the body of knowledge Smokey demonstrated without formal education. We believe he kept a personal library later in life. A solitary man with a brilliant mind would have sought the stimulation of books. Smokey was always on the leading edge of his industry in business trends. Only later in life did he quit reading. His eyesight was failing from a lifetime of welding and there were several pairs of commercial reading glasses in his workshop.

A Social Misfit

Many AS people have trouble with handwriting. Smokey had such a hard time he typed literally everything. We found a few scribbled notations, scraps with numbers and letters, and chemistry formulas. But virtually all his correspondence, notes, and even his shipping labels were typed. However well composed Smokey's narratives are, admittedly exhaustive, he exhibits frequent spelling errors. Some people with an exceptionally strong aptitude in one area lack in others. Take that tendency to the end of the spectrum and it can exclude everything else, in Smokey's case verbal and writing skills.

Smokey was the son and grandson of blacksmiths, although his father turned to cotton farming. Samuel was mechanically inclined and talented with his hands as well. He spent hours with his son working together in a common interest. The difference between an accomplished father and a gifted son's excessiveness was pronounced. Smokey's family was tolerant with his interests and encouraged his endeavors to a degree, at least when he was young. He was allowed freedom to experiment and invent as long as it didn't interfere with chores. His family members repeatedly describe Smokey's preoccupation with machines and tinkering as obsessive.

Smokey increasingly withdrew as an adult. His social contact became less and less over the course of time. He would flash that penetrating gaze he had but then would turn away from someone addressing him. Face recognition is a peculiar problem with AS. We heard from several individuals if Smokey did not want to speak to someone he would turn away and ignore them. When his brother Carmon came to see Smokey in Florida it had been years since the brothers had seen each other, surely not so long brothers would not recognize each other. Still, Smokey said, "You're not my brother."

We at first thought the comment was referring to Smokey's perceived mistreatment. It was really due to AS. He truly did not recognize Carmon. If Smokey saw someone regularly and in the same context he knew who the individual was, such as seeing the postmistress in the Post Office in Noble. O.B. Knott was hard to confuse with anyone. Tall, never without his Stetson hat, and a booming voice Smokey had no trouble identifying his friend. Neither did he have trouble distinguishing Roe from other people seeing and speaking with him regularly, either at the Knott home or at the Noble Mercantile.

In his business relationships with people Smokey's chosen method of communication was by typed letter. To a lesser degree he used telegrams, common for his generation. Even though Smokey was listed in Amarillo city directories not one listed a phone number. Telephone service was readily available in the twenties and thirties in Amarillo. Smokey contracted labor over his lifetime without ever having to use a telephone. He insisted on clinging to his old way of life. Other than that, one reason for not having a telephone might have been right ear dominance, a symptom of AS. After a lifetime around machines and factory noise Smokey's hearing was severely impaired. He was almost completely deaf in his left ear and partially deaf in his right ear. We watched him read lips, which is in conflict with turning away from people, but Smokey did both.

Smokey's use of chemistry and inventing required math skills but he had dyslexia. Many Autistics speak of "counting" visually with mind pictures. Some describe counting in color. It wasn't that Smokey couldn't count. He simply counted differently. Whenever Smokey bought anything at the Noble Mercantile he always placed a $20 bill on the counter regardless of how little it cost. He could not accurately count change without laboring over it. It was easier to produce a bill that would more than cover his purchases so he would not have to count in public. We found rolls of paper tape from an old fashioned lever-style adding machine in his building. We found torn scraps with simple addition and subtraction printed on them repeatedly. The numbers on the tapes, often several feet long, were transposed with variations of the same figures with multiple answers. When Smokey returned to his building after every trip he entered the figures over and over again until he was convinced he was given the correct change.

Smokey's refusal to be touched carried so far he would not hand his money to anyone. He placed his money on the counter and kept one pace away from the counter. O.B., Viola, or Maggie would place his change on the counter and count his change for him slowly.

Smokey fit well into the role he had created for himself as a young man in Spur. He was a talented twenty-four year old man and a successful entrepreneur. He was charismatic, pleasant looking though not considered handsome. What most people remember about him is the look of keen intelligence and self confidence. There was no doubt looking into his face this was a man of profound intellect. One saw intensity, acute awareness, suspicion, and a wee bit of arrogance. There may be family pictures of Smokey in old photo albums but to our knowledge there were never any photographs taken of Smokey after he left home in 1921.

Smokey lived in respectable boarding houses and was a well regarded professional in local society. He was a true workaholic but was admired for it. He did not smoke or drink and would have been perceived as an eligible bachelor.

A Social Misfit

We found nothing to indicate his parents did not have a successful marriage. With this example before him and with so many prospects for a bright future why did Smokey not attract a young woman to marry?

Personal relationships were difficult for him even with his own family. Smokey's eccentric personality evolved as an adult. He was uncomfortable in communicating with people. As his AS became more entrenched his social skills deteriorated. Paranoia and suspicion are common symptoms of AS. Those elusive traits that are characteristic of human experience, love, compassion, trust, empathy, and compatibility were abstracts he could not fathom. This was a man who refused to shake hands, hug, or even let a doctor or barber touch him. The thought of marriage was repulsive to him and impossible to contemplate.

Beyond having AS, a singular existence is not an uncommon characteristic of an inventor. An inventor's grand obsession may replace their pursuit of a spouse. Among a very long list of inventors who did not marry, neither did the Wright brothers, George Eastman, Alfred Nobel, Beulah Henry, or George Washington Carver. One doesn't necessarily exclude the other, but there is a line between being so eccentric one is unable to function in society and the ability to attract a tolerant mate.

Some people with AS do marry but Smokey's self-absorption was total. Even without the misunderstanding between Sophie and Smokey we doubt their relationship could have progressed past companionship. Sophie Roberts was the closest Smokey ever came to a romantic relationship. We must state this name is given to his bookkeeper to make the narrative easier. Smokey would only refer to her as "she" and would not repeat her name. The experience left him with a lifelong suspicion of women in general (including this writer), worse than his ingrained paranoia. I was never able to engage Smokey in conversation and was relegated to being an eavesdropper from the house window. He would shut down when I came within ear shot.

Smokey had two siblings who did not marry; his brother, Ruey and sister, Alta Mae. We know Ruey had milder symptoms of this disorder. This family produced notable offspring who had an admirable work ethic. Ruey was a well-respected cotton farmer in Floydada. Carmon was an equally successful rancher in New Mexico. Gracie and her husband were cattle ranchers in New Mexico. Felix was a steel fabricator at the time of his death in a private airplane crash in 1949. Unfortunately, Alta Mae was committed to a mental hospital in New York sometime between 1943 and 1949 when she was in her early forties. We only mention this as a family fact. A small percentage of AS sufferers have much deeper emotional and mental problems. We do not know if that was the case with Alta Mae but prior to that she was a theater actress. Even so, this was a family of high achievers.

Smokey never established any long-term friendships except with O.B. and Roe. Smokey's persona could be intimidating and did not invite closeness. He had professional relationships and was acquainted with a number of people during his twenty years in Amarillo. After Smokey left Willborn Brothers they thought enough of him to help defend one of his patent claims. Smokey had enough regard for Karl Stello in Florida he used him for several real estate transactions. Still, the only friends Smokey ever claimed were O. B. and Roe.

Smokey was honorably discharged after enlisting in the Army and was described as having excellent character. Such character referrals in WWI were not given lightly in discharge papers. Smokey apparently was able to function in the strict micro-society of the military. And even that was on his terms. Whatever quirks he had must have been tolerated because of the extreme need the Army Air Corps had for qualified mechanics. Smokey was promoted to sergeant during just a sixteen-month enlistment. It illustrated how well such a regimented environment agreed with him. He liked the precision, the dress codes, and the unwavering structure that translated into the military bearing he possessed all his life.

Smokey endured the legendary dust storm of 1934. In November, 1940 he suffered through a catastrophic ice storm that left him house bound for over a week. For a person with AS these were not simple footnotes in weather history but traumatic events. His fragile emotional state was in need of rest. Florida appealed to him after that experience. Smokey moved to Florida with every intention of remaining there. He had the financial resources to establish himself however he chose to and he made a considerable investment in property and improvements. His assets would have allowed him to pursue his interests at his leisure in a mild climate.

Smokey settled with the Treasury Department and in protest abandoned his Welderz Frend manufacturing business in Texas. In doing so he left a lucrative machine shop enterprise as well. Their threats of jail had thoroughly unsettled him, although it would have been unusual for the Treasury Department to actually carry out that threat.

Smokey had a temper bordering on violence. We know his rages were so intense his family feared him. Samuel and Martha literally fled after Smokey threatened them. His tirades in Noble were so alarming people left the store rather than be in his presence. Rage is common in an AS person and has a lot to do with their inability to understand anyone else's perspective. To a person with AS there is no other viewpoint. The only act of violence Smokey committed was killing his mule. Not to justify such a malicious act but Smokey genuinely lacked the ability to perceive the limitations of animal intelligence. He considered it willful disobedience. Killing an animal so brutally is hard to comprehend to a reasonable person, especially today. We could have left this fact out of the book but included the incident as one more facet of Smokey's troubled personality.

When Smokey moved to Florida in the spring of 1941 he built his metal house and workshop with his customary excess. The room-sized house was constructed of 29 gauge galvanized metal and riveted. It had a steel door, a heavy wood floor, and was set and bolted tightly on concrete blocks. Little did he know at the time the house would save his life.

Nothing in Smokey's Texas experience prepared him for the force-four hurricane that swept across southern Florida in August, 1947. He was familiar with Texas dust storms, thunderstorms, and tornadoes but a hurricane was a frightening phenomenon that was unimaginable. The storm was fairly well predicted at the time but given Smokey's isolation he was unaware of the storm. He had rejected his neighbors so many times we know they did not warn them, or, they assumed he knew. Following the first hurricane another traversed the opposite track across the state two weeks later, followed by a tropical storm. For a person with AS shut up in a small room these triple-backed storm events unnerved him completely. It was two weeks before he could emerge from his tiny haven, shaken, and emotionally frayed.

He could not survive such an ordeal again. Smokey had to leave Florida.

Society tends to be more accepting of the Howard Hughes of the world than an old bachelor living in a metal building. Wealth seems to compensate for the acceptance level. Society has set the cultural standard and eccentrics are not tolerated well. Noble was unique in that they allowed Smokey his idiosyncrasies as long as he didn't hurt anyone. They didn't care if he was wealthy, broke, or just plain strange. Smokey was just one more colorful character among many although he topped the list. O.B.'s influence was the main reason Smokey's behavior was tolerated.

Smokey was articulate in describing chemicals or any mechanical function but generally avoided speech otherwise. When he did talk it was a barely audible monotone; again, a common symptom of AS. It is surprising how much Smokey could communicate without uttering a word. If a gesture could accomplish the same task he would not speak at all. So many times Roe would come to an assumption and simply ask him if it were true. Smokey would nod in agreement or shake his head once. This symptom became much worse as he aged. Gestures replaced words almost entirely. His communication was edited to a directional nod, a shake of the head, pointing, and demonstrations. His lack of verbalization may have been more pronounced because he lived in solitude. Smokey would literally go days and weeks without speaking to anyone.

AS people sometimes hear and see things others do not. Many report seeing "auras" about people and things, or they see them in color. Smokey was convinced he had made contact with aliens. For a person so miserably disappointed in the human race it is not surprising Smokey searched elsewhere for some intelligent logic. He told Roe they were coming back after him one day. Smokey's last communication with Roe was a verbal will and testament that whatever was left, was his. Smokey did not plan on dying. He planned on leaving with his aliens.

When we followed Smokey's directions to the thirty-two paces from his window we found a grid of five punctured and drained beer cans. They were spray-painted white, set approximately twelve feet in diameter. They were deliberately placed in a home plate pattern. In retrospect, maybe we should have paid closer attention to where the pattern was pointing. We at first thought this was where Smokey was directing Roe to dig for something. Later we associated it with where Smokey saw his aliens. We believe he positioned the cans as a landing site for his aliens. His crude drawing of aliens was what this AS sufferer saw.

One wonders about the spiritual side of a personality like Smokey. He flatly refused Viola's invitation to church declaring himself a Baptist. The only time Smokey ever entered a church was for O.B.'s funeral. Sitting through a church service would be impossible for someone with Autism; electronic sound with microphones, loud music, clapping, drums, and worse, the close proximity of people. It would have terrified and repulsed him. We were gratified to find religious publications in Smokey's building in Noble. Smokey's spiritual quest had to be in solitude between a man and his God. Who is to judge whether Smokey had a relationship with God or not because he was never seen in church? Not us.

Smokey was adamant no animals could ever stay on his property all his life. He did not want a dog or cat touching him in affection. Many people who live alone enjoy the companionship of a pet, but not Smokey. He apparently mellowed late in life because we found a makeshift shelter outside his workshop for two half-wild cats. We know he bought cat food for them but he would not let them come in his workshop close to him.

As Smokey aged and proved he meant no harm to anyone, people still maintained a healthy distance around him. They did not feel the fear that had people avoiding him in previous years. After all, what could a frail old man do to you? For years after his death people would not enter his property fearing long dormant booby-traps. There may be good reason for that caution.

Every grievous event in his life caused Smokey to be a wary man. He trusted no one and his paranoia was total. Smokey sought a relationship with O.B. and Roe, but it took great effort for him. One had the sense Smokey wanted companionship but was unable to nurture it. On an intellectual level Smokey knew something was wrong with him and he found ways to manage it. He knew the best way to deal with his deeply hidden issues were in solitude. The balm for his troubled mind was his beloved machines and he returned to them constantly for solace. Smokey was comfortable in his narrow environment and he did not question how he lived. This was exactly what he wanted. Solitude. His machines. To experiment. And to work.

We gathered so many negative accounts of Smokey's interaction with people over his life and were surprised people tolerated his behavior as much as they did. Others related agreeable encounters with Smokey and recall an impressive, articulate gentleman.

We can't stress enough how charismatic Smokey was as an individual. He could be rude, threatening, unpleasant, and yet acquaintances were still impressed with him. Smokey had a commanding presence and people seemed to be drawn to him, regardless.

A Social Misfit

Knowing an individual is investigated by the FBI because of their seeming capability of harm would be noteworthy, but two well documented times is amazing. He was that striking.

Smokey's eccentric nature was the essence of his personality. He made no apologies for his behavior or lifestyle and was completely indifferent to public opinion. He was well aware of the sense of fear associated with him and he made no attempt to quiet those fears. He even intentionally promoted it. Smokey kept a distant and abiding peace with the village he chose to live his last years in. He was left to himself and that was all he ever wanted. Second and third generations of children are still regaled with tales of Smokey's escapades in the same light as one telling ghost stories over a campfire.

Was Smokey happy? We hope so. Maybe content is a better word. Few people can say they lived their life exactly how they wanted to. Still, we wonder if at night did he listen to the laughter that drifted across the pasture from the Knott's front porch during summertime domino games? Did he watch two cotton-headed boys playing with their dogs in the backyard and long for children of his own? On Sundays did he see the half dozen cars parked in the front yard and regret losing touch with his own family? We doubt Smokey was capable of such reflection. He was too busy with his machines.

The mystery surrounding this man is finally lifted. Herbert Glen Irwin left his contribution to industry and agricultural history. Smokey was not a German spy. He never entertained the thought of building a bomb or conspired to hurt a soul. Other than underreporting his income, to our knowledge he never cheated or took advantage of anyone. He was not politically radical, mentally ill, or deviant in any manner. He wasn't weird: *he was symptomatic.*

We are satisfied Asperger's Syndrome explains Smokey's personality quirks and the remarkable life he chose to live. Smokey found a way to work with his disability and to a degree, capitalize on its unique benefits. He never felt sorry for himself. His worst crimes were frustration and anger. We can understand, perhaps justify his negative traits, and see what a struggle his daily existence was. For that we have nothing but admiration for him. A person who has survived such devastating problems, financial, professional, emotional instability, addiction, family estrangement, and a neurological disorder – we could understand anyone crumbling under such weights. But Smokey never had the look of a defeated man. Never.

Mr. Irwin, we didn't *know*. With this book, Roe is delivered of his responsibility. Herbert Glen Irwin's story is told. Roe can finally say to his old friend, "Yours truly."

Photographs

Photographs

Maggie Cross and Viola Knott in the Noble Mercantile, 1951

Photographs

Smokey's 1941 Ford Panel Truck, photo taken in 1975

Photographs

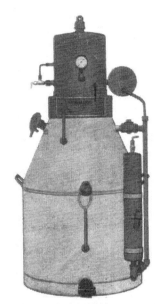

Portable Model

"IT'S THE BEST I EVER HAVE SEEN"
Ask the welder who is using one and he will tell you.

(OVER)

Circular advertising the Welderz Frend, late 1920s. The reverse side gave a narrative of the benefits of this welder over others.

Photographs

O.B. Knott in front of the Knott home, about 1954.

Photographs

Patented Inventions

Appendix

Patented Inventions

Herbert Glen Irwin's thirty-nine patents spanned from 1918 to 1964. Smokey's concentration was focused in five categories: engines, agriculture, oxyacetylene welding, wind power and energy, and to a lesser and more personal degree, foods. His overall contribution was in improvement to existing machinery, new technology, and reduction of labor in contemporary machinery. He manufactured some of his inventions himself. We were unable to verify exactly how many were licensed or sold directly to other manufacturers.

Seven patents were registered in his father's name, Samuel D. Irwin, but we know from other documentation, letters, and interviews they are the work of one lone inventor, Herbert G. Irwin. Members of the Irwin family were surprised any inventions were listed in Samuel D. Irwin's name, knowing him to be only a cotton farmer. Those reasons are noted in Chapter Four.

Smokey had a business partner early in his career, Stephen E. Johnson Jr. Mr. Johnson's input to the inventions is acknowledged but it is unknown to what extent. These exceptions are noted.

This list is chronological by date of submission, followed by the date the patent was granted. Depending on its complexity, each patent consisted of several pages of drawings which Smokey drew himself with his companion text. Smokey's narrative is sometimes exhausting and this appendix is an attempt to summarize them. Most, but not all Smokey's patents can be viewed in detail on the U.S. Patent Office website.

In defending two of his rejected claims (#22, #33) Smokey hired and subsequently fired both patent attorneys. He was successful in having them patented through his own efforts. Those letters written to patent examiners, one consisting of twenty-five pages, the other six, are priceless narratives of logic, systematic argument, and profound assurance of his position. Few attorneys could have done as well. They also give unique insight into Smokey's character.

Every patent attorney Smokey used was based in Washington DC. We know he communicated with patent researchers independently of his attorneys because Smokey quoted other patents, internationally and domestically, in defending his own claims. Given the era, we were amazed at his knowledge of general industry.

The "A" designates those submissions Smokey used an attorney. After so many patents he was well versed enough in the process and was comfortable submitting them without an attorney.

Smokey's life was one of constant innovation. Not all his inventions were patented or even submitted. We were particularly intrigued with his simple rubber "wind stop" on his doors. He invested countless hours of experimentation to arrive at his conclusions and spent years on some projects, simply for his own pleasure and use.

Considering the current emphasis on wind power as an alternate energy source, pollution and chemical exposure, food safety and purity, alternate fuels, and economical living, one can see a modern thinker ahead of his time.

Patented Inventions

Submitted by:

* Samuel D. Irwin
** Samuel D. Irwin and Stephen Elbert Johnson Jr.
*** Samuel D. Irwin and Herbert G. Irwin

1) Vacuum-Energized Make and Break Spark Plug #1,268,719
A, Jul 26, 1917, Jun 4, 1918

2) Vacuum-Operated Make and Break Spark Plug #1,306,667
A, Sep 11, 1917 Jun 10, 1919

Both spark plugs were an improvement of those on the current market. The second spark plug was an improvement on the first. These reduced carbon buildup for a cleaner functioning ignition and smoother running engine. Smokey experimented with alternate fuels in developing his spark plugs, such as distillate benzol (benzene) and other hydro-carbonated fuels.

3) Vaporizing Attachment for Internal Combustion Engines # 1,290,208
A, Dec 3, 1917 Jan 7, 1919

Carbonization was characteristic with early engines. The vaporizing attachment allowed a "decarbonizing" agent to be introduced into the cylinders of the engine. The narrative implies additives or alternate fuels other than gasoline were added with this attachment but the attachment itself was the invention.

4) Device For Cleaning Electrodes Of Make And Break Spark Plugs #1,275,035
A, Dec 3, 1917 Aug 6, 1918

The device was designed to remove carbon from the Make and Break Spark Plug without removing it from the engine. Most spark plugs had to be removed for cleaning.

5) Vacuum Operated Make And Break Spark Plug #1,285,199
A, Dec 3, 1917 Nov 19, 1918

This was a slightly different design and improvement over the earlier Make And Break Spark Plug.

6) Cotton-Bur Separator ** #1,276,370
A, May 20, 1918 Aug 20, 1918

Cotton was manually picked over late summer into the fall. A frost will open a bur slightly but the lint must be removed from the bur before a gin can process it. Closed burs represented considerable loss of lint. Cotton was sometimes picked with dew on the dried bur, which further caused machinery problems in a gin. The separator broke up the bur with blades and flung the pieces against a conveyor belt. Gravity separated the heavier burs from the lighter lint. The lint was caught by brushes and moved to a conveyor belt.

7) Battery Mud-Extracting Device * #1,296,961
A, Jul 1, 1918 Mar 11, 1919

This device was used on storage batteries to deal with the normal "sloughing off" of the active material of electrode plates. It was specifically designed for easy removal of battery "mud" without disassembling the unit. It had two attached containers, which allowed a liquid to be passed through the battery to wash and remove the sediment caused by acid.

8) Vacuum Distributor For Internal Combustion Engines * #1,297,855
A, Aug 28, 1918 Mar 18, 1919

This was a distributor to automatically and successively fire the Make And Break Spark Plugs while infusing controlled air flow into the distributor.

9) Method Of Repairing Aluminum Castings * #1,309,033
A, Nov 26, 1918 Jul 8, 1919

More of a technique, alloy and aluminum is sandwiched in a composite plate. It is fused together by welding and then the plate is formed against a fractured metal casting. High heat is applied through welding, which in turn fuses the alloy and aluminum to the metal casting. The opposite side of the fracture is braced by asbestos and removed after the repair. The method allows for iron, copper, or any metal with a high fusing point.

10) Cotton Bur Separator And Suction Fan ** #1,322,020
A, Dec 6, 1918 Nov 18, 1919

This was an extremely large device consisting of an intake and outlet, with a pneumatic fan to lift and feed cotton from a wagon through a separator into the gin. In the process the burs and debris were separated from the lint through blades, a crusher, and a conveyor.

11) Rotary Cultivator *** #1,322,447
A, Jul 12, 1919 Nov 18, 1919

A cultivator resembling a large drum with protruding spikes, the spikes are adjustable to prevent damage to young plants, and are pitched forward at such an angle to lift and break up crusted earth.

12) Powder-Sprayer * #1,360,642
A, Dec 15, 1919 Nov 30, 1920

A garden-sized sprayer resembling fireplace bellows with a receptacle to hold insecticide powders. Useful for plants or animal application, a nozzle fed the insecticide from the receptacle inside the bellows. When squeezed open and shut, the powder sprayed outward through the tip.

13) Insecticide Dispensing Receptacle #1,370,110
A, Dec 22, 1919 Mar 1, 1921

A simplistic folded rectangular box made from heavy weight Manila paper for use as a disposable container for insecticide. The consumer is instructed to prick a hole in the folded end of the box and squeeze the paper box causing the insecticide to be sprayed through the puncture. Smokey became leery of insecticide use, desiring a disposable unit so the individual would not be exposed to insecticides.

14) Insecticide Holder #1,377,077
A, Dec 22, 1919 May 3, 1921

A large cylinder design, one side being a collapsible bellows that lessened as the insecticide was fed through a nozzle. The nozzle was centrally placed to allow a continuous feed no matter now little insecticide remained in the holder. The tension springs securing both ends of the holder were firmly held to provide an airtight seal. After experimenting with and being exposed to insecticides in his development of these inventions, he became convinced of the harm of insecticide use with food products and livestock.

15) Heating Primer #1,454,929
A, Jun 15, 1920 May 15, 1923

This is a primer to heat a quantity of fuel to start cold internal combustion engines. The fuel was electrically heated in a chamber by the vehicle battery, regulating fuel consumption by gravity.

16) Cotton Picker #1,500,992
A, Sep 1, 1920 Jul 8, 1924

A truly mechanical cotton picker, this was a spindle-type picker employing some of the same elements of Smokey's cotton bur separator. The cotton picker was pulled by mules through the field. The gears and sprockets connected to the wheels provided the energy to rotate two drums with protruding burred spindles. The revolving spindles plucked the dried cotton plant, extracting lint and burs, and crushed the burs to allow further extraction of the lint. The lint and a relatively low amount of debris were propelled through a sleeve onto a platform for manual removal.

Patented Inventions

17) Heading Machine #1,531,293
A, Feb 24, 1921 Mar 31, 1925

Seven pages of illustrations and nine pages of text were necessary to explain this elaborate heading machine. It was specifically designed for Milo maize (sorghum) and Kafir corn. This large mower-sized machine amplified the energy produced through its metal wheels as the header was pulled through a field by mules. It used a complex system of cogs and sprockets to transfer energy to power a circular blade of deep teeth, which functioned as a rotary sickle. A large wooden trough was centrally placed to guide the corn, or other stalk into position. The stalk was simultaneously cut under the head of grain and slightly above the ground leaving a uniform stalk that fell to the ground. The head of grain was dumped into a hopper where a turning spiral conveyor lifted the head of grain over the top into a receptacle. The header utilizes chain, gears, sprockets, transfer cogs, several conveyors, and board feeders with multiple adjustments to allow for harvesting different stalked crops. The operator sits on the side of the machine to make adjustments in the field. We found a near identical heading machine in the yard of the Dickens County Museum, with only minor alterations. The manufacturer of the invention was International Harvester.

18) Push Bar Attachment For Tractors #1,420,106
A, Aug 5, 1921 Jun 20, 1922

This first mention of a tractor with his agricultural patents, the push bar attachment allowed a farmer to push an implement rather than pulling one, thus performing two functions in one sweep of a field. Depending on a narrow or wide row, the push bar attachment allowed for adjustment to the left or right. The push bar was designed to attach to any of several models of tractor bodies and axels.

19) Valve Controlling Mechanism For Acetylene Generators #1,491,702
A Dec 12, 1921 Apr 22, 1924

The first of eight patents for oxyacetylene generators that made up the welder Smokey marketed as the Welderz Frend. This valve mechanism controlled the flow and equalized the rate of consumption of gas, resulting in constant pressure. It not only was original to his design but could be adapted to other acetylene generators.

20) Rotary Crust Breaker #1,498,378
Jan 3, 1922 Jun 17, 1924

This was an improvement over his earlier cultivator using a design that had opposing and overlapping revolving spikes. This design allowed for a more complete soil penetration and break up. Especially useful with dried crusted soil resulting from drought.

21) Vehicle Wheel Repair Washer #1,446,422
Feb 24, 1922 Feb 20, 1923

A very simple answer to a common problem with wooden wheels. The spoke is inserted into the shoulder of a wheel (the felloe). Because of the nature of wood, the spoke would shrink and leave a loose joint (tenon). These were two half washers that were positioned against the spoke. The inside edge of the washer had an incisive edge. The washers could be hammered into the shoulder of the wheel holding the spoke tightly in place.

22) Carbide Agitator For Acetylene Generators #1,727,981
Jan 26, 1925 Sep 10, 1929

It took four years and ten claims before this invention was patented. Smokey initially submitted the invention without a patent attorney. Later he hired one because of the repeated rejections and then fired that attorney, defending the patent himself. We have a marvelous 25-page dissertation of his appeal. At the time, the innovation was so unique the patent examiner stated, "it cannot possibly work." The document lists several other patents to argue his claim in principle, plus attached notarized letters from Willborn Brothers stating they had personally witnessed the action of the agitator. The "agitator" was an automatically controlled valve regulating the gravitation of granular carbide from its container to the water container. The carbide was agitated in the vicinity of the feed valve to prevent banking or clogging. Thus, the feed was constantly maintained and uniformly generated acetylene in proportion to the rate of the consumption of carbide.

23) Shield For Carbide Feeds In Acetylene Generators #1,857,456
May 19, 1927 May 10, 1932

An improvement over numerous splash shields and drip rings in the interior of acetylene generators. Portable generators commonly became clogged in the acetylene feed from moisture by splashing of water in the carbide passageway. Lime deposits were also a problem. The shield and drip ring were self-cleaning.

24) Carbide Agitator For Acetylene Generators #1,797,264
Aug 6, 1927 Mar 24, 1931

A refinement of Smokey's first agitator with the introduction of a diaphragm to further control the flow of a thin stream of well regulated carbide through the automatic feed. The design overcame the variance of two to five pounds of gas pressure.

25) Hand Feed For Acetylene Generators #1,799,589
Aug 18, 1927 Apr 7, 1931

For use with acetylene generators with an automatic feed valve, the hand feed could be used independently. The advantage of using the hand feed raises the initial gas pressure after recharging the generator. Using the hand feed wears away lime deposits in the feed valve and hopper bottom, thus keeping the mechanism clean and safer.

26) Feed Valve For Acetylene Generators #1,748,069
Aug 25, 1927 Feb 25, 1930

A diaphragm controlled feed valve design that could be taken down for cleaning without disassembling the unit. This design had a separable hopper bottom and removable feed valve.

27) Acetylene Generator #1,763,890
Aug 22, 1927 Jun 17, 1930

This was an improved generator of the carbide-to-water type with an automatic control valve. The opposed gas pressure feed-type valve was an improved appearance and simplified the contour with an internal pressure tank. This was more of an improved arrangement and appearance of the different elements of his previous generators.

28) Carbide Feed For Acetylene Generators #1,825,066
A, Aug 23, 1928 Sep 29, 1931

A further improvement to reduce carbide residue cake adhering to the bottom of a carbide-feed hopper and automatic valve, the design also guarded against obstructive residue deposits and soft deposits around the carbide feed outlet.

29) Wind Power Machine #2,152,963
A, Oct 26, 1936 Apr 4, 1939

Note: with one exception Smokey did not use a patent attorney (and later fired) for any of his welding patents but began using them again with this invention. The wind power machine was designed for use in supplying power for a large or small electric generator to charge storage batteries. The design contained an automatic adjustment for expansion and contraction of the belt with varying weather conditions.

30) Wind Power Machine #2,181,658
A, Jul 14, 1938 Nov 28, 1939

An improved design which limited the speed of the generator drive in gale winds. The generator was covered by

Patented Inventions

a housing which supported an exterior rotor blade. The wheel shaft and belt drive allowed for easy replacement and repair.

31) Belt Tightener Of The Spring Type #2,221,479
A, Feb 2, 1940 Nov 12, 1940

An adjustment device to stop the vibration and jerking of the action of a wind powered generator and maintain tension on drive belts. It combined rigidity with spring tension to provide a back-movement to stabilize the generator or motor against back-pulling pressure.

32) Wind Power Machine #2,224,052
A, Feb 5, 1940 Dec 3, 1940

An improved wind power machine more easily maintained which allowed simplified adjustment.

33) Smoke Absorbent Smoker #2,611,311
A, Dec 6, 1946 Sep 23, 1952

This invention was rejected six times. Smokey fired his patent attorney and defended his claim himself. This is a self-contained smoker for inside use on a stove or heating element. It is designed for smoking fresh meat, fowl, or fish with wood or other smoke-producing material. Included in the text is a detailed list of things one would normally not consider for smoking or flavoring meats, such as barley. Such was Smokey's sensitive palette.

Note: The following patents show a pronounced digression in Smokey's intellectual facility. There is an endless spread of his statements of purpose and rambling descriptions. The texts of these patents illustrate an individual who consumed untold hours of experimentation. We do not know if his heroin use was affecting Smokey's neurological condition, his obsessive personality, or it was overshadowing his intellect; possibly a combination of all. Neither can we dismiss the affect of lifelong carbide exposure. The narrative is often hard to follow and excessively detailed. The remainder of his patents were submitted after the FL hurricanes, which definitely affected his mental equilibrium.

34) Fishhook Bait #2,555,088
Jul 1, 1949 May 29, 1951

This was an unassuming muslin pouch secured by a wire clamp and drawstring to hold bait that attracts fish by sight and smell. The intent was to use artificial bait that did not resemble any animal and would attract fish with daytime feeding habits. Changing the ingredients within the pouch the bait would attract bottom feeding or night feeding fish. Three pages of text discuss the assorted compounds and variety of design elements that would still pertain to the patent. The puncture of the pouch by a fishhook is the means to dispense the aroma of the bait. Smokey experimented with a combination of ingredients that would absorb water and change the shape of the pouch. He discusses at length the changes in color and texture with an exhaustive list of ingredients. The narrative also considers using the bait in combination with spinners or wigglers in fishing or trawling for game fish.

35) Arrow Shooter #2,664,078
Dec 20,1952 Dec 29, 1953

Patented Inventions

Fifty individual illustrations and six pages of narrative explain this arrow shooter, which is basically a crossbow. This was a highly accurate crossbow.

36) Archery Bow #2,816,537
Dec 3, 1956 Dec 17, 1957

Twenty-four illustrations and three pages of text, this was an archery bow design with a guide bar and a finger slide. The arrow is anchored in a position to allow steady and accurate shooting.

37) Arrow Shooter #2,926,650
Mar 1, 1957 Mar 1, 1960

Twenty-seven illustrations and three pages of text illustrated a modified design of his first crossbow.

38) Gaseous-Condiment Generator #3,117,510
Jun 8, 1960 Jan 14, 1964

Forty-two individual illustrations and six pages of text were necessary to explain a self-contained pressurized "frying pan" that simultaneously cooks, flavors, and tenderizes meats. It has a mind-boggling series of elaborate gauges, joints, tubing, and adjustable valves to allow for the variety of meats, sizes, and various combinations of spices. An attachment to the generator resembles a hand tire pump that provides the pressure to the cooker.

39) Gaseous-Condiment Generator #3,139,023
Jun 4, 1962 Jun 30, 1964

Patented Inventions

This patent contained forty-five illustrations and six pages of modifications of his earlier model. This is the first time an electrical cord appears on any of Smokey's illustrations or is associated with him.

Patented Inventions

Made in the USA
Lexington, KY
11 March 2010